The Merchant of Venice

ARDEN STUDENT SKILLS: LANGUAGE AND WRITING

Series Editor

Dympna Callaghan, Syracuse University

Published Titles

Antony and Cleopatra, Virginia Mason Vaughan
Hamlet, Dympna Callaghan
King Richard III, Rebecca Lemon
Macbeth, Emma Smith
Much Ado about Nothing, Indira Ghose
Othello, Laurie Maguire
Romeo and Juliet, Catherine Belsey
The Tempest, Brinda Charry
Twelfth Night, Frances E. Dolan

Forthcoming Titles

King Lear, Jean Howard
A Midsummer Night's Dream, R. S. White

The Merchant of Venice

Language and Writing

DOUGLAS M. LANIER

THE ARDEN SHAKESPEARE
LONDON • NEW YORK • OXFORD • NEW DELHI • SYDNEY

THE ARDEN SHAKESPEARE
Bloomsbury Publishing Plc
50 Bedford Square, London, WC1B 3DP, UK
1385 Broadway, New York, NY 10018, USA

BLOOMSBURY, THE ARDEN SHAKESPEARE and the Arden Shakespeare
logo are trademarks of Bloomsbury Publishing Plc

First published in Great Britain 2019

Copyright © Douglas M. Lanier, 2019

Douglas M. Lanier has asserted his right under the Copyright, Designs
and Patents Act, 1988, to be identified as the author of this work.

Cover image © The British Library Board (G.11631, 3:2:135–43)

All rights reserved. No part of this publication may be reproduced or transmitted
in any form or by any means, electronic or mechanical, including photocopying,
recording, or any information storage or retrieval system, without prior
permission in writing from the publishers.

Bloomsbury Publishing Plc does not have any control over, or responsibility
for, any third-party websites referred to or in this book. All internet addresses
given in this book were correct at the time of going to press. The author
and publisher regret any inconvenience caused if addresses have changed
or sites have ceased to exist, but can accept no responsibility for
any such changes.

A catalogue record for this book is available from the British Library.

A catalog record for this book is available from the Library of Congress.

ISBN:	HB:	978-1-4725-7149-6
	PB:	978-1-4725-7148-9
	ePDF:	978-1-4725-7151-9
	eBook:	978-1-4725-7150-2

Series: Arden Student Skills: Language and Writing

Typeset by Integra Software Services Pvt. Ltd.
Printed and bound in Great Britain

To find out more about our authors and books visit www.bloomsbury.com
and sign up for our newsletters.

CONTENTS

Series Editor's Preface vii
A Note on Editions ix

Introduction 1

1   Shakespeare's Stylistic Resources 11
    Historicizing Shakespeare's language 12
    Rhetorical patterning 16
    Metre 19
    Imagery 24
    Wordplay 28
    Writing matters – writing criticism 30

2   Language in Print I: Texts from Texts 35
    Sources 35
    Allusions 41
    Shylock and the Bible 42
    Christians and classical myth 46
    Writing matters – using sources 53

3   Language in Print II: Two Shylocks, Two Portias 57
    The two Shylocks 57
    The two Portias 67
    Writing matters – form, sequencing, proportion 74

4 Language in Print III: Bonds 79
Resonance 79
Bond as commercial contract 80
Bond as connection, constriction, covenant and seal 81
Bonds of hate and love 83
Words as bonds 89
Writing matters – abstraction and nuance 91

5 Language in Dramatic Context 97
The casket scene (*MV* 3.2) 98
The trial scene (*MV* 4.1) 105
Writing matters – context 114

6 The Language of Racial and Ethnic Humour 119
Portia 120
Lancelet Giobbe 127
Shylock 133
Writing matters – asking analytic questions 138

7 The Language of Comedy 143
Rings 144
Music 153
Writing matters – conclusions 160

8 Language through Time: Adaptations and Performance 163
Print editions 165
Performance 171
Adaptations 178

Notes 189
Further Reading, Listening and Viewing 195

SERIES EDITOR'S PREFACE

This series puts the pedagogical expertise of distinguished literary critics at the disposal of students embarking upon Shakespeare Studies at university. While they demonstrate a variety of approaches to the plays, all the contributors to the series share a deep commitment to teaching and a wealth of knowledge about the culture and history of Shakespeare's England. The approach of each of the volumes is direct yet intellectually sophisticated and tackles the challenges Shakespeare presents. These volumes do not provide a shortcut to Shakespeare's works but instead offer a careful explication of them directed towards students' own processing and interpretation of the plays and poems.

Students' needs in relation to Shakespeare revolve overwhelmingly around language, and Shakespeare's language is what most distinguishes him from his rivals and collaborators – as well as what most embeds him in his own historical moment. The Language and Writing series understands language as the very heart of Shakespeare's literary achievement rather than as an obstacle to be circumvented. This series addresses the difficulties often encountered in reading Shakespeare alongside the necessity of writing papers for university examinations and course assessment. The primary objective here is to foster rigorous critical engagement with the texts by helping students develop their own critical writing skills. Language and Writing titles demonstrate how to develop students' own capacity to articulate and enlarge upon their experience of encountering the text, far beyond summarizing, paraphrasing or 'translating' Shakespeare's language into a more palatable, contemporary form. Each of the volumes in the series introduces the text as an act of specifically literary language and shows that the multifarious issues of life and history that Shakespeare's work addresses cannot be separated from their expression in language. In addition, each book takes students through a series of guidelines about how to develop viable undergraduate critical essays on the text in question, not by delivering interpretations but rather by taking readers step by step through the process of discovering and developing their own critical ideas.

All the books include chapters examining the text from the point of view of its composition, that is, from the perspective of Shakespeare's own process of composition as a reader, thinker and writer. The opening chapters consider when and how the play was written, addressing, for example, the extant literary and cultural acts of language, from which Shakespeare constructed his work – including his sources – as well as the generic, literary and theatrical conventions at his disposal. Subsequent sections demonstrate how to engage in detailed examination and analysis of the text and focus on the literary, technical and historical intricacies of Shakespeare's verse and prose. Each volume also includes some discussion of performance. Other chapters cover textual issues as well as the interpretation of the extant texts for any given play on stage and screen, treating, for example, the use of stage directions or parts of the play that are typically cut in performance. Authors also address issues of stage/film history as they relate to the cultural evolution of Shakespeare's words. In addition, these chapters deal with the critical reception of the work, particularly the newer theoretical and historicist approaches that have revolutionized our understanding of Shakespeare's language over the past forty years. Crucially, every chapter contains a section on 'Writing matters', which links the analysis of Shakespeare's language with students' own critical writing.

The series empowers students to read and write about Shakespeare with scholarly confidence and hopes to inspire their enthusiasm for doing so. The authors in this series have been selected because they combine scholarly distinction with outstanding teaching skills. Each book exposes the reader to an eminent scholar's teaching in action and expresses a vocational commitment to making Shakespeare accessible to a new generation of student readers.

Professor Dympna Callaghan
Series Editor
Arden Student Skills: Language and Writing

A NOTE ON EDITIONS

All citations from *The Merchant of Venice* are taken from John Drakakis's edition of the play for the Arden Third Series (London: Bloomsbury, 2011). Citations are noted parenthetically by act, scene and line number. Citations from other Shakespeare plays are taken from the Arden Third Series editions of each play, which can be found in the list of texts in the bibliography. In the discussion of the *Gesta Romanorum* in Chapter Two, I have lightly modernized spelling to aid the reader.

Introduction

The Merchant of Venice is one of Shakespeare's most unsettling and provocative plays. For modern audiences especially, it is all the more unsettling because it's not entirely clear what kind of provocation Shakespeare intended. Its subject matter is hardly what we expect of a comedy, focusing on some of the more troubling aspects of human experience – bigotry, hypocrisy, mercenary business practices, marital infidelity, the impulse to revenge. Though the play contains some of the most compelling speeches on compassion and empathy in the English language, it is a historical fact that *The Merchant of Venice* has been used in the past to reinforce virulent prejudices against Jews. For some, Shylock has come to serve as a dramatically compelling instance of the worst kind of anti-Semitic stereotype, the devious, money-hungry Jew who secretly longs to kill innocent Christians. Indeed, the very name 'Shylock' has become offensive slang for a moneylender who charges extortionate rates, a ruthless businessman or, most nasty of all, simply a Jewish man. For many, the play simply cannot escape the charge of being anti-Semitic. Just to take one example, in 2016, in the wake of the Folger Shakespeare Theatre staging *The Merchant of Venice* along with a revisionary adaptation of *District Merchants*, one outraged writer took to the pages of *The Washington Post* to call for a moratorium on producing the play.[1] Even, he argues, if we grant that Shakespeare's portrayal of Jewish stereotypes and use of racist slurs simply reflect the prevailing prejudices of Renaissance England and not Shakespeare's personal views, the fact that this play gives voice to such bigoted language and continued life to such troubling stereotypes allows it to perpetuate reprehensible lines of thinking. Perhaps, we might reply, in the end Shakespeare is interested in showing the ugliness of such bigotry – a view which many other commentators and producers have entertained. But *The Merchant of Venice* can't easily escape the long history of anti-Semitism and racism in which it has wittingly or unwittingly participated. Elements of the play's language are inescapably racist. And taking such concerns very seriously is all the more urgent given the horrors to which anti-Semitism eventually led – the Holocaust – and the recent resurgence of racist and anti-Jewish sentiment in American and European alt-right movements. *The Merchant of Venice* belongs on a list of Shakespeare plays – *The Taming of the Shrew*, *Othello*, *The Tempest* – that portray the 'Other' – women, people of colour, non-Christians, native peoples – in ways many modern spectators find blinkered or repellent. How then to perform this play without contributing to a long history of prejudice or breaking faith with Shakespeare's text? Should we even perform or study it at all?

That said, it's just as important to acknowledge that *The Merchant of Venice* also features some of the most compelling speeches on cross-cultural empathy and mercy in the English language. The phrase 'hath not a Jew eyes' has come to stand for the possibility of recognizing and identifying with the common humanity of someone not like oneself, and Portia's 'quality of mercy' speech has long been regarded as one of the great articulations of the Christian principle of mercy (even though this speech incorporates Jewish ideas about mercy too). It may be that the characters who utter these lines do not practise what they preach, but Shakespeare goes to some length to voice these moral ideals in the play and to make them poetically memorable. What is more, even though Shylock may seem to conform to anti-Semitic stereotypes, nowhere more so than when he seems intent upon killing Antonio, Shakespeare goes out of his way to give him a compelling backstory. The history of abuse he suffers at the hands of his fellow merchants, a history that culminates in their taking of his daughter Jessica and their theft of his gold, helps explain and perhaps even mitigate his desire to take revenge upon his Christian tormentors. Shakespeare gives us reasons, in other words, to see Shylock as more sinned against than sinning by portraying him as a sympathetic victim of society-wide Christian prejudices. What's more, Shakespeare tips in little details – Shylock's mordant sense of humour, the sentimental detail about his wife Leah's ring, his friendship with Tubal, his railing against Christian hypocrisy in the trial scene – that complicate any effort to see Shylock as a simple Jewish villain or inhuman monster. Given these and other elements we will examine, it is hard to see *The Merchant of Venice* as endorsing in any simple way the anti-Semitism of the play's Christian characters, even though that anti-Semitism is given considerable stage time.

The play's romance plotline is equally unsettling and provocative. On its surface it seems like the stuff of fairy tales. Portia, something of a fairy-tale princess, awaits a suitor who can pass the test of virtue set by her father, who dictates the terms of her love life from his grave. Bassanio, the once feckless but now earnest man of her dreams, the least of Portia's princely suitors, undergoes the trial of the three caskets and, unlike his rivals, he passes the test, much to Portia's delight. Though he professes undying love for his new bride, before the two can live happily ever after, he must save his friend from death, a task with which his new wife secretly helps. Bassanio's speech on 'ornament', the speech with which he solves the puzzle of the three caskets, lays out in eloquent detail two more key virtues in the play, the capacity to see beyond mere appearances (or the letter of the law) and the need to risk it all in hopes of garnering a great reward. Portia's realm of Belmont, a world away from Venice with its gritty business and legal dealings, has the faraway, idealized feel of a fairy-tale kingdom where gold is endlessly bountiful and aristocratic langeur is the order of the day.

The reality of courtship in this play, however, is more complicated than that, particularly for modern spectators who might assume that love should trump economic considerations. Bassanio is interested in Portia – he himself announces early on – because her great wealth will allow him to settle his many debts, and despite his later declaration of love for Portia, it's never clear whether he's entirely moved on from his original gold-digger motivation. His friend Antonio, the 'merchant of Venice' of the play's title, is deeply attached to Bassanio, perhaps homoerotically so, and he takes up a loan from Shylock on Bassanio's behalf to maintain their relationship at a moment when Bassanio is leaving to pursue Portia. With Bassanio, Portia stresses her emotional vulnerability in their relationship, but she uses her money and trickery to assert power in their marriage. Indeed, Bassanio's behaviour during and immediately after the trial scene suggests that he is not as committed to Portia as he earlier professed himself to be, and so it falls to Portia to engineer a coercive readjustment of Bassanio's attitude – under threat of cuckoldry – with the rings trick.

The relationship between Jessica and Lorenzo provides an even more troubling portrait of courtship. Theirs is a very conventional Renaissance plotline, one we see in, say, *Romeo and Juliet* – a young couple outwit a father figure who blocks their marriage. Like *Romeo and Juliet*, *The Merchant of Venice* even features a balcony scene where Lorenzo and Jessica declare their love for one another. But Shakespeare includes elements that undermine the romance of this exchange. Jessica seems just as intent on escaping her father's house and converting to Christianity as she does in making a love-match; indeed, she repeatedly speaks of Lorenzo as her ticket to becoming a Christian by proxy. As she leaves her father's house, she brings with her caskets of gold, allowing us to believe that Lorenzo may be motivated by money as much as by love. (Jessica's mention of a 'casket' of gold in this scene is one of several links between the two courtship plots.) Jessica's trading of her mother's ring for a pet monkey portrays her in a very poor light – as a spendthrift more interested in frivolous pleasures than family legacy. And there is some evidence that by the final scene the relationship between Lorenzo and Jessica has gone cold – or at least lost its initial fire. In both courtship narratives, then, Shakespeare pointedly juxtaposes professions of true love with transfers of property and gold and indications of decidedly mercenary motivations. It is the mixture of these ideal and somewhat sordid elements and Shakespeare's refusal to resolve the portrayal of love definitively in one direction or another that give the romance plots a disquieting quality.

Even the genre of the play causes us some trouble. In Shakespeare's day the play was classified as a comedy. On the first page of the 1600 edition it is specified as a 'comical history', and when the play was included in the First Folio, the first collected edition of Shakespeare's works published in 1623, it was listed among the comedies. Superficially the play does conform to the definition of dramatic comedy common to the English Renaissance – a play that ends with a return of the play's community of characters to proper social order after a period of tumult or misunderstanding, that proper order often marked by the promise of a marriage and/

or a communal feast. In *The Merchant of Venice* we do indeed get a return to social order in the play's final scene. After the elimination of the threat of Shylock, the main characters gather at Belmont, that ideal realm, to enjoy the fruits of their victory as the dawn of a new day breaks; Portia and Nerissa sort out the problems with their less-than-faithful husbands with the ring trick, enabling the joys of the nuptial bed; Antonio has his lost ships and wealth magically restored to him; and the play even ends on a bawdy bit of wordplay so that the audience might leave with a smile.

Yet Shakespeare includes elements calculated to complicate any notion of a 'happy ending'. An element of melancholy pervades the beginning of the first and last acts of the play, a dwelling upon loss and the potential for tragedy. More important, in the course of the play we have gotten to know Shylock, the play's ostensible antagonist. We have had access to the history of indignities and bigotry he has endured, all of which motivate his pursuit of Antonio. When, then, Shylock is destroyed in the trial scene, using an argument that is perhaps dramatically satisfying but clearly legally bogus, the triumph of the Christians over him – the very basis of the play's 'happy ending' – may very well seem morally tainted, yet one more example (and in this case a horrific one) of anti-Semitic abuse, this time not just reported to us but enacted before our eyes in all its sordid detail. The comic resolution at the end of the play, the restoration of a sense of harmonious community, comes at great cost to a character Shakespeare has humanized to some extent, and so the harmony enabled by Shylock's public humiliation has seemed for many commentators haunted by the cruel treatment he is given at court. For those who find Shylock a particularly sympathetic character, the play is more of a tragedy, Shylock's tragedy, than a comedy. This may be why the play's final scene occurs largely in the night-time dark. When in the final scene Portia sees candlelight in the windows of her house, an obvious symbol of comic harmony, the happy return home, she remarks, 'How far that little candle throws his beams! / So shines a good deed in a naughty world' (*MV* 5.1.90–1). Yes, the little candle shines bright, but the wider world in which it shines remains 'naughty', suggesting the persistence of disorder, cruelty and evil despite what Portia sees as her great 'good deed' of crushing Shylock. And the 'comic' resolution of the marriages, we should not forget, turns upon moments of trickery that involve humiliation of Bassanio and Gratiano, a technique with perhaps uncomfortable analogies to Portia's treatment of Shylock (though, clearly, in a more lighthearted key). *The Merchant of Venice* does reach a comic resolution at play's end, but that resolution comes with a high price and has seemed to many not as 'happy' as it first might appear. Nor has it seemed entirely complete. Early in the final scene Jessica falls silent and remains so until play's end, the text leaving us unclear as to how she fits into the play's comic order. These disturbing components are the reason some critics have labelled *The Merchant of Venice* a 'problem comedy', that is, a play which does not easily fit into a conventional definition of a comedy and even includes elements more appropriate to tragedy. In the middle years of his career Shakespeare wrote several plays that have been called 'problem comedies' – *All's Well That Ends Well*, *Measure for Measure*, *Troilus and Cressida*, perhaps *The Winter's Tale* – but *The Merchant of Venice*, written much earlier than these plays, is the first comedy in which he mixes in these darker themes and qualities and allows them to trouble us to the end.

I should caution you from the start that this book will not solve these and other interpretive problems posed by this disturbing play. These questions are part of what makes the play so perennially compelling, along with the sad persistence to this day of many issues it addresses – the ways in which money can shape relationships, hatred can breed more hatred, racism can distort the operation of the law. The play's great power springs precisely from its willingness to juxtapose very different, even contradictory views of money, love, religion, race, justice and comedy without fully resolving them into some neat interpretive package. This book proceeds from the conviction that making sense of Shakespeare's purposes in telling such an intriguingly complicated tale requires our paying special attention to the intricacies of his language. By wrestling with the script's many details we wrestle with the questions Shakespeare asks us to address in all their disconcerting complexity, and we can get a better idea of how and why he has shaped our dramatic experience of this story. Of course, a Shakespearean script is not a play, no more than a musical score is music or a recipe is food. A Shakespearean script is a set of directions for making a Shakespeare play, and like a recipe, it almost certainly will be altered in the making – one may add ingredients and leave out others, particular flavours may be brought forward, and the dish may be deconstructed or reimagined. A point I will be making in the final chapter is that when this play – or any Shakespeare play – is experienced in performance, the choices made by actors and directors shape how we see the issues that the play raises and even sometimes resolve what Shakespeare leaves open. The recipe for *The Merchant of Venice* – Shakespeare's script – can provide a wealth of information about how the playwright designed this particular dish, and that information we need first to master before tinkering with the recipe.

The eight chapters of this book seek to provide you with several different approaches to understanding the language of the play. They are all founded upon the principle of 'close reading', that is, paying very close attention to Shakespeare's specific choices of wording and phrasing. The first chapter addresses Shakespeare's basic poetic toolkit, his techniques for expression. Shakespeare often writes in a heightened poetic style, a style meant to deepen the significance and emotional power of what his characters are saying, and so it is important to understand what the basic building blocks of that style are and how they work: rhetorical patterning of language, iambic metre, imagery and wordplay. In the second chapter, we will take up how Shakespeare works with his sources. Shakespeare is, we should always remind ourselves, typically working from some prior source – he is a masterful adaptor rather than a creator of original stories – so tracing how he reshapes his raw materials allows us to see more clearly what original mark or new thematic emphasis he is putting on his sources. This chapter will also discuss Shakespeare's allusions to classical or Biblical texts, another technique he uses to elevate his dialogue and to suggest by analogy relationships between his story and characters and other well-known tales and figures. Chapter Three addresses Shakespeare's presentation of the two central characters of the play, Shylock and Portia. My argument is that Shakespeare offers us two very different portrayals of these two characters, a divided portrayal that is interpretively complicated, but my central concern is to discuss how Shakespeare uses language in the service of characterization, one of his crowning achievements as a playwright. In Chapter Four, we turn to one of the key themes of the play, the idea that economic considerations and emotional relationships are troublingly intertwined in this play. Shakespeare, I will be arguing, often uses a single suggestive word or phrase to encapsulate his main themes, and here we will be examining the resonant word 'bond' to explore its ramifications throughout the play.

With Chapter Five, we turn to thinking about how dramatic context shapes the meaning of Shakespeare's language. Rather than considering a piece of Shakespeare's language in isolation, we will examine how the meaning of a speech is coloured by the specific circumstances in which it is uttered – by the person who speaks, the person to whom it is spoken, the history they share, the particular situation they occupy. Our study examples will involve two of the most important speeches in the play, Bassanio's 'ornament' speech in the casket scene (*MV* 3.2.73–107) and Portia's 'quality of mercy' speech in the trial scene (*MV* 4.1.180–201). The next two chapters, Chapters Six and Seven, address the question of comedy. In Chapter Six, we will examine the issue of humour in the play, a feature we might expect to see in a comedy. One of the things that most troubles modern readers of *The Merchant of Venice* is the play's anti-Semitic, racist and ethnic joking, and so rather than simply being scandalized, we ought instead to analyse just how those jokes work, what they might tell us about the characters' mindsets and how they seek to shape audience responses. Humour, however, isn't the same thing as comedy, at least as far as Renaissance audiences understood the idea of comedy, and so Chapter Seven examines the comic resolution of the play, focusing upon the play's long final scene. Of special interest to us will be the ring episode, one of the mechanisms by which Portia creates a harmonious relationship with Bassanio and Antonio, and the theme of music, a long-standing symbol of the kind of social harmony we expect from a comedy. In this chapter we will be using many of the concepts we've addressed in the book as a whole: imagery, allusion, characterization, key words, contextual meaning and humour (in this case, sexual humour), in addition to considering the nature of comedy itself. The book's final chapter focuses on adaptation, the uses to which the language of Shakespeare's script has been put by latter-day printers, editors, directors, actors and adaptors. We will look at such matters as the editing and printing of Shakespeare's plays (which are, after all, forms of adaptation), performance practices and adaptations that use Shakespeare's language and those that don't. This kind of adaptation, I suggest, is crucial to Shakespeare's continued vitality in culture over time, and so adaptation of his language – in print, on stage and in new forms – is not something to be lamented but a fact to be understood and celebrated.

Each chapter, with the exception of this introduction and the final chapter, is followed by a short section addressed to writing about Shakespeare. I've tried to key these sections on writing to the topics of chapters where I can, and the book is designed so that each writing section dovetails with the critical discussion that precedes it. If you are interested only in being introduced to *The Merchant of Venice*, you can read the chapters without reading the writing sections, and you can read just the writing sections if you are interested in getting tips on how to construct a critical paper on the play. My writing advice emphasizes the importance of the writing process – freewriting, forming a thesis, planning, drafting, quoting, concluding – and so there is an implied sequencing of tasks built into the order of the writing sections. Of necessity I may not be addressing your particular writing assignment, so you may want to modify my advice (or even toss it out) depending upon your specific circumstances. But nevertheless I hope you'll find these suggestions – classroom-tested over many years – to be helpful as you tackle the challenge of writing on this frustrating, fascinating, magnificent play. I firmly believe that writing about *The Merchant of Venice* (or any Shakespeare play) is one of the best ways to get to know it well, to force yourself to take a position on the many issues it raises, to appreciate the extraordinary artfulness of Shakespeare's manipulation of language, to engage with the characters in great depth, and in short, to make the play truly yours.

CHAPTER ONE

Shakespeare's Stylistic Resources

Shakespeare's language is and is not our own, as any casual reader will quickly recognize. On the one hand, the words Shakespeare uses are for the most part recognizable as English to any competent speaker of the language. In fact, it's a commonplace that many of the words and phrases we use daily were invented or popularized by Shakespeare. The phrases 'bated breath' and 'blinking idiot', to take just two examples, originate with *The Merchant of Venice*. On the other hand, early modern English, and the ways in which Shakespeare manipulates it, differs markedly from everyday modern English in several important ways. Early modern English uses, for example, a different system of pronouns and verb endings than does modern English, and it includes some bits of once-common vocabulary that have fallen out of active use. It also allows for a more flexible syntax (or word order) so that, for instance, inverted word order and sentences with long-delayed main verbs are not uncommon. Learning a bit about these characteristics will ease some of the initial difficulties readers encounter with Shakespeare's language.

Even more important is how Shakespeare takes full advantage of the creative possibilities of early modern English. His plays are written largely in dramatic verse, so Shakespeare makes the most of various elements of Renaissance verse technique – rhetorical patterning, metre, metaphor, imagery and wordplay. These are the stylistic resources on which he draws, the basic building blocks of his art, and knowing a bit about each of them will help you comprehend more and appreciate his extraordinary achievement. What makes Shakespeare's verse particularly special among Renaissance playwrights is the density of meaning Shakespeare manages to pack into a line, his willingness to experiment with word effects of all sorts and the ways in which his lines convey the impression of a character's thought in motion, but most special of all is his very evident delight simply in the aptly chosen, resonant word and well-wrought phrase. Clearly Shakespeare loved language for its own sake – he is something of a connoisseur and inventor of words. But it's reasonable to assume that he loved language also because his audiences paid good money to savour skilfully crafted writing spoken well. With his dramatic verse Shakespeare is catering, in other words, to a public market for eloquent speech, an audience eager for stories told in luxurious, extravagant language. If modern audiences, scions of a predominantly visual culture, love to see movies that push film techniques to their very limits, Shakespeare's audiences, products of an oral and (to a lesser degree) written culture, appreciated stylistic craftsmanship and flair with the English language. What modern audiences sometimes experience as Shakespeare's overly formal, extravagant, wilfully complicated writing style, Renaissance audiences experienced as thrillingly novel and inventive, the verbal equivalent of complex cinematic special effects. Helping to kindle some appreciation for poetic skill and flamboyant eloquence is the ultimate goal of this chapter.

Historicizing Shakespeare's language

First, some technical preliminaries. For modern readers the occasionally unfamiliar vocabulary of early modern English poses the most immediate obstacle to understanding Shakespeare's plays. We may stumble if we don't know, for example, that in the Renaissance the word 'his' can mean either 'his' or 'its', or if we don't recognize that 'tis' is the typical early modern contraction of 'it is'. We need to know that the Renaissance English pronouns 'thee' and 'thou', and their possessive forms 'thy' and 'thine' (like the French 'tu' or the German 'du'), are forms of 'you' appropriate for someone with whom you are familiar or intimate ('you', not 'thou', is the more respectful alternative). Using 'thou' to address someone not close to you may sound presumptuous or insulting, unless you are addressing someone absent, a ghost, a spirit or God. For that reason, paying attention to moments when a character uses 'thou' or 'you' with another character may give some hint as to the nature of their relationship, though Shakespeare is by no means rigorous in how he deploys these pronouns. In fact, characters may occasionally switch from one pronoun to the other when addressing the same person and even within the same speech. Verb endings too can pose a challenge. The ending '-eth' is an equivalent of the third-person present tense ending '-s'; the verb ending '-est' and the verbs 'art', 'wilt' and 'wert' (for modern 'are', 'will' and 'were') are only used with the pronoun 'thou'. These pronouns and verb endings have a churchy ring to the modern ear because of their survival in religious rituals and Biblical translations, though they would not have evoked such an aura of reverence in Renaissance playgoers.

Just as pesky are those words that have fallen out of once common use, such as 'an' (meaning 'if'), 'hither' and 'thence' (meaning 'to here' and 'from there'), 'wont' (meaning 'predisposed or accustomed'), and 'fie' and 'go to', expressions of mild disgust. When Shylock after being summoned to dinner at Antonio's asks 'but wherefore should I go?' (*MV* 2.5.12), he is not confused about directions. The archaic word 'wherefore' means not 'where' but 'why', and so Shylock is pausing to ask himself why he should attend a meal where he knows he will not be truly welcome. It also takes a bit of effort to master vocabularies for arenas of Renaissance life that now have largely passed into history. For instance, nearly everyone in early modern England came into daily contact with horses, and so there was a substantial body of words and phrases familiar to all – bay, jade, roan, groom, pasterns, fetlocks, bit, rein, Dobbin, Barbary, to name a few – upon which Shakespeare could draw with assurance that his audience could follow. Old Giobbe's remark to his son Lancelet that 'thou hast got more hair on thy chin than Dobbin, my thill-horse, has on his tail' (*MV* 2.2.88–9) would have been a more immediate joke to Shakespeare's audience, since they would know that a thill-horse (or fill-horse) was a horse attached to a cart, and Dobbin a conventional name for an old horse, one likely to have a thinning tail. As one might expect, *The Merchant of Venice* is especially rich in the vocabulary of trade and finance, since Venice (like London) was an international commercial mecca and Londoners were likely to know basic business terms. The words 'bond', 'rate', 'worth', 'credit', 'venture', 'hazard', 'owe/own', 'fortune', 'commodity', 'use', 'thrift', 'sum', 'commodity', 'convert' and 'prodigal' all belong to the realm of early modern trade, and Shakespeare taps into the multiple meanings of these words to suggest how economic ways of thinking pervade the relationships, values and behaviour of the play's characters, even in areas of life seemingly far removed from business dealings.

Particularly interesting to students of the English language – and most troublesome for modern audiences of Shakespeare – are those words that in Renaissance English had quite different shades of meaning. These require us to adjust our modern expectations. When, for instance, Portia claims to the Prince of Morocco that 'in terms of choice I am not solely led / By nice direction of a maiden's eyes' (*MV* 2.1.13–14), by 'nice' she means 'foolish', perhaps 'lusty', maybe even 'precise', with a negative connotation of prissiness, all meanings current in Shakespeare's day. What she doesn't mean is 'pleasant' or 'kind', meanings not attached to the word 'nice' until the eighteenth century. It's important that we modern readers be aware of those historical semantic differences, lest we misinterpret. At the trial scene, the Duke's opening plea to Shylock that he show mercy ends with the line, 'we all expect a gentle answer, Jew!' (*MV* 4.1.33). The word 'gentle' certainly encompasses the modern meanings 'mild' and 'polite', but we miss the full meaning of the passage if we don't recognize that the primary meaning of 'gentle' in Shakespeare's day was 'noble' or 'aristocratic', with a play on the word 'gentile'. With that one word, the Duke's remark associates mercy not merely with kindness but with the ruling classes and Christianity, with the implication that Shylock's insistence upon justice is 'un-gentle' in every sense, cruel, vulgar, impudent and un-Christian.

Without some historical knowledge of language and the cultural practices that underlie it, we can also miss some of the sly humour of Shakespeare's writing. Note this little bit of banter between Lorenzo and Lancelet:

LORENZO
　Then bid them prepare dinner.
LANCELET
　That is done too, sir; only 'cover' is the word.

LORENZO
    Will you cover then, sir?
LANCELET
    Not so, sir, neither; I know my duty. (*MV* 3.5.45–9)

The comedy of this exchange is lost if we don't know that the word 'cover' refers to, among much else, laying down a tablecloth (a key prelude to a meal) and putting a hat on one's head, a potentially disrespectful gesture, since one was required to remove one's hat in the presence of one's social betters. The *Oxford English Dictionary* provides a reliable guide to the history of the meanings of words. It arranges definitions chronologically, with the earliest meanings of a word first and so on, along with examples that suggest the historical range within which each definition was current. In any case, it's important not to assume that words in *The Merchant of Venice* have the same meaning as they do in contemporary English. Historicizing one's sense of what even familiar words mean is a crucial skill to develop. If your reading of a passage rests upon a particular meaning of a word or phrase, it would be wise to check that the particular meaning was one that Shakespeare had access to, or you will be building your interpretation on a foundation of sand.

    All of these are obstacles to the first-time reader of Shakespeare, though Shakespearean English still shares enough with modern English that we can follow it with a little effort and some background on specific differences. However, what most divides us from Shakespeare's early modern audiences, I think, is our very different attitude towards poetically heightened language. By poetically heightened language, I mean language distinguished from everyday usage by its rhetorical patterning, elevated vocabulary, elaborate metaphors and imagery, and formal register. The language of most modern pop culture tends to be colloquial, informal and plain-spoken. The typical dialogue of mainstream film and television aims for maximum transparency and immediacy for a broad audience; the stress falls upon simplicity, clarity, contemporaneity, verisimilitude, minimalism and the appearance of spontaneity. Modern audiences have come to associate this plain style with sincerity and authenticity and to regard poetically heightened language as over-calculated, artificial, old-fashioned, snobbish, exclusionary or insincere (even though we modern audiences are more than willing to embrace very complex forms of visual expression).

For audiences of Shakespeare's play, however, attitudes towards poetically heightened language could not have been more different. Evidence suggests that Renaissance audiences, their ears trained by sermons and public speeches to take in long, rhetorically complex forms of discourse, came to plays expecting to hear sophisticated, elevated, poetically elaborate language. Writers played to their apparent delight in linguistic experimentation and wordplay. Spectators believed that poetical sophistication heightened and ennobled the drama's emotional content, deepened its intellectual power, and intensified its capacity to persuade and move the heart. Such assumptions were founded upon practices of classical poetry from Greek and Latin antiquity, the reigning model for literary excellence in the day. To hear grand, eloquent language was in great part why audiences attended the theatre, even for those who had little formal schooling. Lancelet and his father's malapropisms in 2.2 offer an important clue to attitudes towards elevated language in Shakespeare's theatre. Their misuse of grand words like 'infection' (for affection), 'frutify' (for certify), 'impertinent' (for pertinent) and 'defect' (for effect) is comical because they fail to measure up to the standard of verbal sophistication that rules elsewhere in the play. What's more, their elevated vocabulary may hint at the class aspirations that lie behind the desire to hear poetically sophisticated language: to go to the theatre was to experience verbal luxuriousness. Whether these rustics' mistakes indicate their own intellectual failings or witty mockery at their betters' expense is a question to be asked. In any case, to appreciate Shakespeare's artistic achievement we modern spectators must first bracket out our ingrained response to heightened language and embrace a different set of expectations – no easy task.

Rhetorical patterning

Shakespeare uses myriad techniques for supercharging his language, but four are of special interest to us here: rhetorical patterning, metre, imagery and wordplay. To illustrate these techniques in action, let's turn to the first few moments of the play. Shakespeare opens *The Merchant of Venice* with a mystery, Antonio's melancholy, a motif Shakespeare will repeat when he introduces Portia in the scene that follows. This melancholic note is an odd way to begin a comedy, and it is all the more odd because Antonio's melancholy has no clear motivation, as he himself observes:

> In sooth I know not why I am so sad.
> It wearies me; you say it wearies you;
> But how I caught it, found it or came by it,
> What stuff 'tis made of, whereof it is born,
> I am to learn; and such a want-wit sadness makes of me,
> That I have much ado to know myself. (*MV* 1.1.1–6)

At first glance this passage looks rather unartful, but it is a fine example of Shakespeare's poetic technique. Though Antonio's language is flat, almost entirely monosyllabic, without flash or flourish, that very flatness is entirely appropriate to Antonio's mopey mood. As a man who presents himself as serious (another meaning of the word 'sad', a meaning which Gratiano will pick up on soon enough), Antonio doesn't use poetic imagery in this passage. But his lines are nevertheless artfully patterned, with the word 'it' at the heart of various parallel phrases. That unspecific 'it', repeated again and again, underlines the naggingly unknown nature of the sadness Antonio is feeling, adding to the mystery of what 'it' is and where 'it' has come from. The short parallel phrases also have an obsessive quality about them, miming the way in which Antonio is running over versions of the same thought in his mind until he reaches the phrase that breaks the repetitive pattern and ends the sentence with the long-delayed main clause, 'I am to learn'. In the sentence which follows, the repeated 'm's, examples of alliteration, draw our attention to key words – 'makes ... me ... much ... myself'. The alliterative 'w' of 'want-wit' picks up important words from earlier in the speech – 'wearies ... wearies ... what ... whereof'. The verbal craft of this passage is hardly flashy. In fact, it is a good example of the classical aesthetic ideal, *art est celare artem* – the best art hides its artfulness. Nevertheless, we can see that the language has clearly been enhanced in ways appropriate to the topic. This speech provides an apt portrayal of the state of Antonio's mind and an intriguing introduction to a darker element that will become important to the play's complex notion of comedy.

This passage reminds us that Shakespeare need not use elevated vocabulary to heighten his dialogue, though he can do so to good effect. For an example of elevated language, we might look ahead in the first scene to Bassanio's conversation with Antonio, where he first introduces the idea of pursuing Portia. There Bassanio provides a glimpse into his past:

> 'Tis not unknown to you, Antonio,
> How much I have disabled mine estate
> By something showing a more swelling port
> Than my faint means would grant continuance.
> Nor do I make moan to be abridged
> From such a noble rate, but my chief care
> Is to come fairly off from the great debts
> Wherein my time, something too prodigal,
> Hath left me gaged. To you, Antonio,
> I owe the most in money and in love,
> And from your love I have a warranty
> To unburden all my plots and purposes
> How to get clear of all the debts I owe. (*MV* 1.1.122–34)

We learn much here: that Bassanio spent up his inheritance and went into debt to live beyond his means, that he has depended most of all upon Antonio's generosity, that he is now determined 'to get clear from all the debts I owe' with a plan that requires Antonio's help. This is the behaviour of a prodigal, one who squanders his family fortune in pursuit of aristocratic glory, a familiar Renaissance type. The prodigal is also a Biblical type, the protagonist of one of Jesus's parables. In that parable, the prodigal son, after spending all of his birthright and ending up in squalor, returns home to ask for his father's forgiveness. Unlike Antonio's fairly direct approach in his opening speech, Bassanio expresses himself here in an elevated vocabulary – 'disabled mine estate', 'grant continuance', 'abridged / From such a noble rate', 'a warranty / To unburden all my plots and purposes'. Perhaps his ornate way of speaking is intended to express respect to a friend to whom he owes money, but it also seems rather euphemistic, as if he is out to soften his sense of shame or evade full responsibility for his prodigality. The negations and equivocations with which he peppers his speech – 'not unknown to you', 'something showing a more swelling port', 'Nor do I make moan', 'something too prodigal' – only add to the impression of evasiveness. To some extent this is a non-confessional confession of past sins. By contrast, in a line that stands out for its directness of expression, Bassanio is crystal clear about his special relationship with Antonio: 'To you, Antonio, / I owe the most in money and in love'. The syntactic parallel between 'money' and 'love' lays out one of the central themes of the play, the ways in which economic considerations and emotional attachments are intertwined. In Venice and in Belmont, love is a means to get money and money a means to get or express love, something quite evident from Bassanio's trading upon Antonio's good will in the past. And this principle colours the conduct of many relationships in the play. The pursuit of love, like the pursuit of commercial profit, ends up involving issues of relative value, ownership, obligation, risk in the hopes of reward and the potential for loss.

Metre

Though even the most experimental modern drama is rarely versified, metrical verse is a regular feature of Shakespeare's drama, closely associated with the formal register. Not only does metre make dialogue easier to remember (as we all know from song lyrics), but it also serves, so Renaissance literary theorists had it, to elevate the ideas and deepen the emotions expressed in it, and it can provide clues to guide actors' performances. Because of this, we need some rudimentary knowledge of the basic mechanics of writing in poetic metre to understand Shakespeare's artistic choices in *The Merchant of Venice*. In English verse drama, to write metre is to establish a regular pattern of unstressed and stressed syllables into which dialogue can be set, something akin to the beat of a drum beneath a musical melody. For Shakespeare (and his contemporaries as well), the preferred rhythmic pattern was iambic pentameter. The basic iambic rhythm is of an unstressed syllable followed by a stressed syllable (da DUM); five iambic beats (da DUM da DUM da DUM da DUM da DUM) make up each single pentameter line. The opening line of *The Merchant of Venice* is an example of a perfect iambic pentameter line: 'in SOOTH i KNOW not WHY i AM so SAD'. To write good iambic pentameter verse, one must respect the native pattern of stressed and unstressed syllables in multisyllable words – one must say 'SYL la ble', not 'syl LA ble'. What's more, one must respect the typical ways in which speakers tend to stress words within sentences. In the first line of the play, notice how the stress falls naturally on the most important words within the line. If the writer fails to respect the native stress patterns of words or sentences, the result will sound clunky and strange, as if the metre were artificially imposed upon the line. The art of writing dialogue in iambic pentameter, then, is the art of choosing words that fit the metre and ordering them skilfully within the sentence so that the native stress patterns line up with the iambic rhythm, while at the same time conveying the sense clearly and economically and providing speech that sounds relatively natural. From a sheer technical point of view, Shakespeare's achievement as a writer of hundreds of lines of compelling verse dialogue is amazing. Knowing about the demands of metre and about the somewhat more flexible word order allowed by Renaissance English (an influence from Latin), we can account for many of Shakespeare's stylistic choices.

One risk of writing in metre is that it can become predictable and so dull. A merely competent drummer knows how to keep the beat and little else; a great drummer knows how to imply a regular beat while providing little variations – a cymbal accent, a syncopated fill on the snare – that keep things fresh and accent musical details. We can see Shakespeare address the multiple demands of rhythmic regularity and rhythmic variety in Antonio's opening speech:

> In sooth I know not why I am so sad.
> It wearies me, you say it wearies you.
> But how I caught it, found it, or came by it,
> What stuff 'tis made of, whereof it is born,
> I am to learn; and such a want-wit sadness makes of me,
> That I have much ado to know myself. (*MV* 1.1.1–6)

These lines are in mostly flawlessly regular iambic metre, which works to establish in the audience's ear the basic verse rhythm of the play. In line 4, for example, Shakespeare contracts the first 'it is' to ''tis' in order to maintain the iambic beat, but he leaves the second 'it is' alone. This sort of contraction is called elision, and it is one of the basic tools of the Renaissance verse writer. Notice too how in line 5, Shakespeare changes the word order of the more conventional 'sadness makes such a want-wit of me' to the phrasing 'such a want-wit sadness makes of me' in order to maintain a regular iambic rhythm. This technique, familiar from the line 'Columbus sailed the ocean blue', is known as inversion, another common trick.

At the same time, Shakespeare provides variety in this passage first of all by varying the lengths of phrases, placing pauses (indicated by commas) at different places within the ten-syllable lines. In line 2, the pause (called a *caesura*) falls after the fourth syllable in the line; in line 3, there are two pauses (*caesarae*) falling after the fifth and seventh syllables; in line 4, a single pause after the fifth syllable. Two lines in Antonio's speech break with the basic rhythm in different ways. Line 3 is hypermetrical; that is, it contains more syllables (eleven) than a regular iambic pentameter line does, a small metrical variation. More interestingly, line 5 is a fourteen-syllable line. In fact, some editors print it as two lines – the four-syllable 'I am to learn' and a very regular ten-syllable 'and such a want-wit sadness makes of me'. It's possible that something got lost in the transmission of Shakespeare's text, but as it stands that short phrase seems to demand a much longer pause at its end, as if what is absent here metrically echoes Antonio's lack of knowledge about his own sad state. That is, this metrically incomplete line seems to provide the actor with important information about how Shakespeare intended it to be delivered.

The first line of Salarino's reply to Antonio – 'Your mind is tossing on the ocean' (*MV* 1.1.8) – is another instance of a metrically irregular line, with nine syllables rather than the expected ten. In this case, by leaving the line incomplete and ending on an unstressed syllable, Shakespeare nicely conveys with rhythm the idea of mental restlessness and irresolution that Salarino suggests is the source of Antonio's melancholy. Imagine how different the effect would have been if Shakespeare had written 'Your mind is tossing on the windswept sea'. In the eighteenth century, editors often sought to correct Shakespeare's lines in the mistaken belief that metrical irregularities were mistakes or evidence of Shakespeare's inartistry. However, there is good reason to believe that Shakespeare's violations of a strict iambic pentameter beat are often intended and extraordinarily skilful.

Unrhymed iambic pentameter (called *blank verse*) is an exceptionally flexible metrical form, well suited to dialogue in English, but it is not the only metrical poetry that appears in *The Merchant of Venice*. The little ditty sung to accompany Bassanio's selection of a casket (*MV* 3.2.63–72), a passage to which we will return in Chapter Five, is in rhymed iambic tetrameter (four iambs to a line). The scrolls in the caskets are also in rhymed iambic tetrameter, the heavy beat at the end of each line landing squarely on the repeated rhymes and creating a sing-song effect appropriate to the fairy-tale plot. Shakespeare extends the rhymes on the scrolls for the gold and silver caskets, using the same one for nine and seven lines respectively. Besides being a bit of poetic bravado on Shakespeare's part, this extended rhyme contributes to the mocking tone of the words, evoking the kind of satirical verse pioneered by the Tudor poet John Skelton. After reading their scrolls Morocco and Aragon pick up this rhymed tetrameter in their replies, as if they were tacitly accepting their roles as comic losers by involuntarily speaking in the verse form of the scrolls. The verse form in Bassanio's case is quite different. The scroll for the lead casket is less obsessive in its rhyme scheme and so loses much of its sarcastic tone. After reading his scroll Bassanio responds not in sing-song tetrameter but in the more noble iambic pentameter. His reply is in rhymed couplets, but the elegant phrasing of the two long sentences he speaks cuts across the rhymes and gives a properly formal quality to his comments about Portia's ratifying kiss.

We might note here that Shakespeare uses rhyme for a variety of purposes in *The Merchant of Venice*. By convention a rhymed couplet signals the audience that a scene has ended, something necessary in a theatre where there is no curtain to close a scene. But as we've seen Shakespeare can also use rhyme as a means for shaping our impressions of character or tone. It can underline the proverbial quality of a thought, making it more quotable, as in Portia and Nerissa's mocking response to Aragon's departure:

PORTIA
    O, these deliberate fools! When they do choose,
    They have the wisdom by their wit to lose.
NERISSA
    The ancient saying is no heresy:
    'Hanging and wiving goes by destiny'.
(*MV* 2.9.79–82)

Rhyme can also subtly establish a link between characters. Bassanio ends his speech choosing the lead casket with a rhymed couplet – 'Thy paleness moves me more than eloquence, / And here choose I; joy be the consequence' (*MV* 3.2.106–7) – which gives his decision an added heft and finality. The fact that Portia's substantial aside (*MV* 3.2.108–14) is also in rhymed couplets connects the two characters. The formal echo underlines stylistically how her joy flows directly from his correct choice. And rhyme can be used to fine-tune tone. Gratiano, frustrated that Nerissa is peeved he gave away her ring to a clerk, offers his excuse in rhyme – 'Would he were gelt that had it, for my part, / Since you do take it, love, so much at heart' (*MV* 5.2.144–5). This passage, opening up the ring trick that ends the play, works to establish the comic nature of the conversation about rings that follows, a comic tone reiterated in Gratiano's three rhyming couplets that end the play.

Not all of *The Merchant of Venice* is written in verse. In prose are the initial exchange between Portia and Nerissa, Shylock's initial exchange with Bassanio, most scenes involving Lancelet Giobbe, and most notably the entirety of Act 3, Scene 1, where Shylock gives his most famous speech. It's an old commonplace that prose is reserved for lower-class characters and rustics, but it's evident from this list that this isn't quite the case. Why write these passages in prose? What do they have in common, if anything? The conversation between Portia and Nerissa and the Lancelet scenes are comic routines, somewhat detached from the main plot of the play. Their tone is informal, the humour mocking, unrefined; the rhetorical ennoblement that poetry might provide would be inappropriate and counterproductive.

The case of Shylock in 3.1 is more complex. That scene opens with an exchange between Solanio and Salerino mocking Shylock (*MV* 3.1.20–38), a passage not unlike Portia and Nerissa's mockery of the suitors. In both cases, these sequences trade in ethnic stereotypes. But the scene continues in prose as Shylock ominously warns that Antonio should 'look to his bond' (*MV* 3.1.42) and asks 'Hath not a Jew eyes?' (*MV* 3.1.53), and it continues in prose through his conversation with Tubal. This is emphatically not a comic scene. Why, then, is it not in verse, to lend tragic dignity and depth to what is the clearest articulation of Shylock's victimhood? Does this scene *need* the rhetorical heightening that verse might add? Is Shakespeare implicitly pairing Shylock with Lancelet Giobbe as outsiders excluded from the magical circle of the Venetian and Belmontian elite? Does Shakespeare deny Shylock poetry here because the comic genre demands that we not empathize with the villain who eventually must be defeated? Even so, we shouldn't fail to notice that even though it is not versified, Shylock's speech deploys to great effect the sort of rhetorical patterning and concatenating sequences of parallel phrases we saw in Antonio's opening speech. In Shakespeare's formal choices for this key scene, we see yet another indication of a divided attitude towards Shylock in *The Merchant of Venice*, a tension between the eloquent power given to Shylock's most important speech and the demands of stereotyping and comedy.

Imagery

Antonio's opening speech creates a mystery that his compatriots Salarino and Salario immediately try to solve. Their surmises illustrate for us another of Shakespeare's stylistic resources, imagery. Salarino's opening line, 'Your mind is tossing on the ocean' (*MV* 1.1.7), offers a theory that he and Salanio elaborate in the speeches that follow. In fact, Salarino's theory – 'you are worried about your goods at sea' – is itself expressed in terms of a compressed comparison – 'your worried thoughts are ships on an unsettled sea'. This draws on the long-standing symbolic association of the tempestuous ocean with uncertainty and potential danger (as opposed to the land, which is firm and safe). This direct comparison of two unlike things, Antonio's mind to a bobbing ship, is a *metaphor*, a poetic figure Shakespeare often deploys. Notice that he doesn't say 'Antonio's mind is a ship' even though he unmistakably implies it. This is a rather characteristic way that Shakespeare introduces metaphors.

Salarino then goes on to flesh out the comparison:

> Your mind is tossing on the ocean,
> There where your argosies with portly sail
> Like signiors and rich burghers on the flood,
> Or, as it were, the pageants of the sea,
> Do overpeer the petty traffickers
> That curtsy to them, do them reverence
> As they fly by them with their woven wings. (*MV* 1.1.7–13)

He likens Antonio's grand ships ('argosies') to successful merchants ('signiors and rich burghers'), and the sails billowing in the wind to the fat ('portly') bellies of those men. Other smaller ships are likened to minor tradesmen ('petty traffickers') who watch with awe and respect as Antonio's magnificent argosies sail away. Even the tiny detail that the ships 'fly by' reveals that they are apparently unladen with goods, leaving port empty rather than returning heavy with merchandise. In this case, Salarino's comparison of Antonio's ships to Venetian nobles is indirect, not direct, for he says that 'your argosies with portly sail' are '*Like* signiors and rich burghers' (1.1.8–9, my emphasis). Such a comparison using 'like' or 'as' is a *simile*, another favoured poetic figure of Shakespeare. And we might see the speech as a whole, where each new detail fleshes out the comparison between ships and signiors, as a dramatic version of an *epic simile*, a figure in which an indirect comparison is elaborated at some length. It is called an *epic* simile because this kind of extended comparison was a favourite of ancient epic poets.

Beautiful and visually compelling as Salarino's elaborated image is, what is its purpose in the scene? Why is this image developed, and what issues does it introduce? Salarino here introduces a major theme of the play, the element of risk involved with sending out ships onto the restless sea in search of exotic merchandise from which to profit. In the course of the play, Shakespeare will attach key words to this kind of risky enterprise – 'hazard', 'venture' – and develop the theme at great length, but here the idea is introduced in terms of a memorable image. Salarino suspects that Antonio's melancholy springs from worry about the potential loss of his investment, and his image clarifies what is at stake – not just Antonio's profits but also the potential loss of his social status, what makes him the envy of lesser merchants. With brevity and imaginative power, then, Shakespeare communicates to us Antonio's high standing, Salarino's perception of Antonio's attachment to superiority and the submission of others, and perhaps even a bit of Venetian social division into grand merchants and 'petty traffickers', a division that soon plays into the division between Christian merchants and Jewish usurers. The quasi-angelic detail of Antonio's ships 'fly[ing] by' on 'woven wings' may even put into play some subliminal association between Antonio's status as merchant and Christian holiness that Shakespeare can later develop.

Shakespeare often follows a poetic passage with a less florid speech or line that clarifies the idea he's just introduced. That, it would seem, is the function of Salanio's comment, 'Believe me, sir, had I such venture forth, / The better part of my affections would / Be with my hopes abroad' (*MV* 1.1.14–16). Salanio follows this with a couple of concrete examples – using a blade of grass to determine the strength of the wind, poring over maps to recheck his fleet's route. Salanio also introduces a key word in the play, 'venture', repeating it twice. This notion of taking a commercial risk in search of potential profit here applies strictly to Antonio's ships, but Shakespeare will soon expand upon that idea, extending it to the tale of the test of the three caskets, Portia's giving of the ring to Antonio, and Shylock's all-or-nothing insistence upon his bond.

By commenting that 'every object that might make me fear / Misfortune to my ventures, out of doubt, / Would make me sad' (*MV* 1.1.19–21), Salanio sets the stage for Salarino's long speech that follows. In it Salarino offers a poetic elaboration of ideas we've just heard. He suggests that Antonio's blowing upon hot soup to cool it would put him in mind of a strong wind at sea, threatening his ships; the sand in an hourglass would remind him of the unseen sandy shoals upon which a ship might become grounded and eventually swamped; the stony facade of a church would remind him of rocks upon which a ship might be dashed to pieces. In each case, some mundane detail – breath, sand, stone – triggers an image of disaster in Antonio's mind and causes him distress. This sort of thinking, where one detail is closely associated with another by contiguity, is akin to another poetic figure oft used by Shakespeare: the *metonym*. A metonym evokes an idea by naming one part of it, as in 'wave' for 'ocean' or 'bread' for 'meal', or by naming something commonly linked to it, as in 'crown' for 'monarch' or 'press' for 'journalism'.

As is Salarino's wont, he poetically embellishes the metonymic associations he raises, offering additional details that make the imagined disasters all the more concrete. In the case of the ship run aground, he pictures the 'wealthy *Andrew*' (the name of the ship) flipped topsy-turvy in the sand, with 'her high top' 'vailing' to 'kiss her burial' (*MV* 1.1.26–8), that is, stooping to the low place where it has become buried. For a Renaissance audience keenly attuned to questions of status, this image suggests a terrible loss of social standing. Antonio's ship, likened just a few lines earlier to a wealthy signior, is now lowering its 'high top' like a hat 'lower than her ribs', an act of humiliating submission where once it provoked reverence from 'petty traffickers'. In the case of the ship on the rocks, the image is even more dire. The rocks 'touching but my gentle vessel's side, / Would scatter all her spices on the stream, / Enrobe the roaring waters with my silks' (*MV* 1.1.31–3). This image would seem to suggest a sudden sword attack upon an unsuspecting 'gentle' victim, after which the wounded ship bleeds expensive merchandise upon the waves. If we recall that the act that kills Christ on the cross is a spear wound to his side, there is perhaps reason to see a quasi-religious association lurking in the background. In any case, both images picture the threatened ship in human terms, making it easier for Antonio to identify with it. Salarino sums up this portrayal with the memorable line 'but even now worth this, / And now worth nothing?' (*MV* 1.1.34–5). The parallel phrases, the stark contrast between 'this' and 'nothing', the sense of sudden disaster underlined by the two 'now's, and the extended meaning of the word 'worth' which now has more than a financial meaning – all of these details underline the frightening sense of commercial, social and even bodily vulnerability that Salarino thinks Antonio's venture has invited. Little wonder he confidently declares, 'I know Antonio / Is sad to think upon his merchandise' (*MV* 1.1.38–9).

Salarino and Salanio's opening conversation illustrates the power of metaphor, the ways in which compelling comparisons and images can guide (or misguide) our train of thought. This opening sequence also shows us how economic ways of thinking can invade every part of human experience, the characters' thoughts, emotions, ways of speaking, relationships with others, even in this case their imaginations, in ways they don't consciously recognize. A visit to church, the place where we might seek spiritual solace, escape from the workaday world and put the pursuit of wealth in perspective, instead can remind us of our precarious commercial involvements. Even the image of Christ's sacrifice for mankind's salvation turns into just another thought-prompt for the possible loss of one's merchandise on the unpredictable sea. Shakespeare's writing is unusually rich with metaphor and imagery, and he often layers or compresses images in dazzling fashion, as he does in these speeches. It's this metaphorical and imagistic density, perhaps more than any other single quality, that characterizes Shakespeare's writing, and it's that quality that seems to challenge modern audiences most, accustomed as we are to a much plainer verbal style. Knowing this may help you, with some practice, become a more adept reader of Shakespeare and help you appreciate his artistry.

Wordplay

In his reply to Salerino and Salanio, Antonio firmly denies that business concerns are the cause of his melancholy. Even so, the terms of his denial – he has diversified his ventures – suggest that he has been thinking about his potential financial risk and has hedged against it. In his denial, in fact, Antonio twice uses another key word that epitomizes the connection between economic concerns and the unpredictability this opening sequence dwells upon. That word is 'fortune', meaning both 'wealth' and 'chance or fate', and it can have either meaning both times Antonio says it: 'I thank my fortune for it', 'nor is my whole estate / Upon the fortune of this present year' (*MV* 1.1.40, 42–3). Antonio's repeated use of this word reminds us of how fully commerce and chance are intertwined. Interestingly enough, Antonio himself may not yet appreciate this fact. That is to say, Shakespeare may put this word 'fortune' in his mouth to offer us some ironic commentary on his confident denial, if we are attuned enough to language's richness to hear it.

Modern readers tend to think of wordplay like puns or *double entendres* as the stuff of adolescent humour, the lowest form of entertainment, and it's true that Shakespeare finds it hard to resist a good 'quibble' in his comedies, as the eighteenth-century critic Samuel Johnson famously grumbled. Certainly Shakespeare and his original audiences appreciated a good verbal joke. When old Giobbe, thinking Lancelet is dead, laments that 'the boy was the very staff of my age, the very prop', Lancelet has some fun with the literal meanings of 'staff' and 'prop': 'Do I look like a cudgel, or a hovel post, a staff, or a prop?' (*MV* 2.2.61–4). The joke is all the funnier if we remember that Lancelet's name includes the word 'lance', that is, 'spear'. He may not look like a staff or prop, but he is named like one. But Shakespeare often uses wordplay to more serious ends – to highlight key themes, to suggest a conceptual affinity between different ideas, to introduce irony or layers of meaning the characters may not be aware of. In his conversation with Bassanio later in this opening scene, for example, Antonio speaks of devoting 'my purse, my person, my extremest means' (*MV* 1.1.138) to Bassanio's financial redemption. The pun on 'purse' and 'person' isn't meant to elicit a chuckle so much as to suggest a deep link – both at the level of sound and at the level of ideas – between Antonio's financial resources and his very body. That link will soon become a central issue when Antonio's investments are lost at sea and he is faced with losing a pound of flesh. What's more, Antonio's offer of his person along with his purse indicates an intensity of emotion that hints he may be feeling more than the typically close bond of Renaissance male friendship. That suggestion of homoeroticism is all the more viable if we pick up on the bawdy associations of 'purse'. The link between money and personhood plays out in *The Merchant of Venice* in all kinds of ways – in Bassanio's exploitation of Antonio's friendship, in Bassanio and Portia's relationship, in the ways that religious identities are allied with attitudes towards different kinds of profit-taking, in the connection between Shylock's daughter Jessica and his ducats, in the link between the taking of Shylock's wealth in the trial scene and the destruction of his Jewish identity. Here Shakespeare establishes that key idea with a memorable bit of wordplay before exploring its many ramifications.

I've dwelt upon the opening scene of *The Merchant of Venice* as a way of illustrating several basic facets of Shakespeare's poetic technique, elements we will be returning to again and again throughout this book. Shakespeare draws upon a handful of simple but powerful resources – rhetorical patterning, iambic verse, metaphor and imagery, and wordplay – to achieve complicated and nuanced effects, to reveal facets of characters' personalities, to shape our moment-by-moment experience of the action, to lay out key issues. As readers or viewers, we can best understand the artistry of Shakespeare's writing by keeping a close eye on each of these poetic elements, always asking ourselves how he is using them and to what purpose, and we should look for those moments, phrases or even single words that encapsulate the issues he puts in motion.

Writing matters – writing criticism

The art of writing well about Shakespeare ultimately rests upon a single skill – your ability to read closely. It's crucial, then, to develop an eye for stylistic details and patterns and to learn how to ask interesting questions about them. One advantage of reading over hearing *The Merchant of Venice* is that you can slow down the pace for those patches where imagery is especially dense or places where Shakespeare's sentence structure demands extra time to work out. Better yet is to combine both approaches at once: pair your reading with listening at the same time to an audio version of the play. Reading will focus your mind on details of Shakespeare's text, while hearing the language performed will often clarify the meaning and tone of passages, as well as help you develop an ear for the spoken texture of Shakespeare's language and speed up your comprehension. To be sure, viewing film and video performances can also be useful in understanding the text, but those performances, because they engage the eyes as well as the ears, can push Shakespeare's language into the background, particularly when you are first encountering the play. Just keep in mind that many audio performances of Shakespeare work from abbreviated scripts.

What to pay attention to as you read? Keep an eye (and ear) out for repeated words, images or metaphors that seem to serve as a focus for a given passage; phrases in parallel construction or in strong contrast; oddities of metre, rhyme or sentence structure; and moments where the dialogue exploits multiple meanings of a word or toys with similarities in sound between words. All are ways Shakespeare signals to his audience what is most important in a passage, and taken together, they establish patterns of meaning that extend throughout a scene or plotline. Mark these stylistic features as you read, and try to give a label to or description of the details you've isolated. Though mastering basic terminology for stylistic features of Shakespeare's writing may seem tedious, learning those terms will actually help draw your attention to the features they name and make your analysis of them more precise. As you collect details of language for analysis, it's helpful always to place them in historical perspective. What, as best as you can determine, did that word or image mean to Shakespeare and his audience? It's here that a little research in the *Oxford English Dictionary* or other sources can protect you from the sin of anachronism, that is, of unwittingly projecting onto *The Merchant of Venice* meanings from the present which didn't yet exist. To be sure, directors and adaptors often introduce anachronisms in their works in an effort to make Shakespeare's work relevant to the present, but typically they do so consciously, as an act of adaptation. Attending to the meaning of the script as Shakespeare's original audience might have construed it requires you to become more sensitive to the history of the English language and more cognizant of the different shades of meaning it makes available, both now and in Shakespeare's day. Anyone who's learned a musical instrument knows that at first there's a learning curve, sometimes even a steep one, but with practice you develop a more finely tuned sense of the instrument's basic characteristics and subtleties. So too with Shakespeare's language.

Isolating details of style and giving them labels, however, is not enough, interesting though those details may be in themselves. Your ultimate object is to identify patterns across those individual details and create a claim about the significance of those patterns. A pattern might consist of a recurring word or image that points to the same issue or theme, consistent pairing of two elements (say, Shylock's daughter Jessica and ducats), repeated contrasts (say, between the language of mercy and the language of justice), an element of structural or stylistic design (say, the association of Lancelet with prose or the casket scrolls with iambic tetrameter), a sequence of words or images that indicate a character's change from one state to another (say, the changing ways that Bassanio refers to Portia's ring) or something else. You begin to build your case by collecting many noteworthy details and thinking about what characteristics or meanings they share. You're certain to find several patterns among the stylistic features you're examining. Think of what you're doing as teasing out the thematic or stylistic threads of the play, and of course you should expect there to be many of them. Not every detail will be relevant to every pattern you will notice, so expect to do some sifting as you analyse, discarding this detail as less significant, highlighting that detail as especially revealing or dense with meaning.

I find it helpful to keep these questions in mind as I analyse what I've found: since Shakespeare might have told this tale in any number of ways, why did he choose to tell it *this* way? Why use this word or phrase or image or metaphor, and not another? How does this set of details point to some larger concept, some overarching issue raised by the play? How are these details *significant* (all of them may not be)? And not all details are created equal: which among them is a particularly substantial example of the theme, idea, controversy or stylistic strategy you've isolated? The latter, a *telling detail*, should provide you with lots of material to work on and reward especially close analysis. Analysis of a telling detail is often a good place to begin the body of your essay or to end it. It's a good idea to try to work inductively, from a pattern of details outwards to its larger implications: what can the patterns you've identified tell us about, say, Antonio's developing mindset, Portia's understanding of love, Shakespeare's perspective on the issue of 'ornament', the nature of comedy in the play's final acts, or the like?

In order to practise the skills you'll need to develop, choose a passage or a single scene from *The Merchant of Venice* you find intriguing, puzzling or compelling. Reread your selection several times, each time focusing on just one of the elements discussed in this chapter – patterned language and sentence structure, metre and rhyme, imagery and metaphor, and wordplay. Typically (though not always) you'll find several examples of each if you've selected a substantial passage. Mark what you find, and after you've made four passes make a list of what you see as the most significant details. The aim here is to slow down your reading speed and concentrate your attention on each sort of stylistic feature. With a bit of practice you'll ferret out these features more intuitively, but at first it's helpful to proceed slowly and methodically, just as practising scales and simple melodies gives a musician the skills eventually to play naturally from finger memory. After you've compiled your list of details, stand back and look for patterns – some shared idea or issue, a noteworthy contrast, a sequence indicating an arc of development. Why say it *that* way? Not every detail you've identified will contribute to the pattern, but put a check by those that do. Then think a bit about which of the details seems to you most important or which best illustrates the idea that emerges from the evidence you've gathered. Think of this as an anchoring detail, one you'll want to expand upon when you come to it in your essay.

This exercise springs from a very fundamental article of faith about Shakespeare's method – that the content and style of *The Merchant of Venice*, indeed all of Shakespeare's writing, are artfully wedded to each other. That is, Shakespeare closely coordinates what he wants to say and how he chooses to say it so that he can boost the visceral impact and intellectual sophistication of his work. That's why attending to nuances of his verbal style – his turns of phrase, his choice of words, his elaboration of images – is so very essential to understanding the content of his writing.

CHAPTER TWO

Language in Print I: Texts from Texts

Shakespeare is not an 'original' writer in the usual modern sense of the word. Only rarely does he create a plot or a character entirely out of whole cloth. Rather, he is a master of the venerable art of making texts out of others' texts. This is not in any way to denigrate Shakespeare's creativity or achievement. As anyone who's enjoyed the music of a master DJ can tell you, a great work of art can be made by remixing someone else's materials. Such is the case with *The Merchant of Venice*, the main sources of which were tales that appear in two collections, Giovanni Fiorentino's *Il Pecorone* and the anonymous *Gesta Romanorum*. In addition to these and other sources for his main plots and characters, Shakespeare often alludes to myths and famous figures from a variety of works known in his day. We can learn much about Shakespeare's artistic methods and intentions by tracing how he reshaped the tales from which *The Merchant of Venice* is taken and how he deployed stories, images and references from the cultural archive of his day.

Sources

Il Pecorone and *Gesta Romanorum*, from which Shakespeare probably took the central plot motifs for *The Merchant of Venice*, are collections of medieval romances, sprawling tales of adventure and the fantastic. The bond with a treacherous Jew comes from *Il*

Pecorone (*The Sheep*, that is to say, *The Fool*), an Italian collection of tales by Giovanni Fiorentino written in the late fourteenth century but not issued in a printed edition until 1558.[1] Fiorentino's collection is modelled roughly on Boccaccio's famous collection *The Decameron*, in which multiple tales are told on successive days. It is the first story told on the fourth day upon which Shakespeare draws. For the motif of the casket test, Shakespeare turned to the 39th tale in the *Gesta Romanorum* (*Deeds of the Romans*), an anonymous compilation dating from the turn of the fourteenth century and a perennially popular book. Shakespeare probably knew this tale from a much-republished English version by the printer Richard Robinson, a version known as *Certain Selected Histories for Christian Recreation*. Both source tales are complicated narratives rich with supernatural events, friendship and treachery, voyages and shipwrecks, and happy endings after the protagonists have endured some suffering. In both cases, Shakespeare takes up only part of the source plots, though he also lifts various names, personality types, relationships between characters and key details (such as the pound of flesh, the ring test, and the inscriptions and metals of the caskets). Tracing what Shakespeare saw fit to use, how he spliced plots together and reshaped them, and what he thought necessary to change or omit can help us identify more precisely what Shakespeare saw as crucial to his purposes.

Interestingly, both of these sources involve marriage tests, a common romance motif and perhaps what prompted Shakespeare to combine these plots. Kenneth Muir suggests that the plotline of one source helped address the defects of the other.[2] In *Il Pecorone* the Lady of Belmonte is a widow who promises to marry any suitor who succeeds in sleeping with her; if he fails to do so, however, her penalty is to take his goods and send him on his way. What we discover is that she has rigged the test by drugging her potential suitors before bed. Though bits of her challenge remain in the provisos of the casket test – losing suitors must give up not their goods but their rights to woo in the future – the Lady's behaviour was too risqué for the Elizabethan stage. So Shakespeare substituted the more demure plotline from the *Gesta Romanorum*, changing the Lady from a widow into a maiden and the test from one of the suitor's sexual prowess to one of his concept of value.

Shakespeare makes many changes small and large as he shapes his raw materials into a coherent play, but I will focus on just three, leaving the rest for you to explore: the relationship between the Antonio and Bassanio characters, the nature of the casket test and the characterization of Shylock. In *Il Pecorone* Giannetto is the third son of a wealthy merchant family, who upon the death of his father Bindo is left without a legacy. (Giannetto's situation is typical of the time, for the eldest sons inherit all the family's wealth.) Before his death Giannetto's father arranges for his son to be raised by his godfather Ansaldo, a wealthy merchant of Venice who provides Giannetto the wealth to become an admired Venetian gentleman. Giannetto is the model for Shakespeare's Bassanio, Ansaldo for Antonio. However, Shakespeare significantly alters the character of each and the relationship between the two. Fiorentino's Giannetto wisely uses the wealth provided by Ansaldo to build a reputation for gentlemanly honour and courtesy that 'almost everybody in Venice thought well of him, seeing him to be so prudent, agreeable, and unusually courteous'.[3] Only later in the tale does Giannetto lose Ansaldo's fortune in pursuing the unnamed Lady of Belmont, the crafty widow who twice tricks him out of treasure before Giannetto manages to wed her. Shakespeare's Bassanio, we might remember, is at first presented as a prodigal. He confesses that he has squandered his own inheritance and got himself into debt by pursuing 'a more swelling port / Than my faint means would grant continuance' (*MV* 1.1.124–5). This bit of information complicates Bassanio's character considerably. From the start Bassanio is eager for redemption, yet Shakespeare leaves his motives unclear: is he seeking moral reform or just a path out of debt? Does his wooing of Portia spring from love or legacy-hunting? The effect is that the pursuit of love and money is far more intertwined in Shakespeare's version of the tale, as is their uncertain relationship to virtue.

Shakespeare alters Ansaldo's character even more. Fiorentino's Ansaldo is resolutely cheerful, pious and loving, enduring Giannetto's repeated loss of his goods with patience. Shakespeare's Antonio, by contrast, is plagued by unexplained melancholy, and his treatment of Shylock, though apparently motivated partly by faith, is troublingly savage. Though Ansaldo wants Giannetto to see him before he goes under the Jew's knife, just as Antonio does, he does not engage in the guilt-tripping that saturates Antonio's letter to Bassanio, nor does he speak of himself in the self-pitying way that Antonio does, as 'the tainted wether of the flock, / Meetest for death' (*MV* 4.1.113–14).

Most notably, Ansaldo's feelings for Giannetto are explicitly those of a father for a surrogate son. Antonio's relationship to Bassanio, that of an older friend for a younger, is in many ways more intense and less clearly defined. Indeed, the bond Antonio strikes with Shylock seems a means by which Antonio can bind himself to Bassanio as Bassanio leaves to pursue a new lover, Portia, a dynamic entirely absent from Fiorentino's tale. Many commentators have seen in Antonio's behaviour elements of an unrequited homosexual desire for Bassanio or perhaps the hint of a past relationship that ended in ambiguous friendship. Such homoerotic desire, impossible for Antonio to express publically in Christian Venice (or in Shakespeare's England), might explain much about his behaviour: his odd melancholy; his vehement denial that his 'sadness' springs from love; his tearful goodbye to Bassanio reported in *MV* 2.8.36–50; the hints at emotional blackmail in his relationship with Bassanio; the element of self-loathing in his gestures towards martyrdom; perhaps even his cruel treatment of Shylock, which we might see as his projection onto Shylock of his sense of his own sin. If this is the case, Antonio's desire for a bond with Bassanio is fulfilled at the trial when Bassanio declares his willingness to sacrifice Portia (and himself) to save Antonio, a declaration that then prompts Portia to renegotiate the place of herself and Antonio in Bassanio's affections through the ring trick. Nothing in Fiorentino's version corresponds to this. Indeed, when Giannetto reluctantly gives the lawyer his ring, he is very clear about his absolute commitment to his wife: 'I love her better than anything else in the world ... She is as beautiful and wise as anyone Nature ever made' (Bullough, vol. 1, 474). The theme of intense male-male attachment seems solely Shakespeare's addition, one that complicates Shakespeare's consideration of the nature of love and its relationship to money.

Some echoes of vocabulary suggest that Shakespeare takes the casket test relatively directly from Richardson's version of the *Gesta Romanorum*,[4] though in the *Gesta* it is a woman's virtue being tested, not a man's. Shakespeare clearly lifts the inscriptions on the three caskets for use in his own play, but the small changes he makes do much to reveal his reconception of the casket test. In Richardson's version, the inscriptions on the gold and silver caskets are, respectively, 'Whoso chooseth me shall find that [what] he deserveth' and 'Whoso chooseth me shall find that [what] his nature desireth'.[5] In the allegorical gloss included with the *Gesta*, the gold casket is said to represent 'some worldly men, both mighty men & rich' (*Gesta Romanorum*, 103v) who eventually discover that their worldly achievements mean nothing to God and so deserve damnation. The silver casket represents 'some Justices & wise men of this world' (*Gesta Romanorum*, 103v) who learn that their intellectual skills won't allow them to argue their way into salvation. In the tale itself, the heroine – known only as 'the Maiden' – rejects both caskets, associating the gold one with deceptive appearances and the silver with 'the lust of the flesh' (*Gesta Romanorum*, 100v). Instead, she chooses the unpromising lead casket, which bears the inscription, 'whoso chooseth me, shall find that [what] God hath disposed for them' (*Gesta Romanorum*, 100r). As the Maiden makes clear, the lead casket symbolizes a simple faith in God or, as the allegorical gloss puts it, 'a simple life and a poor, which the chosen men choose, that they may be wedded to our blessed Lord Jesu Christ by humility [and] obeisance' (*Gesta Romanorum*, 104r). In the *Gesta*, then, the casket test examines one's ability to reject the attractions of this world in favour of religious devotion. The Maiden's correct choice demonstrates her fitness to be a proper Christian wife.

In *The Merchant of Venice*, Shakespeare makes some significant changes. He reassigns the 'desireth' label to the gold casket and the 'deserveth' to the silver so that gold becomes the symbol of an object of worldly desire and silver a symbol of aristocratic merit or 'desert'. In the *Gesta Romanorum*, the choice of caskets tests one's Christian faith, but in Shakespeare's play, the philosophical speeches of Morocco and Aragon indicate that the choice tests how each suitor assigns value to an object. In Morocco's case, he contemplates who else might desire each symbolic casket; in Aragon's case, he judges in terms of how much he thinks he should merit each casket. We can see this change in the nature of the test most clearly in the substantial change Shakespeare makes in the inscription on the lead casket. In the *Gesta Romanorum*, that inscription reads, 'Whoso chooseth me, shall find that [what] God hath disposed for them' (100r); in *The Merchant of Venice*, the inscription reads, 'Who chooseth me must give and hazard all he hath' (*MV* 2.7.16). Shakespeare replaces the *Gesta*'s reference to God with the notion of 'hazarding', that is, taking a huge risk without ensuring a guaranteed return. To be sure, hazarding bears some resemblance to Christian faith – both involve trusting in a happy outcome despite appearances – but hazarding is an economic principle, not a religious one, one that locates an object's value in how much one is willing to risk for it. This small change, then, extends the choice of caskets in new thematic directions central to the play. That choice now tests Bassanio's fundamental system of value in the realms of love, trade and, yes, religion, all linked under the single multivalent term 'hazard'.

Shakespeare's portrayal of Shylock departs significantly from that of the Jew in *Il Pecorone* and indeed from the portrayal of stage Jews in most of the plays that preceded *The Merchant of Venice*. In *Il Pecorone*, the Jew who engages Ansaldo in a bond for a pound of flesh is quite clear about his reason for enforcing it – 'he wished to commit this homicide in order to be able to say that he had put to death the greatest of the Christian merchants' (Bullough, vol. 1, 472). Fiorentino's depiction accords with the stereotype of the bloodthirsty Jew whose hatred for Christians is simply a given. At the trial the Jew – he is never named – offers no justification for his actions other than they are his legal right. By contrast, Shakespeare gives Shylock a substantial biography. We learn that Shylock has long endured abuse by Antonio and that his daughter has eloped with a Christian and taken with her his money and jewels, a history of Christian mistreatment that provides potentially sympathetic motives for his actions. His allusions to Biblical precedent and his references at trial to having made a covenant suggest that Shylock operates (or seems to operate) out of religious principle and that the trial is a contest not just between hero and villain but between Jewish and Christian ideals, justice and mercy. Yet Shakespeare also goes out of his way to introduce moral ambiguities. In Shakespeare's version, Shylock first presents the bond as a 'merry sport' (*MV* 1.3.141), a preposterously good deal offered to gain Antonio's friendship, though it's entirely possible Shylock presents the matter as a joke so as to trick Antonio into thinking the penalty for default isn't serious. In Fiorentino's version, the Jew is explicit that the bond gives him the right to 'take a pound of flesh from any part of [Ansaldo's] body he pleased' (Bullough, vol. 1, 469). There is no suggestion that Ansaldo is deceived as to the danger of this bargain. As in *The Merchant of Venice*, the trial scene in Fiorentino's tale involves the Lady of Belmont in disguise as a lawyer, the Jew's unwillingness to take more than the principal in payment, the awarding of the pound of Ansaldo's flesh with the stricture that the pound be exact and no blood be shed, and the lawyer's insistence that the Jew take the pound of flesh or nothing. The jeering of the crowd makes explicit the moral of the episode: 'he who lays snares for others is caught himself' (Bullough, vol. 1, 474).

Shakespeare, however, takes the judgement much further. Defeated, Fiorentino's Jew simply tears up the bond and storms out of the courtroom and the story. Shakespeare, however, extends the judgement of Shylock, Portia using legal manoeuvring to deprive him of his livelihood, his legacy and his religion, forcing him to assent to it all by publically admitting 'I am content' (*MV* 4.1.390), one of the most devastating lines in the play. Shakespeare's extension of the court's judgement, the insistence upon not just defeating Shylock but publically humiliating and obliterating him, has suggested to many a response all out of proportion to the offence, another example of cruel Christian bigotry masquerading as a neutral administration of the law. Shakespeare's addition raises all over again the ethics of Christian behaviour in the play, particularly regarding the Venetians' treatment of the Jews.

Allusions

Allusions are one of the time-honoured poetic resources Shakespeare uses to flesh out the meaning of his works. Allusions offer him a means for linking his story with other stories, adding authority, resonance and symbolic texture to plot and characterization. Shakespeare depends upon his audience having a working knowledge of famous figures and tales from his own day and from history. To be sure, over time many of these references have fallen out of cultural memory, and so some of Shakespeare's allusions now pose a significant barrier to the modern reader. The problem is even greater for those reading Shakespeare outside of an Anglo-American context. But this problem hovers over all cultural production. Think about it: who in a hundred years will be able to follow an episode of *The Simpsons* without a bit of study? And who could deny that it would be worth the effort? Necessarily, then, to study Shakespeare is to study other texts upon which he draws, just as it is for almost all other works of art.

Allusions to specific events, landmarks or people allow Shakespeare to establish a time frame or setting with great economy. Shylock's repeated reference to the Rialto, a main bridge over the Grand Canal and one of the city's famous architectural marvels, does much to situate the play firmly in Venice. This was particularly so since the bridge had just been rebuilt in 1592, only a few years before Shakespeare wrote his play – it would have been a landmark fresh in the minds of those who were well travelled. Since the Rialto was (and is) lined with shops, reference to it also helps to emphasize the city's reputation as a major mercantile and banking hub and to place Shylock at its centre. To take another example, we are told that Balthasar, the law clerk whom Portia impersonates at the trial scene, is from Padua. Why this city? Certainly Padua is convenient to Venice, within a day's horseback ride. But more important was Padua's formidable reputation as a college town and intellectual centre.[6] Its university was the second oldest in Italy, originally founded as a law school, and it boasted such famous alumni as Dante and Copernicus. Galileo taught there. In *The Taming of the Shrew* Lucentio arrives in Padua with the intention of studying philosophy, and in *Much Ado about Nothing* Benedick is said to be from Padua, a hometown befitting his witty personality. It is telling that Doctor Bellario, the learned lawyer who endorses Portia/Balthasar's credentials, would be from Padua, a town recognized as a place of formidable learning. The allusion to Padua, then, is not just a random bit of local colour. It establishes Portia/Balthasar's intellectual authority and perhaps smooths the way for accepting the twisted legal logic she uses in the trial scene – since Balthasar is from Padua, so the courtroom might think, 'his' legal reasoning must be sound. These examples illustrate how allusion to a single name can provide us with considerable information, if we dig into the associations it might have for Shakespeare's audience.

Shylock and the Bible

Shakespeare also uses allusion to famous works of the past to give his writing added authority and greater poetic depth. Two of his favourite touchstones in *The Merchant of Venice* are the Bible and classical mythology, and how he uses such references is crucial for understanding the mindsets of his main characters and the themes of his play. A particularly illuminating allusion, one often perplexing for first-time audiences, is Shylock's discussion of Jacob and Laban's sheep in 1.3. When Antonio expresses his hostility to charging interest for loans, Shylock offers this story in response:

> When Laban and himself were compromised
> That all the eanlings which were streaked and pied
> Should fall as Jacob's hire, the ewes, being rank,
> In the end of autumn turned to the rams;
> And, when the work of generation was
> Between these woolly breeders in the act,
> The skilful shepherd peeled me certain wands,
> And, in the doing of the deed of kind,
> He stuck them up before the fulsome ewes,
> Who, then conceiving, did in eaning time
> Fall parti-colour'd lambs, and those were Jacob's. (*MV* 1.3.74–84)

Shylock's tale is taken fairly directly from Genesis 30. Jacob, weary of mistreatment by his uncle Laban and yearning to return home, asks Laban for the wages he is owed. When Laban says 'name your price', Jacob asks for the pied and striped animals of his flock, that is, the one with the less desirable wool, the impure ones. Ever the unscrupulous uncle, Laban then removes all the pied and striped animals from his flock and puts them under the care of his sons, depriving Jacob yet again of his just deserts. Undeterred, Jacob hatches a plan: he will force the remaining animals to give birth to pied and striped offspring by putting up peeled branches before the animals as they breed. His plan depends upon the folk belief that what one sees at the moment of conception influences the appearance of one's young. By viewing peeled, that is, speckled or striped branches as they breed, the animals yield pied and striped offspring that Jacob can then claim as his own, thereby thwarting his uncle's intention to cheat him of what he is due.

What is the purpose of this odd tale? First of all, it establishes a pattern that holds throughout the play – consistent with his status as 'the Jew', Shylock is consistently associated with Biblical allusions from the Torah or Old Testament. He swears by 'Jacob's staff' (*MV* 2.5.35) and imputes bastardy to Lancelet by calling him 'the fool of Hagar's offspring' (*MV* 2.5.42); his former wife, we learn in 3.1.110, is named Leah, a name associated with the Jacob story; in the trial scene,

Shylock praises Portia's performance as judge by comparing her to Daniel, the wise prophet (*MV* 4.1.119). One function of the Jacob story, the first of the play's Biblical allusions, is to establish Shylock's devotion to the Jewish tradition, the fountainhead of his sensibility. Shylock is especially partial to Jacob, in part because of Jacob's cleverness in making profit, in part because of Jacob's special place in the Jewish patriarchy – 'this Jacob from holy Abram was, / As his wise mother wrought in his behalf, / The third possessor' (*MV* 1.3.68–70; i.e., Abraham was Jacob's grandfather and the third Israelite to strike a covenant with God). Shylock also knows the New Testament well enough to use references to it as a weapon against the Christians. He expresses his disgust for pork (a forbidden food in Jewish dietary law) by snarkily alluding to the tale of Jesus casting demons into a herd of swine[7] – 'Yes, to smell pork, to eat of the habitation which your prophet the Nazarite conjured the devil into' (*MV* 1.3.30–1), and when raging against Bassanio, Gratiano and his rebellious daughter he refers to the criminal who was pardoned instead of Christ in the crucifixion story – 'These be the Christian husbands! I have a daughter: / Would that any of the stock of Barabbas / Had been her husband than a Christian' (*MV* 4.1.291–3).[8]

More important is Shylock's deployment of Biblical allusion to defend his practice of usury. Loaning money for interest was officially forbidden for Christians because of Christ's words condemning it: 'And if you lend to those from whom you expect repayment, what credit is that to you? Even sinners lend to sinners, expecting to be repaid in full. But love your enemies, do good to them, and lend to them without expecting to get anything back' (Luke 6.34–5). For Jews, however, usury was not forbidden by scripture. Deuteronomy specifies that Jews could charge interest to those outside the faith but not to those within it: 'You may lend to a foreigner upon interest; but you shall not lend to your brother upon interest' (Deuteronomy 23.2). Because Jews were legally barred from most other professions in Christian Europe, they provided the economic service Christians could not, usury. It was a service the new expansion in trade demanded, since one needed capital to finance voyages that might turn a profit. Yet even so usury remained stigmatized, regarded (officially at least) as ungodly, uncharitable and especially unnatural in its making money from money, rather than making money from selling goods or labour. Of course, this distinction tries to dodge a crucial question: in the end, what is the real ethical difference between making a profit and taking interest? The central difference, as we shall see, is risk or 'hazard', an economic and moral principle the Christians claim to embrace, and engaging in risk involves having faith in the operation of providence and being willing to endure loss.

Shylock's allusion to Jacob addresses the stigma of usury. Like Jacob's clever strategy with the ewes, Shylock suggests, usury manipulates money's capacity for 'breeding', for making profit. Shylock sees 'skilful' Jacob's ingenuity in reaping profit in this fashion as Biblically sanctioned, even as a sign of God's blessing – 'This was a way to thrive, and he was blest: / And thrift is blessing, if men steal it not' (*MV* 1.3.85–6). So, the implication runs, is Shylock's charging of interest a blessed way to thrive. Shakespeare makes sure we make the connection between this story and usury. To Antonio's question 'is your gold and silver ewes and rams?', Shylock jokes, 'I make it breed as fast' (*MV* 1.3.92). There is even a faint wordplay between 'ewes', 'use' and 'Jews'. Shylock's formulation gives us our first indication of how Shylock intertwines his religious values with the pursuit of 'thrift': 'he was blest' in this case means both 'he was made holy, a chosen child of God' and 'he was made rich'. Unlike those fussy Christians who won't charge interest for loans and who look down upon those who do, Shylock's only moral stricture about the pursuit of profit is that 'men steal it not'. Once Laban 'compromised' (that is, co-promised, made a bond) with Jacob for the pied and striped animals, Jacob was free to benefit from the deal in any way he might, short of theft. The analogy anticipates Shylock's mercenary response to Antonio's default on his bond and also Shylock's moral outrage at the Christians' theft of his ducats and daughter.

Even so, Shylock's Biblical allusion can be understood in another way, as comparisons so often can. Antonio sees Shylock's reading of the Bible as self-serving, a case of citing scripture for his own purposes. He points out that Jacob's manipulation of the breeding process was 'a thing not in his power to bring to pass, / But swayed and fashioned by the hand of heaven' (*MV* 1.3.88–9). For Antonio, reading the tale from a Christian viewpoint, Jacob violates 'the deed of kind', a process of procreation that ought to be governed by nature ('kind') and God rather than the artificial intervention of man. The bond between Jacob and Laban is set up as a 'venture', that is, a risk that Jacob takes on in hopes of reaping profit, not a deal in which he can engineer results through unnatural means. Antonio recasts

Shylock's analogy between Jacob's flock and Shylock's loans so that it illustrates the 'unkind' nature of manipulating money's capacity to breed. This, in a nutshell, is the Christian position on the proper use of goods: proper Christian behaviour entails 'venturing', that is, risking one's money without the guarantee of a financial return (like interest), trusting nature and God to provide profit. 'Kind' (and the related word 'kindness') emerges as a central word in the scene: though it means 'natural', it also means 'loving and merciful' and 'bonded together by kinship'. This cluster of definitions encapsulates Antonio's conception of Christian values.

All these nuances are in play when later in the scene Shylock offers the 'merry bond' without interest to Antonio, saying 'this is kind I offer' (*MV* 1.3.138). Instead of manipulating 'the deed of kind' as Jacob might, Shylock accedes (or seems to accede) to Christian practices of moneylending in an effort to forge some sort of personal bond with Antonio. As Antonio observes after they strike their bargain, 'the Hebrew will turn Christian, he grows kind' (*MV* 1.3.176). But Shylock's understanding of the Jacob story suggests that when (like Laban) Antonio doesn't fulfil his part of the bond, Shylock (like Jacob) can feel free to manipulate circumstances in his favour, to act with 'unkindness'. Bassanio senses the danger when he declares 'I like not fair terms and a villain's mind' (*MV* 1.3.177), 'fair terms' referring not just to the extraordinarily favourable conditions of the bond but also to Shylock's surprising solicitousness towards Antonio. With remarkable brevity Shylock's allusion to Jacob establishes the extent to which economic and religious values for both Jews and Christians intermingle and shape their very different views of the world.

Christians and classical myth

Since Shylock's primary source for allusions is the Old Testament, we might expect that the Christian characters would often allude to the New Testament. There are indeed moments when the Christians invoke New Testament concepts – most notably, Portia's 'quality of mercy' speech and the discussion of mercy throughout the trial scene. Even so, contrary to what we might expect, the Christians rarely refer directly to the Bible.[9] Instead, their preferred point of reference is classical literature. The Prince of Morocco, apparently a Christian since he boasts of slaying Muslim foes, refers to the sun in classical style as Phoebus and compares himself to Hercules; Salarino speaks of Janus and Nestor, and both Portia and Jessica of Cupid; Bassanio, in his choosing of the lead casket, alludes to Hercules, Mars and Midas, and when he receives the letter from Antonio, he refers to his friend as 'one in whom / The ancient Roman honour more appears / Than any that draws breath in Italy' (*MV* 3.2.293–5); and Lorenzo and Jessica trade classical tales at the opening of the play's final scene. These allusions become a symbolic *patois* they share (and Shylock, Jessica and Lancelet do not), the tribal language of the elite. And the relative absence of direct scriptural allusions from these characters suggests that they may be 'cultural Christians', that is, those who understand Christianity as a set of general moral concepts (like hazarding and mercy) allied with their interests and practices (like trade), rather than specific religious doctrines deeply rooted in scripture. These characters invoke Christianity to their social advantage when need be, but otherwise they think of themselves as heirs to the classical past.

One of the most revealing classical allusions can be found in Bassanio and Antonio's opening exchange, where Bassanio first describes Portia:

> In Belmont is a lady richly left;
> And she is fair, and, fairer than that word,
> Of wondrous virtues: sometimes from her eyes
> I did receive fair speechless messages:
> Her name is Portia, nothing undervalued
> To Cato's daughter, Brutus' Portia:
> Nor is the wide world ignorant of her worth,
> For the four winds blow in from every coast
> Renowned suitors, and her sunny locks
> Hang on her temples like a golden fleece;
> Which makes her seat of Belmont Colchis' strand,
> And many Jasons come in quest of her. (*MV* 1.1.161–72)

There is much to be said about Bassanio's description of Portia. This speech provides crucial exposition. It is here that Belmont is first mentioned, opening out the world of the play to a new setting. We learn that Belmont is a seaside kingdom, since Bassanio tells us that 'the four winds blow in from every coast / Renowned suitors'

(*MV* 1.1.169–70) and he likens Belmont to 'Colchis' strand' (*MV* 1.1.171), the shore of a very rich kingdom on the Black Sea.

It is here too that we first learn of Portia, and Bassanio's description tells us as much about him than it does about her. Bassanio first mentions that she is 'richly left' (*MV* 1.1.161), that is, left with a wealthy inheritance; then he mentions that she is 'fair' (*MV* 1.1.162), that is, beautiful; then, lastly, he suggests that she has 'wondrous virtues' (*MV* 1.1.163). What are we to make of this order? What might it tell us about Bassanio's perception of Portia and thus of his intentions towards her? He begins with mention of her riches, so is his interest in her primarily financial, even mercenary? This line of thinking might be strengthened by the conversation that precedes this speech, laying out Bassanio's prodigal past. But he ends with mention of her virtues, something he calls fairer (more beautiful) than the word 'fair', so is he most interested in her moral integrity, something we might find confirmed when he chooses the correct casket? The language of value that runs throughout the speech – 'nothing undervalued' (*MV* 1.1.165), 'her worth' (*MV* 1.1.167) – raises the crucial question: what is the basis of Portia's value for Bassanio, monetary or moral?

This speech includes two interesting classical allusions. The first is to Portia's classical namesake, the famously virtuous daughter of the Roman senator Cato. This classical Portia was the object of several suitors' attentions, and she eventually married Brutus, a key conspirator against Julius Caesar. When Portia heard of her husband's death on the battlefield, she was said to have committed suicide by swallowing hot coals. Though the allusion allies Portia of Belmont with Roman notions of heroic virtue, Bassanio also situates her exclusively within relationships with men, particularly father and husband – 'Cato's daughter, Brutus' Portia' (*MV* 1.1.166) – perhaps revealing his inability to see Portia as an independent woman, something to which Shakespeare returns in the ring episode. The second allusion is to the tale of Jason and the Argonauts, a Greek epic myth widely alluded to in Latin poetry. Jason and a band of seafaring heroes undertake to steal the golden fleece from the king of Colchis, the ancient Black Sea kingdom; their adventures become the subject of the epic poem *Argonautica*.

The allusion to Jason's exploits runs in several directions at once. First, Bassanio likens Portia's blonde hair (her 'sunny locks', *MV* 1.1.169) to the fleece, suggesting that he sees her primarily as a golden prize, not as a woman. Second, his emphasis on the many other Jasons who 'come in quest of her' (*MV* 1.1.172) provides a heroic veneer to the legacy-hunting enterprise he is engaged in. He is not just exploiting Portia's romantic interest in him; as he frames the matter, he is embarked on a daring epic quest. And the mention of other Jasons puts some pressure on Antonio to finance his quest quickly, lest one of other adventurers succeed in getting Portia's hand.

Bassanio's allusion to the tale of Jason and the Argonauts may also introduce parallels he doesn't have in mind, but which we might be aware of. That is, at work here may be dramatic irony, when a character knows less about the implications of his words or actions than the audience does. What Bassanio doesn't mention is the role of Medea in Jason's success. Medea, a powerful daughter of the king of Colchis and a maker of magical potions, aids Jason in getting past the serpent that guards the golden fleece. After Jason marries Medea, he then cruelly abandons her, an act that leads her in desperation to commit one of the more horrific crimes in classical literature, the killing of her own children in revenge. Certainly Bassanio isn't thinking of these parts of the story as he likens himself to Jason and Portia to the golden fleece, but for those who know the story of the Argonauts well (and it was a famous tale), these details set up less complimentary parallels to Bassanio's behaviour. As we shall soon see, there may be reason to think that Portia may have helped Bassanio pick the correct casket, just as Medea helps Jason procure the golden fleece; Bassanio's commitment to Portia after marrying her is called into question during the ring episode, in ways that parallel Jason's abandonment of Medea; and Medea's revenge, prompted by Jason's cruel treatment, bears some uncomfortable parallels to Shylock's extreme revenge upon Antonio and to Portia's comic revenge upon Bassanio with the rings. It's only as the play unfolds that we may see these darker implications. Yes, it's a small allusion, but Shakespeare doesn't want us to forget it, for later, just after Bassanio wins Portia's hand in the casket test, Gratiano bellows in triumph, 'We are the Jasons; we have won the fleece' (*MV* 3.2.240). Even the sound of the word 'argosy' (meaning 'merchant ship'), used four times in the play, may hint at a connection between Antonio's merchant ventures and Jason's famous ship the *Argo*, even though the word 'argosy' derives from another source.[10]

It would be a mistake to see these classical allusions as Shakespeare simply dressing up his writing. In this case, they serve the purpose of characterization. Besides being appropriate for Bassanio's gentlemanly status, these allusions make his quest for Portia seem grand, allying the circumstances of their courtship with fairy tale and fantastical legend. This suggests more generally how classical allusion functions for many of the Christian characters in the play. These references are examples of the rhetoric of heroic entrepreneurialism, the notion that taking business risks is a bold, noble enterprise, akin to the exploits of classical heroes. This rhetoric is still with us today – how often have you heard business executives like Richard Branson, Elon Musk or Steve Jobs portrayed as courageous adventurers and role models? In *The Merchant of Venice* the Christians often use allusions to classical champions to lend their 'hazarding', either in trade or in pursuit of Portia's hand, an element of heroism and nobility.

Of course, we might view this rhetoric more critically. Bassanio's reference to Jason could be seen simply as his attempt to make pursuit of Portia to clear his debts seem much less mercenary than it might otherwise appear to be. Details undercut the quality of heroic risk he seeks to establish. Bassanio notes that he has received 'speechless messages' from Portia's eyes, a look of erotic interest that Portia will confirm in her conversation with Nerissa in the next scene. She is, Bassanio seems to say, a sure thing, and he underlines the point by ending his speech with the claim, 'I should questionless be fortunate' (*MV* 1.1.176). That claim might be the bravado of an intrepid adventurer, or it might be the confidence of a man who knows he's not really taking a risk at all. Even more important, the circumstances of the speech – he is asking his friend to underwrite the venture – make clear that it is Antonio, not Bassanio, who will bear the financial risk and eventually the mortal threat. In short, though Bassanio's allusions seek to elevate his enterprise, if we read them critically they may end up highlighting rather than hiding his economic motives.

Sometimes Shakespeare depends upon our having a detailed knowledge of classical myth. The Prince of Morocco, for example, invokes Hercules as he boasts his courage in trying his fortune with the caskets:

If Hercules and Lichas play at dice
Which is the better man, the greater throw
May turn by fortune from the weaker hand.

So is Alcides beaten by his rage,
And so may I, blind Fortune leading me,
Miss that which one unworthier may attain,
And die with grieving. (*MV* 2.1.32–8)

Here Morocco melds two tales of Hercules together from classical sources Shakespeare knows well – the tale told by Ovid in *The Metamorphoses* in which Hercules, enraged when his servant Lichas brings him a poisoned garment, tosses him into the sea; and the tale *The Life of Romulus* in *Plutarch's Lives* in which Hercules plays at dice with a temple attendant, agreeing to provide him good fortune if he loses.[11] Morocco's allusion would seem to confuse the two stories, mistaking Lichas for the temple attendant. But is the error Morocco's or Shakespeare's? If Morocco's, the mistake undercuts his use of classical heroic rhetoric and is akin to Lancelet's misuse of Latinate words, marking him as a fool. But it is also certainly possible that Shakespeare nodded. Whoever has made the mistake, here the allusion to Hercules undercuts his heroic stature, for in this version Hercules, when he takes a risk and loses to 'one unworthier', gets angry and dies of humiliation, decidedly unheroic behaviour. Morocco may present himself as a larger-than-life warrior able to 'mock the lion when 'a roars for prey, / To win the lady' (*MV* 2.1.30–1). But his allusion to Hercules, with whom he seems to identify, suggests he doesn't quite grasp the concept of heroic 'hazarding'.

Close knowledge of the classics is also rewarded in the moonlit exchange between Lorenzo and Jessica that opens the play's last scene. There the two lovers trade allusions to what seem like romantic tales from classical literature – Troilus and Cressida, Pyramus and Thisbe, Dido and Aeneas, Medea and Jason. All is not what it seems, however, for Shakespeare depends upon our knowing that each of these tales ends in terrible tragedy. The references may reveal more than these lovers know, foreshadowing the tragic direction of their own love story. Shakespeare hints that this is so when Lorenzo, perhaps with some misjudged teasing, perhaps with a bit of Christian bigotry, inserts himself and his wife into this set of 'romantic' tales: 'in such a night / Did Jessica steal from the wealthy Jew, / And with an unthrift love did run from Venice / As far as Belmont' (*MV* 5.1.14–17). It is possible to play Lorenzo and Jessica's exchange as tongue-in-cheek and affectionate, but if we know something about the classical tales from which they are taken, the allusions that frame their conversation do not bode well for their future.

I've suggested that the Christian characters rarely directly allude to the Bible, but there is a perhaps surprising exception: Lancelet Giobbe, the play's resident 'clown' or rustic fool. Lancelet's comical references to religious language require a good ear and a detailed knowledge of Elizabethan religious culture. For an audience steeped in the Bible, Lancelet's reference to Old Giobbe as 'my true-begotten father' (*MV* 2.2.31) would bring to mind the formula of Jesus as God's 'only-begotten son', and his suggestion that 'the Jew is the very devil incarnation' (*MV* 2.2.24) is a blasphemous garbling of the idea that Jesus is God incarnate. Other allusions are more oblique. Lancelet's question 'do you not know me, Father?' and Old Giobbe's reply 'I know you not' (*MV* 2.2.68–9) have the ring of Matthew 7.22–3, and the kneeling of the son to ask blessing before the blind father (*MV* 2.2.73) is featured in the tale of Esau and Jacob from Genesis 25.19–34. The quips about Lancelet being a 'staff' for his father's old age (*MV* 2.2.61–4) seem to allude to a famous line from Psalm 23, 'Yea though I walk through the valley of the shadow of death, I will fear no evil: for thou art with me, thy rod and thy staff be the things that do comfort me' (Psalm 23:4). Even Lancelet's family name Giobbe is a little Biblical gag, for it sounds like 'Job', the long-suffering prophet of the Old Testament. Lancelet's moaning about his 'suffering' at Shylock's hands becomes all the more comic when compared to Job's truly harrowing trials. Editors commonly change the name from 'Giobbe' to 'Gobbo', but doing so obscures the joke.

Lancelet alludes to other kinds of religious discourse too. The phrase 'I am Lancelet, your boy that was, your son that is, your child that shall be' (*MV* 2.2.79–80) sounds very much like 'as it was in the beginning, is now, and ever shall be', a much repeated line from the *Book of Common Prayer*, a collection of litanies that any church-going Elizabethan would instantly have recognized. In Lancelet's opening deliberation about whether to run away, the comedy turns upon a scenario familiar to audiences of morality plays, those allegorical plays addressed to questions of temptation and redemption. In a morality play, often the protagonist must choose between a character who tempts him to sin and one who voices the righteous way. The irony of Lancelet's soliloquy is that he takes the path suggested by the 'fiend' (to run away) because, so he claims, Shylock is himself 'the very devil incarnation' (*MV* 2.2.24).

We will have reason to return to Lancelet's opening speech in Chapter Six, but for the moment we might ask: what to make of this comic pile-up of religious allusions? They turn upon the pleasure of recognition and the perhaps unconsciously witty ways in which Lancelet misuses the references, but they also make a point about Lancelet's understanding of Christian tenets. Though religious discourse is clearly part of his vocabulary, his understanding of its substance is skin-deep, as is his understanding of the Latinate words he also misuses. How then to evaluate Lancelet's conversations with Jessica in which he insists she is damned for being a Jew? Do these also spring from an inadequate understanding of Christian principles? And should we see Lancelet's superficial understanding as indicating a larger inadequacy in the Christian community or simply his own personal failings? These examples illustrate that Shakespeare uses allusion – and our capacities to read allusions in excess of what characters may explicitly indicate – as a symbolic shorthand. They can communicate with exceptional economy qualities of character, tone and theme if we take the time to examine the sources from which they are taken.

Writing matters – using sources

Writing a research essay on *The Merchant of Venice* can be daunting because so much has been written on the play before (including this very book). Actors face much the same kind of anxiety: how to say something original with your performance about a character who has been played by so many others? Creative writers share this worry too, especially those who like Shakespeare know their classical literary forebears well and learned to write by imitating them. One of the reasons Shakespeare includes allusions to classical and Biblical literature is to draw upon established authorities and give his writing added heft and legitimacy. But Shakespeare, as we've seen, also often reinterprets his sources even as he refers to them. He puts established phrases, motifs, and plots in new contexts, looks at them from a different angle, gives them a new emphasis, extends them in new directions, so that they become part of his own work, fully his own while still lending their authority to his writing.

Shakespeare offers us here a useful model for how to incorporate research into your work: striking a balance between being faithful to your sources and asserting your own voice and perspective.

Your sources provide your thesis with evidence and authority, particularly so your primary source, the play itself. It is crucial, then, to quote your sources accurately. That means not just transcribing them correctly but also choosing direct quotations or crafting paraphrases that give a fair sense of your source's position. If you misquote or misrepresent your source's basic position, you've damaged your own authority rather than enhanced it. One mark of a novice writer of research essays is too much direct citation, especially from outside sources. Artful paraphrase is a skill well worth developing, for paraphrasing forces you to put into your own words the essential meaning of the materials you are using and to look at them critically. Paraphrase, that is, can be a form of analysis. And it helps you avoid a paper which is just a patchwork of citations, the effect of which will be to diminish your own voice. Of course you should sometimes cite directly, especially from the Shakespeare text, to illustrate the points you are making. Too few citations and your argument will seem ungrounded, unauthoritative, overly general, without sufficient ballast. But reserve direct citation for those instances in which you want the reader to look closely and analytically at what you've quoted. Think of citations as ducats: spend them in hopes of substantial return but not too prodigally.

With direct citation, it's critical to remember that no quotation is ever self-explanatory. Every reader will see any passage you quote slightly differently. So you need to guide the reader to what is important in the quotation for your argument – highlight specific features, sketch out its context (who said this? to whom? why?), specify its tone or purpose, explore its implications. For a substantial block citation, it's wise to precede your citation with a short contextualizing remark and follow it with a passage of analysis in which you focus in on important details. Think of this in terms of classic cinema technique: begin with a quick wide shot establishing the basic setting (context), then follow that with a lingering shot of your main subject (citation), then move to a series of close-ups that pick up telling details (analysis), before backing out to another shot of your main subject which we now understand in a new way (conclusion). Once you get comfortable with this structure, you can vary it to suit your needs.

Using secondary sources on *The Merchant of Venice* involves all the above skills and a few more. When you start your paper, the temptation may be to pack off to the library and gather a pile of books on *The Merchant of Venice* or, worse, to engage in a clickfest on the internet. I've done this myself, and what happens is that I tend to fasten on whatever piece of criticism I read first (or that I first understand). In other words, if you begin the research process without first spending some time formulating a focus or hypothesis of your own, you will be prone to becoming too dependent on your sources' ideas and not forming a perspective of your own. It's crucial, then, that you spend some time struggling with the play itself, developing your own ideas and questions about it, narrowing down your focus, before you turn to other critical voices. I typically write down my guiding topic or thesis before I go on a scavenger hunt in the library so that I have mapped out for myself some preliminary sense of direction. Of course, this map only initially orients your journey. Your direction may change as you discover roadblocks, become interested in some side road, learn that the original journey isn't as interesting as you thought it might be or find out that you can't possibly cover all the territory in a short time. But your initial map helps you avoid taking someone else's package tour. Sometimes you need additional factual information to help you refine your initial map. You will be amazed at the number of specialized Shakespeare encyclopaedias and handbooks that provide basic information on all manner of topics. To continue my travel analogy – others have travelled these roads before and have become experts on various specialities of the region, so take advantage of their expertise.

Eventually you will want to consult the array of criticism on *The Merchant of Venice* and use it in your essay. Novice writers tend to search out only those critics who agree with their initial position and ignore those who don't. Certainly you want to support your thesis with outside sources, but if you use only sources that agree with you and you quote from them liberally, you run the risk of diluting your own original voice in your essay. What you end up with is a 'me, too!' essay that feels like you've let others do the hard work of interpretation for you. My experience is that many students underestimate the power of disagreement with other critics. You may, for instance, substantially agree with a critic's view of Portia as a manipulator, and you may want to use that critic's work to support your argument. But it's likely that you part company with her on some issue, even if that issue is small – you read Portia's 'quality of mercy' speech differently than she does, you view Portia's self-assertion more positively than she does, you think Portia has a change of heart when Bassanio reads Antonio's letter whereas she doesn't. Announcing that difference of judgement allows you to assert your own critical voice, and sometimes that difference can point you to your own distinctive view of the play.

In other words, you can use criticism not only to support your argument but also to push against, to assert how your unique perspective on the play differs from that of others. Of course, to make your distinctive perspective convincing, you'll need to return to Shakespeare's script and show how your reading accounts for details others haven't sufficiently addressed. That's the value of disagreement: it sends you back to *The Merchant of Venice* to read it even more carefully. This kind of critical disagreement need not be all or nothing – rarely is a critic utterly right or wrong in every detail. And you should take care to understand a critic's argument well before disagreeing with it – you would hate to have your own ideas misrepresented, so it's important not to misrepresent the ideas of others. You may even find that after reading an article and reviewing the script, you have changed your own perspective on an issue, slightly or substantially. That's part of the to-and-fro process of refining your thesis. Both agreeing and disagreeing with other critics, sifting their arguments carefully while being fair to their perspectives, allow you to refine your own original, nuanced perspective on the play, one you'll want to ground ultimately in details from Shakespeare's script.

CHAPTER THREE

Language in Print II: Two Shylocks, Two Portias

The two Shylocks

The Merchant of Venice provides us evidence for not one but two Shylocks, and divining the relationship between those two quite different characters – if there is a relationship at all – is one of the big interpretive challenges of Shakespeare's play. We meet the first of those Shylocks in 1.3, his first scene in the play. Shylock's initial banter with Bassanio reveals much about the strained relations between Christians and Jews in Venice. Their exchange is a study in mutual passive aggression. Shylock draws out committing himself to the loan, Bassanio takes odd exception to Shylock's reference to Antonio as a 'good man', and Shylock, even as he defends the phrase as a compliment, suggests that Antonio is in fact vulnerable to all kinds of financial disasters and has 'squandered' (*MV* 1.3.20) his ventures abroad. But it is Antonio's arrival a moment later that really sets Shylock off. His first comment, 'how like a fawning publican he looks' (*MV* 1.3.37), suggests that Shylock is repulsed by what he sees as Antonio's hypocritical piety and humility. He equates him to one of those minor – and notoriously corrupt – Roman officials who oppressed the Jews in historical Judea. Throughout his first soliloquy of the play Shylock speaks directly of his secret hatred for Antonio and of his desire to 'catch him once upon the hip' (*MV* 1.3.42), a wrestling term that refers to pulling an opponent into a position so that he can then be pinned. (This is a phrase that Gratiano will repeat in the trial scene, when it becomes clear that Shylock has been defeated by Portia's reading of the bond: 'Now, infidel, I have you on the hip' [*MV* 4.1.330].)

Shylock's ominous comment, 'I will feed fat the ancient grudge I bear him' (*MV* 1.3.43), perhaps the most important line of this speech, offers additional insights into Shylock's state of mind. It tells us that Shylock's antagonism to Antonio is 'ancient', more than merely a personal grudge but something stretching back through time. Shylock's opening and closing comments, 'I hate him for he is a Christian' (*MV* 1.3.38) and 'Cursed be my tribe / If I forgive him' (*MV* 1.3.47-8), seem to place the 'grudge' in the context of a long-standing feud between Jews and Christians, though Shylock makes clear that he also despises Antonio's penchant for loaning money without interest, a practice that undermines Shylock's livelihood as a usurer. Shylock's ominous final line also suggests that he is planning a revenge even at this early point in the play, if only he can put Antonio at a disadvantage. And the metaphor of eating – 'feed fat the ancient grudge' (*MV* 1.3.43) – hints at cannibalism and points towards the bizarre penalty of the bond he eventually strikes with Antonio. We shall return presently to this metaphor.

Shylock's first soliloquy thus characterizes him as a wilfully vengeful Jew, secretly plotting Antonio's downfall from the moment he gets the request for a loan. Details from that speech align Shylock with two conventional literary villains. One is the stage Jew, unfaithful in all senses of the word, miserly and money-grubbing, tricky and merciless in his dealings with those not of his religious tribe. His quasi-cannibalistic bloodthirstiness is linked to the Christian 'blood libel' against Jews, the folk claim that Jews sought the blood of Christian children for use in their religious rituals. This grotesque accusation seems to have originated in medieval England, where in the twelfth century it was included in the saint's life of William of Norwich and from there seems to have spread across the country. Chaucer even includes the libel in 'The Prioress's Tale' in his *Canterbury Tales*, and versions appeared in medieval balladry and drama. This myth fuelled the rise of English anti-Semitism for the next one hundred years and led eventually to the expulsion of the Jews from England in 1290, though some Jews remained in small urban enclaves until officially reinstated in 1657. Christopher Marlowe's over-the-top villain Barabas from *The Jew of Malta* is a good example of this conventional stage type. Barabas is a gleefully Machiavellian Jew who plots the elaborate deaths of Christian rivals when his wealth is confiscated and then faithlessly switches sides against the Turks when it serves his needs. *The Jew of Malta* first premiered in 1592 and remained popular on the stage afterwards. Appearing only a few years before Shakespeare's *The Merchant of Venice* (written between 1596 and 1598), Marlowe's tragedy testifies to the familiarity of Renaissance English audiences with the conniving Jew as a stereotypical villain eager for Christian blood. Many have argued that Shakespeare's play was an answer to Marlowe, providing a less over-the-top version of the stage Jew. Whether Shylock is any less sinister than Marlowe's Barabas is a matter of debate. In Belmont, Jessica reveals to the gathered Venetians that 'when I was with [Shylock], I have heard him swear / To Tubal and to Chus, his countrymen, / That he would rather have Antonio's flesh / Than twenty times the value of the sum / That he did owe him' (*MV* 3.2.283–7). Her comment suggests that Shylock has, in league with other Jews, intentionally trapped Antonio with the bond so that he could have access to his Christian flesh. We never hear this information directly from Shylock's lips, and it is certainly possible that Jessica says this to ingratiate herself with her new Christian companions, but the detail fits with the anti-Semitic image of the conspiratorial, bloodthirsty, devious Jew.[1]

In general outline Shylock also resembles those creatures of the Faerie world who seek to trick unwitting humans into bad bargains that allow them to be kidnapped, controlled, killed or eaten. This kind of behaviour, for example, is typical of ogres and trolls in northern European fairy tales, and it is up to the tale's protagonist to trick the trickster in order to worm his or her way out of an ill-conceived oath and avoid a nasty death. Such is the case in the tale of the Three Billy Goats Gruff, where the three goats must trick the hungry troll who guards the bridge they seek to cross. This motif can also be found in the chivalric romance tradition, medieval tales of knights and nobles. 'The Franklin's Tale' in Chaucer's *Canterbury Tales*, for example, turns upon a wife's foolish vow to marry a suitor if he can clear the rocks from the coast of Brittany, a task he accomplishes with the help of magic. Interestingly enough, the wife is released from the bargain only because the suitor nobly shows mercy and relents, precisely what the court of Venice expects of Shylock and never receives. In the Christian moralist tradition, the part of the ogre was taken up by the devil or Vice figure who works to trick the virtuous if naive protagonist into committing him- or herself to sinfulness that is ultimately self-damning. The Judeo-Christian creation myth, where Eve is bamboozled by Satan into eating the forbidden fruit, is a form of this tale, and this narrative often structures tales of saints confronted by devilish temptation. Christopher Marlowe also used this narrative motif to great effect in his *Doctor Faustus* (between 1588 and 1592), a play built upon German tales. Faustus strikes a literal devil's bargain with Mephistopheles to get magical powers for twenty-four years in exchange for his soul, a bargain Faustus tries unsuccessfully to wriggle out of. In *The Merchant of Venice* this sense of being caught up in a trickster's clever trap extends not only to Antonio but also to the Venetian court, for as both Antonio and Shylock observe, the Duke is constrained by 'the course of law' (*MV* 3.3.25) to enforce the contract. If the court does not follow the law, no contract would be considered binding and international commerce, the lifeblood of the city, would grind to a halt: 'the commodity that strangers have / With us in Venice, if it be denied, / Will much impeach the justice of the state, / Since that the trade and profit of the city / Consisteth of all nations' (*MV* 3.3.26–31).

This Shylock – the sinister trickster, the Christian-hating Jew, the miserly refuser of merriment, the bloodthirsty inhuman devil who shows no mercy and delights in power over his victims, the monster whose defeat we are coaxed to applaud – can certainly be found throughout the text of *The Merchant of Venice*. But there is a second Shylock. This is the man who is a victim of systematic Christian prejudice against Jews, one whose indignation is motivated – and for some readers entirely justified – by a long history of oppression.[2] That history we learn about in Shylock's first scene with Antonio. When Antonio presses Shylock for an answer to his request for a loan – 'Well, Shylock, shall we be beholding to you?' (*MV* 1.3.101) – Shylock reminds him that repeatedly, 'In the Rialto you have rated me / About my moneys and my usances' (*MV* 1.3.103–4) and, worse, called him a dog and spat upon him. Shylock is underlining Antonio's hypocrisy in his asking for a loan and expecting out of a sense of privilege that Shylock, his social and religious inferior, will gratefully comply. Shylock even pictures what Antonio seems to expect – Shylock's 'bend[ing] low', speaking 'in a bondsman's key' (that is, in a slave's tone of voice, with wordplay on 'bond'), 'with bated breath and whispering humbleness' (*MV* 1.3.119–20), humiliating himself in submission before his Christian antagonist. When Antonio objects to even this modest level of self-assertion on Shylock's part, saying that Shylock should lend money to him as if he were 'thine enemy' (*MV* 1.3.130), Shylock dials back the hostility, declaring that 'I would be friends with you and have your love, / Forget the shames that you have stained me with' (*MV* 1.3.134–5). Yet even as Shylock promises to forget the past, he reminds Antonio that his actions have long stigmatized him.

Even so, he indicates his willingness to offer 'kind' (or 'kindness') in the form of a loan without a 'doit [small coin] / Of usance for my moneys' (*MV* 1.2.136–7). As we saw in Chapter Two, 'kind' is an important and resonant word, one repeated throughout the scene and having a variety of meanings in the Renaissance – 'in accordance with nature and natural law', 'akin, appropriate to one's shared relations', 'noble, gracious', 'loving, caring'. Certainly one meaning of Shylock's offer is that he is nobly returning kindness (in the modern sense) for Antonio's ill treatment. Another, even more generous reading is that he is acting out of a sense of shared humanity that seeks to transcend the religious divide between them. It's possible to read Antonio's reply – 'I'll seal to such a bond / And say that there is much kindness in the Jew' (*MV* 1.3.148–9) – as an equivocal acceptance of that shared humanity, though Antonio recalls religious antagonisms between Christians and Jews with his biting reference to Shylock as 'the Jew'. Indeed, after Shylock's exit Antonio continues to think in bigoted terms. He comments, 'Hie thee, gentle Jew. / The Hebrew will turn Christian, he grows kind' (*MV* 1.3.173–4), punning on 'gentle' (meaning noble) and 'gentile' and stressing that it's only Christian behaviour that can be regarded as 'kind' (i.e., generous, natural). For Antonio, Shylock can be 'kind' only insofar as he becomes a Christian or 'gentile Jew'; he conceives of shared humanity ('kind') only within his own Christian frame of reference.

Shylock's appeal to a shared humanity and his sense of it being wronged by Christian abuse is found most famously in his 'Hath not a Jew eyes speech' in 3.1, where he first resolves to enforce the bond against Antonio:

> He [Antonio] hath disgraced me and hindered me half a million, laughed at my losses, mocked at my gains, scorned my nation, thwarted my bargains, cooled my friends, heated mine enemies,

and why his reason? I am a Jew. Hath not a Jew eyes? Hath not a Jew hands, organs, dimensions, senses, affections, passions? Fed with the same food, hurt with the same weapons, subject to the same diseases, healed by the same means, warmed and cooled by the same winter and summer as a Christian is? If you prick us, do we not bleed? If you tickle us do we not laugh? If you poison us do we not die? (*MV* 3.1.49–60)

Underlying Shylock's outrage at his mistreatment is the notion that all human beings share a natural kinship and dignity. That fundamental sense of human 'kind' he locates in our common bodily experience of pain (and, less frequently, pleasure), an experience that ought to lead to identification with or empathy for one's fellow humans. Antonio's campaign of anti-Semitic abuse, Shylock suggests, violates a law of nature. It is as if Antonio were treating Shylock as a member of a different, non-human species rather than someone simply with a different religious heritage.

This shared humanity with Shylock is just what the Christians of the play so often deny when confronted with Jewish difference. Only moments before this speech, Salarino answers Shylock's claim that his daughter Jessica is 'my flesh and my blood' by denying that she, now a Christian, shares anything bodily with Shylock: 'There is more difference between thy flesh and hers than between jet and ivory, more between your bloods than there is between red wine and Rhenish' (*MV* 3.1.34–6). (There is an additional racist dig built into the equivalence between Shylock's flesh and 'jet', that is, black skin.) It is as if, as Lancelet Giobbe twice proposes (*MV* 2.3.11–12, 3.5.9–10), Jessica's true father were actually a Christian, and so she has nothing in common at the level of the body with her putative father Shylock. It's impossible for Salarino and Lancelet to maintain their view of all Jews as inhuman, utterly unlike Christian 'kind', without also maintaining the fiction that Jessica is somehow not descended from Jewish stock.

Shylock's radical answer to Christian efforts to treat Jews as 'un-kind' is to assert his essential humanity and so to highlight the injustice of his mistreatment. His answer is reinforced by a series of ringing parallels: 'He hath disgraced me, and hindered me half a million, laughed at my losses, mocked at my gains, scorned my nation, thwarted my bargains, cooled my friends, heated mine enemies' (*MV* 3.1.49–52). We might notice that Shylock's catalogue of Antonio's abuses focuses primarily on his business relations and his reputation; Shylock seems stung more by being socially ostracized rather than by being physically assaulted (the spitting and kicking we know of from 1.3). The parallels suggest that this is a relentless, organized scheme to ruin him, not just occasional slights. When Shylock turns to assert his shared humanity with the Christians, he again uses a sequence of parallels, this time a series of rhetorical questions: 'Hath not a Jew eyes? Hath not a Jew hands, organs, dimensions, senses, affections, passions? Fed with the same food, hurt with the same weapons, subject to the same diseases, healed by the same means, warmed and cooled by the same winter and summer as a Christian is?' (*MV* 3.1.53–8). The effect is to interrogate the prejudices Salarino and Salanio have put on display but more importantly to confront the assumptions of the audience. It is one of Shakespeare's most moving passages, a compelling indictment of anti-Semitism and a plea for empathy across cultural divides, and it makes a powerful case for Shylock as victim, not villain.

Even so, this famous passage does not occur in isolation. As is so often the case in this play, dramatic context complicates matters. Shylock's argument quickly takes an ominous turn:

> And if you wrong us shall we not revenge? If we are like you in the rest, we will resemble you in that. If a Jew wrong a Christian, what is his humility [i.e., the response he should expect]? Revenge! If a Christian wrong a Jew, what should his sufferance be by Christian example? Why, revenge! The villainy you teach me I will execute, and it shall go hard but I will better the instruction. (*MV* 3.1.60–6)

Here Shylock deploys the discourse of shared human-'kind' to justify his right to inflict pain upon Antonio, on the theory that he is only imitating the skewed principles Christians have adopted towards the Jews. Shylock's catalogue of Antonio's abuses establishes that the Christians have repeatedly violated the principle of shared human-'kind', and so he argues that he is justified in adopting their sense of justice.

The parallelism between all the other rhetorical questions Shylock asks and his question 'if you wrong us shall we not revenge?' would seem to compel our consent. But should it? On the one hand, the conclusion of the speech would seem to spring from Shylock's righteous response to being victimized. He should, as a victim, be able to seek recompense under the law, a recompense based upon the same principles and practices that the Christians embrace. After all, the law ought to treat everyone in the same way, in part precisely because of the principle of shared humanity. If people suffer in the same way, then legal remedies for human suffering should not treat one group in preferential ways. In other words, we might see Shylock's pursuit of revenge as consistent with his status as a victim of Christian privilege. On the other hand, however, we might see this turn in Shylock's argument as evidence of the way in which he can twist praiseworthy ethical principles to justify his long-standing designs against his enemies, what he himself admits is 'villainy' in this speech. Does this moment verify Antonio's observation about Shylock that he is 'an evil soul producing holy witness', 'a villain with a smiling cheek' (*MV* 1.3.95–6)? Is this a version of quoting Scripture to suit his ends, another example of Shylock's slyly villainous nature, justifying his intent to kill Antonio under the veil of moral principle? What makes this key passage challenging is that it complicates all over again the question of whether Shylock is villain or victim or whether the two Shylocks are two parts of a larger psychologically complex whole.

These two characterizations of Shylock are perhaps most difficult to address in the trial scene, where Shylock's behaviour is at its most relentless. There he seems to fulfil the stereotype of the bloodthirsty Jew, the monster who cruelly and remorselessly seeks Christian blood. In Chapter Five we will have more to say about this extraordinary scene, the template – at least in its general rise and fall of action – for nearly every trial scene that has followed it in fiction. For the moment I want to stress how Shakespeare's portrayal of Shylock's behaviour can be read in terms of the two Shylocks, even in this scene. To see how, let's focus on a single sentence, the one that Shylock utters at the end of his first major speech in the scene. The Duke has addressed him with a plea for mercy for Antonio. In reply, Shylock answers that he need not offer a rationale for pursuing Antonio's life:

> So can I give no reason, nor I will not,
> More than a lodged hate and a certain loathing
> I bear Antonio, that I follow thus
> A losing suit against him! (*MV* 4.1.58–61)

This reply would seem to establish unequivocally that Shylock seeks Antonio's life rather than the ducats he is owed. The phrase 'lodged hate' stresses that Shylock's feeling for Antonio is not some passing emotion but a long-simmering enmity that can't be dislodged simply by the Duke's appeal. Shylock refuses even to engage the Duke, stressing that his antipathy for Antonio (and by extension Christians in general) is something primal rather than rational. His examples of similar sorts of revulsion – men who cannot abide a roasted pig, a cat or a bagpipe – are, he argues, forms of 'affection', involuntary inclinations that determine 'what [one] likes or loathes' (*MV* 4.1.49, 51). Notice that Shylock himself has already expressed his Jewish revulsion to pork – he comments on that in his first meeting with Bassanio (*MV* 1.3.30–4) – and his puritanical dislike for the pipe – he warns Jessica about 'the vile squealing of the wry-necked fife' (*MV* 2.5.29); his contempt for cats comes through in his complaint about Lancelet Giobbe: 'he sleeps by day / More than the wildcat' (*MV* 2.5.45–6). In other words, Shylock is here speaking about himself in the third person, and he's insisting that he is naturally, viscerally compelled to 'yield to such inevitable shame / As to offend himself being offended' (*MV* 4.1.55–7). That is, even if it seems shameful (and even if in the case of Antonio it leads to loss of money), Shylock has no choice but to give himself over to irrational disgust when confronted with Antonio's offensiveness. By framing his pursuit of Antonio in this way, Shylock puts himself beyond the reach of legal, rational or moral argument. This speech seems to provide unambiguous evidence that Shylock's hatred for Antonio is monstrously irrational.

And yet might we understand the phrase 'a losing suit' in another way? Traditionally, 'losing suit' has been understood to refer to the worthless flesh that Shylock expects to receive upon judgement. Indeed, when Shylock struck the 'merry' bargain, he stresses that the forfeiture he's proposed will lead to him losing profit: 'A pound of flesh of a man's flesh, taken from a man, / Is not so estimable, profitable neither, / As flesh of muttons, beeves or goats' (*MV* 1.3.161–3). But it's possible that Shylock expects to lose the legal action he's engaged in and expects the court to intervene unfairly on Antonio's behalf. The Duke seems to veer in that direction when, after Shylock insists he will 'stand for judgment' (*MV* 4.1.102), he declares 'upon my power I may dismiss this court' (*MV* 4.1.103) if Bellario has not arrived to offer an intervening judgement. Why would Shylock pursue a suit he expects to lose? One possibility is that should the Duke dismiss the case or summarily decide against Shylock, then Christian injustice, the regime of bigotry under which Shylock has long suffered, will be plain for all to see. And, as both Shylock and the Duke observe, the result of a dismissal for Venetian trade would be disastrous, for no one would be able to count on unbiased enforcement of its contracts or laws. As Shylock puts it, 'if you deny me, fie upon your law: / There is no force in the decrees of Venice' (*MV* 4.1.100–1). Shylock's aim may be less to take a pound of Antonio's flesh than to force the court to rule against him, to 'pursue a losing suit' in an effort to expose Venetian society for what it is, a privileged enclave that persecutes those different than itself and masks its prejudice with hypocritical Christian platitudes. Shylock's suit becomes, like Portia's caskets, a test of values: what do the Venetian power elite value more, the impartiality of the law or one of the most beloved insiders, Venetian commerce or Antonio's life? In this reading, Shylock emerges as a crusader against the system of victimization he has endured, one who is willing to sacrifice so as to force the ugly truth out into the open.

Shakespeare is renowned for the moral and psychological complexity of his characters, and Shylock provides an especially apt example of how he achieves that effect. By presenting us with two different personalities under the same name, Shakespeare prompts us to think in sophisticated ways about who Shylock is and how we respond to Jewish difference. In particular, Shakespeare's approach to characterization forces his audience to think about how Shylock's two personalities relate to one another. Does Shylock develop from victim to villain (and perhaps back again), or does Shylock's personality remain essentially the same throughout the play? If Shylock does develop, what are the crucial events that motivate his change of heart? With Shylock, is Shakespeare portraying the psychology of a victim of bigotry, one whose hatred is enflamed in the crucible of anti-Semitic oppression? Is Shylock's antagonism towards Christians the product of his experience, his own religious piety or a monstrousness born in the blood? Is Shylock a frustrated peacemaker, one who despite his loathing for his tormentor Antonio offers an act of kindness in hopes of reconciliation, only once again to be mistreated and humiliated? Does Shylock become a self-sacrificing warrior against Christian hypocrisy, or does he actively seek Christian blood, hiding his perverse intent behind a veneer of moralistic rhetoric?

We might ask too about how Shakespeare uses Shylock's two personalities to shape our ongoing response to him as a representative Jew. Do we carry memory of Shylock the victim into those moments where he seems to play the villain? Does Shakespeare seek to undermine our initial impression of Shylock, one calculated to confirm the stereotype of the Jewish villain, by building sympathy for him as a victim of anti-Semitism? Or are we to identify with Shylock's appeal to a common humanity, only to be caught up short by his anti-Christian rage and his design upon Antonio's life, reinforcing the idea that any empathy we might have for Shylock is misplaced, even dangerous? How does Shakespeare encourage us to respond to Shylock when he is defeated in court – as a villain cleverly outwitted or as a victim of anti-Semitic conspiracy? Though the problems raised by the two Shylocks are especially difficult in the trial scene, they run throughout the play's main plot and are the reason why *The Merchant of Venice* remains so challenging for its audiences.

The two Portias

As with Shylock, so with Portia. Shakespeare presents us with two quite different personalities under the single name of Portia and challenges us to synthesize them into a coherent whole. We are first introduced to Portia by Bassanio in his glowing description of her in *MV* 1.1.161–6 as a woman of wealth, beauty and most of all virtue. As we learned in Chapter Two, her name brings to mind another Portia, the mythic daughter of Cato the Younger, the great Roman statesman renowned for his moral rectitude. This Portia is a paragon of virtuous martyrdom and by extension passive femininity. There are several moments in *The Merchant of Venice* where Portia exudes this kind of self-sacrificing virtue. She repeatedly expresses her willingness to abide by her father's casket test, a test of virtue, even though she bridles a bit at 'the will of a living daughter curbed by the will of a dead father' (*MV* 1.2.23–4). When Bassanio correctly chooses the lead casket and wins Portia's hand, she speaks of her marriage to him as a virtuous sacrifice of her autonomy and riches:

> But now, I was the lord
> Of this fair mansion, master of my servants,
> Queen o'er myself; and even now, but now,
> This house, these servants, and this same myself,
> Are yours, my lord's. (*MV* 3.2.167–71)

We shouldn't fail to notice, however, that Portia is often able paradoxically to assert her power through this kind of seeming passivity. She accepts the casket test in part because it allows her to fend off suitors she dislikes, something revealed by the brutal send-offs she privately gives to the Princes of Morocco ('a gentle riddance', *MV* 2.7.78) and Aragon ('O, these deliberate fools! when they do choose, / They have the wisdom by their wit to lose', *MV* 2.9.79–80). And her subjection to Bassanio in the passage above is accompanied by her giving of a ring, which she tells him will 'be my vantage to exclaim on you' (*MV* 3.2.174) should Bassanio give it to another. Later in the same scene, the arrival of Antonio's letter becomes an occasion for Portia to forgive Bassanio for pretending to be wealthier than he really is, to demonstrate her concern for Bassanio's friend's predicament and to sacrifice some of her inheritance – 'pay him six thousand and deface the bond. / Double six thousand, and then treble that, / Before a friend of this description / Shall lose a hair through Bassanio's fault' (*MV* 3.2.298–301). Even so, this moment is also an occasion for Portia to assert the privilege and power that comes with extraordinary wealth. One last element to notice here: these instances of Portia's virtuous conduct all occur in public, before an onstage audience of some sort. They constitute an important part of Portia's public persona.

The other Portia is the one we see in private, very often in the company of Nerissa, her maid and confidante. We first meet this Portia in the play's second scene, as she chats privately with Nerissa about her love life. Like Antonio, Portia enters the play complaining of melancholy – 'by my troth, Nerissa, my little body is aweary of this great world' (*MV* 1.2.1–2), though in her case we soon learn her woe, unlike Antonio's, is very certainly a matter of love. Nerissa replies somewhat cheekily, reminding Portia that in fact her melancholy is unjustified by her life of exceptional good fortune. She is one of those people who are unhappy because they have too much, not too little. Nerissa's conclusion is one very familiar from classical philosophy, punctuated by one of Shakespeare's serious puns, on the word 'mean': 'it is no mean happiness, therefore, to be seated in the mean' (*MV* 1.2.6–8). That is to say, a life of virtuous balance, the happy 'mean' that avoids both excess and abstinence, is no small ('no mean') feat to achieve.

Portia's reply is somewhat surprising, given the reputation for public virtue that comes with her name. She declares that Nerissa's little nuggets of moral wisdom, her 'sentences', are all 'good' and 'well-pronounced' (*MV* 1.2.10), a lovely little performance of ethical correctness. The actual conduct of virtue is something very different. We may know intellectually what we ought to do, observes Portia, but given humankind's impetuous nature, actually putting it into practice is rather more difficult: 'If to do were as easy to know what were good to do, chapels had been churches, and poor men's cottages princes' palaces ... The brain may devise laws for the blood; but a hot temper leaps o'er a cold decree' (*MV* 1.2.12–14, 17–19). The exact tone of Portia's remarks here is a little difficult to pinpoint – is she irritated at Nerissa's impertinence, sarcastic about moral ideals, or especially aware of humankind's fallen state? In any case, her private scepticism about the classical ideal of virtue and her unwillingness to acknowledge that her melancholy is, as Nerissa suggests, a first-world problem are surprising, given her public reputation for 'wondrous virtues' (*MV* 1.1.163). In private, this Portia complains about the test of virtue her father has set for suitors. That test, it's clear, is the source of her melancholy ('is it not hard, Nerissa, that I cannot choose one, nor refuse none?', *MV* 1.2.24–5) and, what's more, she rather ungenerously sneers at the suitors who come to woo her. Portia's father's will is a symbol of the power men exert over women's lives in the name of defending Christian virtue, and in public Portia conforms to her father's edicts. In her asides and behind-the-scenes remarks to Nerissa, however, a different, private Portia emerges, one who strikes some distance from the righteousness established by her name and public reputation, a good example of what Karen Newman calls an 'unruly woman'.[3]

In the case of the casket test with Bassanio, we watch an emerging struggle between the public and private personalities of Portia. Note how she interrupts herself in her initial speech to Bassanio, as she begs him to postpone his choice of caskets:

> There's something tells me—but it is not love—
> I would not lose you; and, you know yourself,
> Hate counsels not in such a quality.
> But lest you should not understand me well,—
> And yet a maiden hath no tongue but thought—
> I would detain you here some month or two
> Before you venture for me. (*MV* 3.2.4–10)

This passage nicely demonstrates how Shakespeare gives the impression of immediacy, a mind working out an idea, starting and stopping, becoming self-conscious, changing direction and reformulating the thought in real time as we listen. Her train of thought seesaws between virtuous feminine modesty and silence ('a maiden hath no tongue but thought'), between her proper submission to the casket test and her impulse to assert herself by declaring openly her desire and forcing Bassanio to delay. Much of what Portia says here takes the form of negations ('it is not love', 'I would not lose you'), a rhetorical form that Freud suggests reveals precisely what is being denied ('I'm not thinking of elephants', 'I have no desire for my mother'). Those repeated 'not's allow Portia to bring up topics and make assertions – 'I love you', 'stay with me' – while technically not doing so. She does this partly out of self-protection (after all, she is speaking to the man she really wants), partly out of deference to Renaissance codes for properly modest feminine behaviour. So is Portia's way of speaking here evidence of her struggle to remain genuinely virtuous despite her strong – and not entirely chaste – desire for Bassanio, or is it her conscious and clever strategy for bypassing gender strictures, a way to maintain the impression of feminine virtue while actually resisting its constraints?

The difference between the two Portias emerges most clearly in 3.4, a short scene in which Portia leaves Lorenzo in charge of her estate before leaving Belmont for Venice. The Portia we meet in the scene's first half is the virtuous public figure. Lorenzo singles out for praise her noble 'god-like amity … which appears most strongly / In bearing thus the absence of your lord' (*MV* 3.4.3–4). 'Amity' is a word much associated with classical virtue, designating something between love and friendship, a feeling with the intensity of love without the polluting element of sexual desire. 'Amity' also depends upon a fundamental resemblance or compatibility at the spiritual level, a concept captured by our contemporary phrase 'soul mates'. Interestingly, amity describes the relationship between Bassanio and Antonio as much as it does to the relationship between Bassanio and Portia, and the two relationships are in potential conflict. Under normal circumstances, Lorenzo's comment implies, a wife might be jealous or suspicious of a husband who abandons her immediately after their marriage to attend to a friend, but Portia, at least in public, is so virtuous that she trusts Bassanio and supports him in his aid to Antonio.

Portia's reply underlines her native virtue – 'I never did repent for doing good, / Nor shall not now' (*MV* 3.4.10–11). She goes on to argue that because Antonio resembles Bassanio in virtue, the very condition of 'amity', it is appropriate that she sacrifice to save 'the bosom lover of my lord': 'If it be so, / How little is the cost I have bestowed / In purchasing the semblance of my soul / From out the state of hellish cruelty' (*MV* 3.4.18–21). There is more than a little hint of virtuous, even Christ-like martyrdom at work in Portia's phrasing, as well as a metaphor of financial transaction. Portia's 'cost' here is both emotional (the pain of separation) and monetary (her considerable wealth). It is as if she were buying Antonio's soul out of damnation and, because of her virtuous sacrifice, perhaps buying her own soul too. Even this much discussion of her virtuousness, Portia seems to realize, risks looking immodest, so she cuts herself off – 'This comes too near the praising of myself; / Therefore no more of it' (*MV* 3.4.23–4) – and she turns to giving her charge to Lorenzo. Portia tells him that she intends to 'live in prayer and contemplation' (*MV* 3.4.28) at a nearby monastery until Bassanio's return, a tale entirely in line with her reputation for Christian rectitude. Everything about Portia's conduct in this half of the scene suggests a woman of scrupulous, patient righteousness, willing to sacrifice herself to her husband's needs in service of the principle of virtuous amity.

A rather different Portia emerges, however, when Lorenzo and Jessica exit and the scene becomes private. This Portia is suddenly decisive, all business. Without hesitation she orders her servant Balthasar to take a letter to Padua to her cousin, Doctor Bellario, and to bring the items he provides to her at the Venetian ferry. (Alas, poor Balthasar! His reply, 'Madam, I go with all convenient speed' [*MV* 3.4.56] is his only line in the play, and Portia will soon take his name in the courtroom scene.) These 'notes and garments'

(*MV* 3.4.51), we soon surmise, are the props that she and Nerissa will use to pretend they are men. Portia's comments about their acting as men return us to the sarcastic mode we saw her adopt in her withering comments on suitors. She makes a phallic joke about wearing 'my dagger with the greater grace' (*MV* 3.4.65) and sneers at man's bragging about their sexual desirability, slaying the ladies by denying them their love. This part of Portia's speech, the comedy easily enhanced by some gestures or accents that play up the cross-gender mockery, may suggest why Portia adopts this ruse, seemingly out of the blue. She fears that all men – including her new husband – tell 'puny lies' and are 'bragging Jacks'. Which is to say, she wants to keep her eye on Bassanio, to see whether he is worthy of her trust. She here resists the position of the virtuously submissive woman she has just played. We may be reminded of the Portia in *MV* 1.2 who was well aware of the gap between high-minded moral pronouncements and the realities of hot-tempered human behaviour.

Nerissa's question, 'why, shall we turn to men?' (*MV* 3.4.78), adds another dimension to the exchange. Her astonished tone may mirror our own – where did this Portia come from? More importantly, Nerissa may be reacting to the suggestion of immorality in their adopting male identities and engaging in cross-dressing. One reason that women were forbidden to act on the English public stage was that a woman's public display was widely regarded as inherently lewd, a conspicuous refusal of the modesty, silence and submissiveness appropriate to virtuous feminine conduct. In some moral tracts, women in masculine clothing are described as sexually provocative, especially to other men. A woman publicly attired in male clothing was thus a multiple affront to the gender double standard of the day. Portia's plan that the two parade about 'accoutred like young men' (*MV* 3.4.63) – she supplies no further information about the rest of her plan – may strike Nerissa as shocking or at least very strange. Portia's reply, 'Fie, what a question's that, / If thou wert near a lewd interpreter' (*MV* 3.4.79–80), highlights a second meaning of Nerissa's question, as if the two were going not to turn 'into men' so much as turn their sexual attention towards other men, a meaning that emphasizes the bawdy interpretation of her remark even as she warns against it. Portia's comment tells us that she is capable of thinking in those terms. The private Portia we see here is take-charge, well aware of men's moral failings, resistant to patriarchal norms for women's behaviour, playful and maybe even a little sexually provocative, hardly the paragon of female virtue Lorenzo praises in the scene's opening lines.

Shakespeare's approach to the characterization of Portia, as in the case of Shylock, raises many interpretive questions. Which Portia are we meeting in the trial scene? Is the role of Balthasar merely a means for Portia to express the central principle of Christian virtue in her 'quality of mercy' speech? How to understand Portia's legalistic entrapment of Shylock? We know from Portia's behaviour that beneath the public facade of virtue there are complicated private attitudes of mistrust, contempt and desire. Does our awareness of the gap between public and private colour how we understand the operation of justice in Venice, and particularly Portia's motives for treating Shylock as she does? Can we speak of Portia's character development as a result of her playing the part of the law clerk Balthasar? Does her taking on a male role at the trial allow her to become more assertive, less bound to the public role of the submissive woman as the play goes along? Or do we see Portia return to the public role of the virtuous woman when she returns to Belmont? Is the ring episode at play's end a playful exercise of virtue, a reminder to Bassanio and Gratiano of the moral obligation of their marriage vows, or an assertion of her power within her marriage and household?

We'll have occasion to return to some of the questions in subsequent chapters. For the moment, however, we may want to notice how, with these central roles in the play, Shakespeare provides evidence for at least two (and perhaps more) very different perspectives on the very same characters. You may be able to detect the same approach to characterization at work with other characters in *The Merchant of Venice* – say, with Lancelet, Bassanio or Antonio. How then should we approach the analysis of Shakespeare's characters, long regarded as one of his crowning achievements? Should we view these characters as unified personalities and look for ways of making their different qualities psychologically consistent and comprehensible? It is certainly possible to see Shylock's oscillation between victim and victimizer in terms of the psychology of a traumatized man who lashes out in kind when he is confronted by even more cruelty from his tormenters, and it is also possible to see him as a villain who tries to mask his own dastardly plans by highlighting the hypocrisy of others. Should we understand these perspectives as layers of personality, as, for example, public and private selves in shifting relationship to each other depending upon the situation? Or should we see these characters as disunified? Does Shakespeare present us with a particular view of a character to serve the specific dramatic moment, without an expectation that we synthesize those viewpoints into one coherent personality? In this view, Portia might be a paragon of virtue when the plot demands a spokesperson for mercy, and an assertive, even provocative woman when it's time for Bassanio's comic comeuppance with the rings. Is our sense of psychological complexity just a matter of our bringing to bear the wrong kind of modern expectations? Your answers to these questions might also bear upon how actors might approach the performance of Shakespeare's roles. No matter how you address these intriguing issues, it is clear that Shakespeare uses language with great artfulness to create uniquely multifaceted, complex characters that challenge our interpretive skills and stick in the memory.

Writing matters – form, sequencing, proportion

You've freewritten a bit about the play, you've crafted a working thesis statement, and you've gathered evidence from Shakespeare's script and perhaps from research sources to support it. Now what? Next is to think about the structure of your argument, that is, how you might break your paper into sections and how those sections might relate to each other. This is a crucial part of the planning process and one that should send you back to your working thesis. It is helpful to think about the structure of your argument from three angles: form, sequence and proportion. Of these three, form is the most important, by which I mean the basic rhetorical nature of your argument, the kind of case you seek to make. Rhetoricians have identified several different types of basic arguments used in literary criticism – comparison-contrast, definition, analysis, classification, process analysis, cause-effect argument, problem-to-solution argument, contextualization. In effect all these types of argument boil down to three basic kinds:

- *Analysis*: Analysis papers break down the topic into more specific constituent parts and suggest how the more specific elements help us understand the broad topic. Comparison-contrast papers do this by comparing two items from several different angles; classification papers suggest how your topic fits into some larger classificational scheme of related items (for instance, suggesting how 'usury' fits into a class of sins involving money, a class that includes 'hoarding', 'prodigality' and 'theft'); definition papers often contrast closely related concepts to help make crucial fine distinctions (say, defining 'freedom' by contrasting it with 'liberty', 'independence' and 'abandon'). All of these rhetorical types involve understanding your topic through more specific subtopics.

- *Process*: Process essays analyse changes that occur over time, and so involve breaking down a process into a series of steps and showing how each step follows from another. It might take the form of the 'before-after' essay that traces a single change (say, Shylock's sudden decision to make Antonio 'look to his bond'), or it might trace a much longer process of development or change (for example, Bassanio's evolving understanding of marriage). The 'cause-effect' paper also falls into this category, suggesting how one or more particular causes lead to a specific effect. The trick of these essays is to break the process you're considering into discreet steps or stages and to show how each step leads logically to the next.

- *Contextualization*: This kind of essay puts a passage, character, plotline or metaphor into a particular context to explain it – a historical context, a social context, a psychological context, an artistic context or the like. Often, such an essay uses comparison and contrast between text and context to make the case for the context's relevance and explanatory power. Some contextualizing essays suggest how the context leads to a certain perspective in the text, in 'cause-effect' fashion. The contextualizing essay requires the writer to sketch out the context succinctly, elegantly and with some nuance, so it typically requires some research and, more important, synthesis of your research findings.

What sort of structure, then, does your working thesis statement imply? Are you making an argument in which you are defining a broad concept (say, 'hazarding')? Are you basically comparing and contrasting two items or characters? Are you examining a change or development in the course of the play? Are you setting a character, plotline, theme or metaphor in some sort of context? Are you articulating a problem or question – say, why is Antonio melancholy? – and then suggesting a solution? There are certainly other basic rhetorical forms, and sometimes your thesis may combine more than one of these. Even so, spending some time with your working thesis and thinking about what basic kind of argument it implies will help you find an appropriate structure for your paper.

Let's take the example of the chapter you've just read. My thesis is that two central figures of *The Merchant of Venice*, Shylock and Portia, exhibit a distinct duality in their characterizations. So the basis structure of my argument about these two characters involves comparison and contrast, with emphasis on *contrasting* the two sides of each character. You can easily imagine that I might have adopted a different thesis – for example, that Shylock and Portia *change* from one type of personality into another in the course of the play. If I'd made that argument, I would have adopted a before-after structure for each section of the chapter, emphasizing *how* each character changes, though I might also want to talk a little bit about *why*. Or I might have argued that in Portia's case the crucial context for her behaviour is Renaissance patriarchy, that is, male domination of women in the period, in which case I'd be pursuing a contextualizing argument.

Typically your working thesis will suggest your paper's basic rhetorical form. And identifying that form will help you break your argument into basic sections. For example, with a comparison-contrast paper, you will group like qualities together into separate sections. In my case, I've grouped Shylock's villainous qualities into one section and then followed that with discussion of Shylock's qualities as victim. If I were to write a before-after paper, for example, something regarding Portia's character development, I would need to describe Portia's 'before' state first and then follow it by discussion of her 'after' state, along with analysis of how and why she moves from one state to another. For a contextualizing argument, I would need to start with a short description of the scene or character I'm going to contextualize, follow it with a full explanation of the context itself, and then follow that with an analysis of details of the scene or character within that context. For a problem-to-solution argument, I would need first to establish the problem or central question and then explain my solution. Each rhetorical form suggests a basic way to divide up the argument into logical sections. You can also subdivide those sections as your thesis and your evidence demand.

You'll also want to give thought to sequencing, that is, the order you will present the sections of your paper. Sometimes your argument will naturally suggest a logical order – point A logically leads to point B leads to point C. Some guidelines for sequencing, however, spring from the basic logic of the rhetorical forms. They are as follows:

- If your paper involves a series of specific points explaining a broad claim, put your points in order of ascending importance. That is, end with your most important or compelling point.

- If your paper involves processes of change or development, prefer chronological order for your sections. That is, put your sections in the order the steps occur in time.

- If your paper involves contextualizing Shakespeare's text, explain the context before proceeding to analysis of the text.

- If your paper involves a problem-to-solution or question-to-answer structure, explain the problem thoroughly before offering and explaining your solution.

You can, of course, vary the conventional order of sections – these are guidelines, not rules. But these guidelines do describe the order your reader will expect you to adopt given the nature of your argument. So if you vary the expected sequencing, you'll want to provide explicit signposts in your essay so that your reader won't get lost.

Proportion works hand in hand with sequencing to give a reader a sense of the relative importance of points. Put very simply, the more space you devote to a point, the more important your reader will perceive it to be. It's a very common mistake to write an essay in which you devote lots of time to issues in the opening paragraphs and then, because you are tiring as you write, you spend less and less time analysing and explaining as you go along (leading to shorter and shorter paragraphs). Such an essay gives the impression of the argument just petering out, and often the last point – which should be a point that drives the argument home – seems like an afterthought, ending, to quote T. S. Eliot, not with a bang but with a whimper. For this reason, you should place weaker points towards the start of your paper and devote considerable space to your final, strongest point or piece of evidence. This is especially true of analytic papers, where you may be tempted to begin with your strongest point. In fact, you may want to write that section first and place it towards the end once you've drafted the essay. More generally, think about how much space you want to budget for each of your points so that your essay communicates with its proportions how important each idea is within the overall argument.

Once you've thought about these matters, you're ready to start drafting. One final suggestion: it's very easy to lose track of your central argument as you wrestle with each detail. This is especially true when you draft on a computer, since as you write, your first paragraph or two – where typically you will announce your thesis statement – will scroll up out of view and so your thesis statement will risk drifting out of mind. For that reason, I find it helpful to write my working thesis statement on a post-it and stick it in a corner of the computer screen. That way, I'm reminded of my central argument every time I look at the screen, and it's less likely I'll drop the thread of my basic argument. The post-it also reminds me that I need to tie in each of my individual points and my textual analyses to the thesis. Of course, as you write you may discover that your argument has slightly (or entirely!) changed as you've re-examined your evidence in the course of drafting. Once you've written a draft, test the argument of the essay you've actually written against the thesis on your post-it. If they don't match, you may need to adjust your thesis statement (and perhaps your draft) so that they do.

CHAPTER FOUR

Language in Print III: Bonds

Resonance

One of the qualities that give literary language its sense of depth and richness is resonance. Resonance is somewhat difficult to define with precision. Its roots lie in music. Think of a guitar: musical resonance refers to the way in which plucking one string causes other strings to sound with harmonically related tones (called 'overtones' in musical parlance). In writing resonance designates how an aptly chosen word, phrase or image has multiple significances at once, some literal, some symbolic, some connotative, some by association, some even related to the word's sound or the image's sensual qualities. A resonant word or image sets in motion several themes or ideas at once, and a skilful writer can draw out and develop those multiple qualities in the course of a tale. Shakespeare often uses a single resonant word – or a cluster of semantically related words – to serve as a thematic centre for a play. Such is the case, for example, with 'dream' in *A Midsummer Night's Dream*, 'hand' in *Titus Andronicus*, 'redeem' in *1 Henry IV*, 'blood' in *Macbeth* or 'will' in his sonnets. In *Macbeth*, for example, 'blood' refers literally to the blood of Macbeth's victims, metonymically to the gruesome violence of their murders, metaphorically to the line of succession and to the spirit or soul believed to reside in blood, connotatively to horror, defilement and purgation. As Shakespeare repeats these key words throughout a play, associating them with various actions, images and bit of dialogue, they have the effect of pulling together and mutually amplifying different thematic strands of the play. In *The Merchant of Venice* one such key word is 'bond' and its related words 'bind' and 'bound'.[1]

Bond as commercial contract

One meaning of 'bond' is quite obvious and specific. It refers to a particular kind of financial and legal document essential to the operation of the Venetian state. Renaissance Venice's political might was built upon international trade, and so, as Antonio, the Duke, Shylock and Portia all remark at various moments, the state's power depends upon the legal reliability of its commercial contracts. A bond guarantees payment of funds on loan, with a substantial penalty for a debtor who defaults. Bonds are not the same thing as 'shares', which designate part ownership in a company or enterprise. Someone holding shares takes on the risk of losing their investment: if the company succeeds, they profit, but if the company goes belly-up, they lose money. By contrast, a bond is the sure thing – repayment of the loan is guaranteed, typically along with some interest. Of course, you can agree to a bond and then use the money to buy shares in a company, in hopes of profiting eventually from its ventures. This manoeuvre is risky, however, for if the venture fails you end up defaulting on the loan with ruinous consequences. Indeed, versions of this kind of commercial tactic have led to financial bubbles, such as that of 2008. Antonio is engaged in a form of just this manoeuvre: he borrows money to invest in Bassanio's marriage venture in hopes that Bassanio will profit (through marriage to Portia) and be able to repay him for this and past loans. A version of this procedure – borrowing in order to invest in ventures – was also a new feature of mercantile culture in early modern England, as various trading companies pursued potentially lucrative opportunities overseas, opportunities that involved great risk and required considerable investment up front. Though technically usury was forbidden, Shylock's arrangement with Antonio reflected the reality of Renaissance England's first substantial forays into global trade in the period. English merchants had to borrow at interest to finance their trading ventures. In that sense, Shakespeare was using Venice, already an established trading centre, as a mirror of London's changing business environment. At first, Shylock specifies that his bond with Antonio is a specific type of bond: 'Go with me to a notary, seal me there / Your single bond' (*MV* 1.3.140–1). A 'single bond' (*simplex obligatio* in legal jargon) obligates the borrower (and his heirs) unconditionally to pay what is owed, whereas a 'penal bond' allows the contract to be voided if certain conditions are met (such as a compensatory action or payment). The kind of bond Shylock strikes with Antonio, then, is the more ironclad of the two.

Bond as connection, constriction, covenant and seal

Yet the word 'bond' refers to much more than just the legal contract Shylock insists upon. Those additional meanings and their broader implications resonate throughout the play. 'Bond' (and 'bind') has two general meanings in some tension with one another. On the one hand, 'bond' can refer to a connection, link or union, a coming together of two (or more) characters. In common parlance, a 'bond' typically signifies something deeper, tighter or more profound than our rather bloodless modern term 'relationship'. A 'bond' involves an emotional or historical connection, even in the case of business dealings. In the case of Shylock and Antonio, the 'bond' they seal exceeds simply striking a financial arrangement. Their bond, like many modern business deals, involves sharing a meal that celebrates the dealmakers' camaraderie and mutual trust. (This meal occurs on the night Jessica is spirited away by Lorenzo.) As he and Antonio come to terms, Shylock declares, perhaps disingenuously, perhaps earnestly, 'I would be friends with you and have your love' (*MV* 1.3.134), and Antonio, despite his evident anti-Semitism, seems to soften towards Shylock with his comment, 'the Hebrew will turn Christian, he grows kind' (*MV* 1.3.174).

On the other hand, the word 'bond' also evokes the notion of restriction or mutual obligation, some element of legal, psychological, moral or symbolic force that ties the parties to one another and prevents them from abandoning or abusing trust. This, the *Oxford English Dictionary* suggests, is the oldest meaning of the word. A bond in this sense involves a principle of constraint that limits the potential damage one party can do to another in a relationship. It seeks to put the brakes on aggression, betrayal or selfishness that, contracts so often seem to imagine, lurks around the corner. Shylock memorably articulates this principle of restriction or constraint with the maxim he offers as he leaves his house to join the Christian merchants for dinner. 'Fast bind, fast find', he tells Jessica, 'A proverb never stale in thrifty mind' (*MV* 2.5.52–3; 'fast' here means both 'quickly' and 'securely'). His immediate concern is the securing of his house and fortune from theft, but the more general principle at work, one to which Shylock subscribes, is that tightly 'binding' one's goods (or daughter or business partner), restricting them physically or contractually, assures one's control over them, one's ability to 'find' them later and prevent their loss. This principle governs not just Shylock's housekeeping but crucially his business relationship with Antonio, in which he uses the contract and the law to prevent Antonio from wriggling free of responsibility, making sure that he is literally bound over for trial and judgement. The word 'bond' and its cognates both name the coming together of two parties and a means for restricting their coming apart. Since a bond involves an affective link, its constraints are in part designed to protect the parties against emotional vulnerability.

The word 'bond' is also linked to the central place of covenant in Jewish theology. Covenant in its religious sense refers to the contract between God and his chosen people, the Jews, a bond sealed with an oath and involving stipulations and mandates on human conduct, the ritual practices and moral tenets of Judaism. Jews understood the covenant between God and man, the foundation of their faith, as the model for covenants between human beings. It's notable, then, that when urged to break the bond in the trial scene, Shylock proclaims, 'An oath, an oath, I have an oath in heaven! / Shall I lay perjury on my soul? / No, not for Venice' (*MV* 4.1.224–6). Here Shylock explicitly ties his bond with Antonio to his covenant with God. To walk away from the bond would be more than merely violating his personal pledge; it would be tantamount to violating a key principle of his faith.

One last sense of the word 'bond' takes us out of the realm of abstraction. We often mark the bonds between people with some physical object that embodies both the connection between individuals and the constraints upon it, a marker ratified by legal authority or by its being struck in public before witnesses. Here the obvious example is the paper contract between Shylock and Antonio, an important prop in the trial scene. Shylock puts particular stock in his bond having official status. In *MV* 1.3, he insists that the bond be notarized with a seal. In answer to Gratiano's taunts at the trial, he replies confidently, 'Till thou canst rail the seal from off my bond / Thy offend'st thy lungs to speak so loud' (*MV* 4.1.138–9), suggesting that the ratifying seal has more rhetorical force than do Gratiano's words. The seal gives the words of Shylock's merry bond the force of law, a force that can be used in Shylock's favour but which, he soon learns, can also be turned against him. In the case of marriage, the physical marker of the 'bond' of marriage is the ring Portia gives Bassanio, the counterpart of the kiss with which Portia ratifies his choice of the correct casket (*MV* 3.2.147–8), given to him before they take their vows in church. The ring marks their bond of love and Portia's ceding of her property to her new husband, but it also publicly binds Bassanio to her and spells out her penalty for his parting with the ring, making it tantamount to his betraying her romantically. When he gives the ring away to Balthasar the law clerk (Portia's alter ego), he violates their marriage contract, an offence akin to Antonio's default on Shylock's loan, and the meaning of the ring, like the meaning of Shylock's bond, takes on a new significance. There is a second ring in the play, the ring given by Shylock's wife Leah to him before the two were married, a symbol of the bond of love between the two. It is potent enough emotionally for Shylock that he keeps it and never sells it, even after Leah's death. The play does not make clear whether Shylock gives the ring to Jessica, perhaps as part of her inheritance from her mother, or she simply takes it as part of the spoils she steals when she elopes. In any case, by so casually trading the ring away for a monkey, Jessica pointedly breaks the bond between herself, her father and family and aligns herself with the Christian patricians. Indeed, it may be Jessica's act of violating the marital and familial bond that hardens Shylock's resolve to 'have the heart of him [Antonio] if he forfeit' (*MV* 3.1.115).

Bonds of hate and love

The Merchant of Venice explores several different kinds of 'bonds' between characters: bonds of love (and hate), bonds of friendship, familial bonds, bonds between masters and servants, social or tribal bonds, even bonds between humankind and God. What interests Shakespeare is the way in which various qualities of the 'bond' between Shylock and Antonio, the central bond of the play, resonate in different ways with other characters' relationships. One way we can see the connection between Shylock's bond and bonds between characters is the way in which the language of property, mercantilism and contractualism appears throughout the dialogue, often in contexts far afield from business dealings. Such language suggests that concerns about relative value, money and property, profit and risk, emotional bonding and binding obligation, all concerns operating in Shylock's bond, are also in play in characters' relationships with one another.

To take one of the more obvious examples, in the trial scene Shylock confronts Christian hypocrisy regarding mercy with a searing speech about slavery. The logic of his takedown turns on property and people. Why, Shylock asks, don't Christians show mercy to their slaves by freeing them, welcoming them into their families or offering them creature comforts? Their answer, he notes, is that 'you bought them', and with the claim 'The slaves are ours' (*MV* 4.1.92, 97) comes the right to do with one's possessions as one likes. Slaves are to be treated as property, not people; property rights trump human rights or any appeal to mercy. So too, Shylock argues, it is with Antonio: 'The pound of flesh which I demand of him / Is dearly bought; 'tis mine, and I will have it' (*MV* 4.1.98–9). Shylock's bond allows him to own Antonio, to put him into legal bondage, to treat him not a person but a piece of meat, to do with him as he likes. And, Shylock underlines, this contractual protection of property rights and its enshrinement in Christian practices is at the very heart of the Venetian state: 'if you deny me, fie upon your law: / There is no force in the decrees of Venice' (*MV* 4.1.100–1). Shylock's appeal to the law over mercy, he suggests, is no different than Christian practice, which, for all its high-minded appeals to mercy, depends upon property law, that is, the power of bonds, to underwrite the bondage that makes Venetian privilege possible. It's notable that the Duke has no good answer for Shylock's argument. He immediately calls for Bellario, ostensibly to get him out of this ideological dilemma.

The language of property and contractualism is particularly strong in the case of the marriageable women of the play. Shylock conflates the loss of his daughter Jessica with the loss of ducats, if we are to believe what Salanio mockingly reports of Shylock's lament in the street, 'My daughter! O, my ducats! O, my daughter' (*MV* 2.8.15). Three scenes earlier when he leaves Jessica alone to attend Antonio's dinner, Shylock tells her to lock herself away in the house with the miser's command 'fast bind, fast find' (*MV* 2.5.52). The proverb covers both his relationship with his property and his daughter – both are to be hoarded. And he is not alone in thinking of Jessica as if she were property. When she elopes with Lorenzo, Jessica asks her husband-to-be 'whether I am yours' (*MV* 2.6.32) before tossing down the first of several caskets of Shylock's fortune. This suggests *quid pro quo* at work in their relationship, a money for love transaction, with Jessica as much a stolen commodity as are Shylock's chests of gold. In a terrible irony Jessica, in an effort to escape a father who thinks of her as property, elopes with a man who may at some level share those thoughts. Even though Lorenzo emphasizes his love for Jessica's wisdom, beauty and truth in his speech about her, before Jessica appears at the balcony he speaks to his compatriots about 'play[ing] thieves for wives' (*MV* 2.6.24). The parallel with Bassanio's pursuit of Portia, especially his speaking of her as the stolen 'golden fleece', reminds us of these husbands' mercenary financial motives.

Even here, at the moment of Jessica's romantic triumph, Shakespeare includes language that suggests her unease with being aligned with stolen property. As she tosses down the casket of gold to Lorenzo, Jessica says, 'I am glad 'tis night you do not look on me, / For I am much ashamed of my exchange' (*MV* 2.6.35–6). The context suggests that Jessica is referring primarily to her disguise as a boy ('exchange' can mean 'change'), but the word 'exchange', with its commercial connotations, may also signal that she is feeling guilty about the money-for-love bargain she fears she has struck. That guilt is clearly at work in her exchange with Lorenzo at the start of the play's final scene. As the two trade 'in such a night' references to mythic love stories, Lorenzo adds their own tale to the list:

> In such a night
> Did Jessica steal from the wealthy Jew,
> And with an unthrift love did run from Venice
> As far as Belmont. (*MV* 5.1.14–17)

The word 'steal' (meaning both 'leave secretly' and 'rob'), along with mention of Shylock's wealth and her own 'unthrift' ('overly generous', 'prodigal') love, reminds Jessica of the questionable financial conditions of her romantic bond with Lorenzo. Annoyed or ashamed at the word 'steal', Jessica fires back with her own version of their story:

> In such a night
> Did young Lorenzo swear he loved her well,
> Stealing her soul with many vows of faith,
> And ne'er a true one. (*MV* 5.1.17–20)

Here Jessica places responsibility for the theft with Lorenzo, not herself, and she suggests the crime involves not property but her very heart and soul, casting Lorenzo as one who has spirited her away under false pretences, at best a romantic cad, at worst a soul-stealing devil. The tone of this exchange depends upon how it is performed – it can be playful or increasingly tense. But however it is played, the language points to trouble when bonds between men and women become intertwined with questions of property.

The same intermixing of romantic and financial bonds haunts the relationship between Bassanio and Portia and surfaces in their language. Early in the play Bassanio tells Antonio of his intention to woo Portia in a speech redolent with financial vocabulary – 'richly left', 'nothing undervalued', 'worth', 'golden fleece', 'thrift', 'fortunate' (*MV* 1.1.161, 165, 167, 170, 175–6). For all his talk of her 'wondrous virtues', Bassanio sees his courtship as a commercial venture. Of course, the casket test is designed precisely to weed out suitors who desire Portia only for her inherited wealth or status, but Bassanio passes the test by ignoring the precious metals gold and silver and risking everything by choosing lead. In his first scene with Portia, Bassanio is understandably careful not to use terms that evoke a financial motive. Yet when he greets Lorenzo, Jessica and Salerio upon their arrival afterwards at his moment of romantic triumph, it is as if that vocabulary involuntarily surfaces: 'welcome hither, / If that the youth of my new interest here / Have the power to bid you welcome' (*MV* 3.2.219–21). 'Interest' suggests not only Bassanio's emotional attachment to Portia but also the commercial profit he has made from the match.

Even so, it is, perhaps surprisingly, Portia's speech that is most coloured by financial terminology. When Portia gives herself to Bassanio after he has chosen the lead casket, she speaks of wanting to be 'trebled twenty times myself, / A thousand times more fair, ten thousand times more rich' so that she might 'stand high in your [Bassanio's] account' (*MV* 3.2.153–5). In this case, Portia seems interested in converting financial vocabulary back into a romantic vocabulary. She wants Bassanio to see her worth as grounded in her status as a woman, 'an unlessoned girl, unschooled, unpractised', a 'gentle spirit' (*MV* 3.2.159, 163), not as a wealthy prize, this even as in the very same speech she transfers ownership of herself and her estate over to her new husband. For all of her public sealing of her love bond with Bassanio, Portia is well aware of her loss of power in this transfer of property, and so she controls that loss with the conditions that accompany her giving of the ring:

> ... when you part from, lose or give away,
> Let it presage the ruin of your love,
> And be my vantage to exclaim on you. (*MV* 3.2.172–4)

The ring, like a financial contract, is her means for imagining the possibility of breaking their bond even at the moment they make it and to dictate the terms of that break. This is the first of several indications that Portia is in more control of her relationship with Bassanio than it might first appear. When she hears of the amount of Antonio's loan, she responds with a privileged shrug, 'what, no more?' and promises to supply Bassanio with 'gold / To pay the petty debt twenty over' (*MV* 3.2.297, 305–6). Perhaps even more telling, in an effort to cheer Bassanio up, she makes a joke about the loan that financed Bassanio's courtship of her: 'since you are dear bought, I will love you dear' (*MV* 3.2.312). With this line she forgives him for presenting himself as richer than he actually was, but she also pointedly asserts herself as the dominant party in their relationship, the buyer and not the bought.

By reminding Bassanio of how costly he has been for her to 'buy', Portia highlights another way in which financial bonds and human bonds intersect. Financial bonds involve webs of obligation into which are woven emotional agendas. The relationship between Antonio and Bassanio provides a case in point. When we first encounter Antonio with Bassanio, we learn that they have had a long relationship, one that has involved Antonio loaning him money so that Bassanio could maintain an aristocratic lifestyle he could ill afford. That debt, Bassanio notes, involves not just a financial obligation but an emotional one – 'To you, Antonio', he says, 'I *owe* the most in money and in love' (*MV* 1.1.131, emphasis added). When Bassanio goes on to declare his intention 'to get clear of all the debts I owe' (*MV* 1.1.134) by courting Portia, then, this is a significant problem for their relationship, particularly so for Antonio, whose deep attachment to Bassanio is not clearly reciprocated in kind. Debt has been a means for Antonio to keep Bassanio financially and emotionally obligated to him, and so Bassanio's intention to clear his debts, particularly by striking up a relationship with Portia, presents an emotional crisis for Antonio. The awful paradox is that Bassanio is asking his friend to finance the breaking of their relationship. This circumstance may explain why Antonio is willing to take on the bond from Shylock despite its dire terms – it reinforces Bassanio's emotional obligation to him. When Shylock decides to enforce the terms of the bond, Antonio uses his own peril to oblige Bassanio to return to Venice and to wring from him a declaration of his love. In what looks at first glance like noble selflessness, Antonio's letter in 3.2 masterfully leverages his sacrifice of purse and person to urge Bassanio to see him once more. His promise to clear all debts between the two upon his death emotionally binds Bassanio all the more tightly to him, and the element of guilt-tripping in the letter's final lines – 'use your pleasure; if your love do not persuade you to come, let not my letter' (*MV* 3.2.319–20) – turns Antonio's plight into a test of the strength of Bassanio's feelings for him.

At the trial Antonio extends this strategy of obligation, insisting on sacrificing himself when Bassanio offers to substitute his own life (*MV* 4.1.110–12). And in what threatens to be his final speech before his death, Antonio twice stresses that he is paying his friend's debt by braving Shylock's knife, holding Bassanio's hand as he does so. That paying of Bassanio's financial debt involves him incurring an emotional debt to Antonio, and Antonio uses that debt to push Bassanio into clarifying his commitment to him:

> Say how I loved you, speak me fair in death,
> And, when the tale is told, bid her [Portia] be judge
> Whether Bassanio had not once a love. (*MV* 4.1.271–3)

In the end Bassanio gives Antonio just what he desires, a declaration that he would sacrifice 'life itself, my wife and all the world' (*MV* 4.1.280) to save his beloved friend. Portia's legerdemain with the ring in the final scene allows her to renegotiate the terms of what has become a love triangle, with Antonio allowing himself being 'bound again' (*MV* 5.1.251), this time as the guarantor for Bassanio's future fidelity to his wife. In this way, Antonio is able to maintain his bond with Bassanio (along with the emotional obligation), but it becomes incorporated into the marital bond between Portia and Bassanio. The dynamics in these characters' relationships, their emotional bonds, mirror the network of debts and obligations we find in financial bonds. Indeed, in Antonio's case, loans become a means for him to express his love and to extract it from his beloved.

Words as bonds

Shakespeare is fascinated by the way the meaning of a bond can be reversed and still be binding. This quality of the bond is related to wordplay. Shakespeare especially delights in banter that involves one character taking another's words and turning their meaning in some unexpected direction, as a way of gaining rhetorical advantage. This is, for example, the point of Gratiano's bawdy quip with Nerissa regarding a bet 'stake down' in 3.2 or Lancelet's exchange with Lorenzo about preparing for dinner in 3.5. In both cases, the first speaker remains bound to the words he or she has spoken, even though the second speaker redefines them in some unexpected way. The result is a loss of face or power, in the cases above momentary and humorous, more substantial and serious elsewhere in the play. The way in which a verbal bond's meaning can be turned on its head is central, of course, to Shylock's comeuppance in the trial scene. Shylock thinks that he can treat seriously language in the bond he had earlier presented as 'merry', that he can legally bind Antonio to words he had earlier agreed to but whose new meaning Antonio had not foreseen. Portia's judgement in the trial scene uses the same rhetorical tactic, but to Shylock's disadvantage. She fastens on the word 'flesh' and interprets it in a literalistic way Shylock does not anticipate (flesh but not blood), and then she binds tightly him to that language, to Shylock's legal disadvantage. She does the same with the word 'pound', which she treats as an exact measurement, rather than a euphemism for a small amount. When Shylock refuses Bassanio's offer of payment in court, this too becomes a verbal bond. Shylock simply doesn't appreciate the full force of his words until the case begins to go against him.

The reversible force of bonds also operates when Bassanio gives away Portia's ring to Balthasar after the trial. In this case, he gives the ring intending to recognize the clerk's 'deservings' (*MV* 4.1.446) as the vanquisher of Shylock. (We might also ask why Antonio encourages Bassanio to give away his wedding ring, particularly since he claims it will let 'my love withal / Be valued 'gainst your wife's commandment' [*MV* 4.1.446–7].) Yet once Portia receives the ring, it becomes a symbol of Bassanio's potential for abandoning his commitment to her if opportunity arises. When Portia reveals it in the final scene, claiming that 'by this ring the doctor lay with me' (*MV* 5.1.259), the original meaning of the ring is reversed, turned upon Bassanio. When Portia first gave him the ring, she did so in recognition of her proper submission to him as a dutiful wife (*MV* 3.2.166–71). Back in her hands the ring now signifies her potential independence, her power to make him a cuckold and so to undercut his masculine reputation. Portia routes the ring's return through Antonio, so that in the end it now also signifies Antonio's formal recognition of the primacy of Portia and Bassanio's relationship, with an oath even more binding and serious than his bond with Shylock: 'I dare be bound again: / My soul upon the forfeit, that your lord / Will never break faith advisedly' (*MV* 5.1.251–3).

In much the same way, the emotions attached to a bond can also be reversed and yet still remain binding. We can see this most clearly in the case of Shylock and Antonio, where Shylock's initial attempt at being friends with Antonio through the 'merry bond' curdles into hatred when Shylock senses he has been betrayed. Hatred becomes a perverse sort of bond between the two men. When Shylock repeatedly cries 'I'll have my bond' in *MV* 3.3 and 4.1, he is referring not only to his legal contract but to the loathing he has for his enemy. And that bond of hatred bears upon how we understand the meaning of the 'pound of flesh' Shylock insists upon at trial. Even as he is seeking to destroy Antonio, is Shylock pursuing or even strengthening his bond with him? If we think of the cutting of Antonio's flesh as a symbolic circumcision (as many critics have suggested), is Shylock perversely trying to erase the difference between himself as Jew and Antonio as Christian in order to bring them closer together? Is Shylock's focus on taking the pound of Antonio's flesh from 'nearest his heart' (*MV* 4.1.250) a perversely literal way of bringing himself close to his enemy's heart? If we recall myths of the Jews as consumers of Christian blood, does Shylock's bloodlust reveal a desire to ingest Antonio, to assimilate him into himself? In other words, is Shylock's insistence upon his bond with Antonio a way for Shakespeare to explore how the desire for revenge involves an emotional bond with the thing one hates, a bond with surprising resemblances to love?

Weirdly enough, Antonio's 'merciful' judgement upon Shylock also smacks of this paradoxical love-hate bond. Why doesn't Antonio advocate for Shylock's death, as Gratiano repeatedly encourages him to do? By specifying that Shylock be baptized, Antonio's explicit intent is to destroy his foe's faith and livelihood (as a Christian Shylock cannot loan money for profit). But baptism also makes Shylock one of Antonio's Christian 'tribe', a person he is obligated by his own faith to treat as a brother, even to love. This is not to minimize the destructive effect of Antonio's 'mercy', only to note that bonds of friendship and hate, mercy and malice, become perversely intertwined as the play goes on.

Writing matters – abstraction and nuance

As this discussion of 'bond' suggests, choosing the apt word or phrase – what the French call the *bon mot* – is an important ideal to keep before you as you draft your argument, particularly your thesis statement. Nothing delights a reader more than encountering a word or phrase that perfectly and succinctly captures an idea. It's one of the reasons I love to read a great movie or theatre review – I savour the kind of phrase that exactly describes an actor's performance or the camerawork of a director, something that just begs to be put to memory and quoted. The *bon mot* has a persuasive effect as well. We're more likely to find an idea convincing when it is expressed in carefully crafted, precise language, and we tend to be sceptical of wording that is vague or ill-chosen. Lancelet Giobbe and his father undermine their attempts at persuading Bassanio of Lancelet's fitness for aristocratic service by using learned words they are not in control of. By contrast, Lancelet is at his comic finest when he expertly exploits the multiple meanings of a word like 'cover' to get the best of Lorenzo. It's very easy to counsel you to choose your words carefully, but like Portia says to Nerissa, 'if to do were as easy as to know what were good to do, chapels had been churches, and poor men's cottages princes' palaces' (*MV* 1.2.12–14). So in the paragraphs below, I want to take up two specific elements of word choice that, after years of marking papers, I've seen many a student struggle with. Those elements are abstraction and nuance.

First, abstraction. It's obvious to say, but language lets us refer to the same object in the world with very different degrees of specificity or generality. I might refer to myself, for example, as Douglas M. Lanier, as a Shakespearean, as a professor, as a man, as a person, as a creature or as a thing. The list I've just given ascends a ladder of abstraction from most specific to most general. You can do this with any word. Look around the room and try creating your own list using anything you see. Adjusting the level of abstraction up or down helps us see different qualities of the 'same' object or idea. In my list, each time I go up a rung on the ladder of abstraction I am grouping myself with an ever-larger set of things that share one quality. But with each move upwards I also lose some of the particularity that makes me a specific, unique being. Shakespeare often shifts between an abstract vocabulary and concrete, specific words. To use a cinematic analogy: we might think of him as shifting between close-ups that focus on the particularity of individual objects and long shots that place those objects in some wider context or put us at a contemplative distance from them. A good example can be found in the opening lines of Portia's 'quality of mercy' speech:

> The quality of mercy is not strained:
> It droppeth as the gentle rain from heaven
> Upon the place beneath …
> 'Tis mightiest in the mightiest; it becomes
> The thronèd monarch better than his crown.
>
> (*MV* 4.1.180–2, 184–5)

In both cases Shakespeare begins with a generalization and then shifts to something more concrete. In the first case the gently falling 'rain' simile explains the phrase 'not strained'; in the second case the 'throned monarch' offers a specific example of the phrase 'the mightiest'. Being aware of levels of abstraction helps you chart how Shakespeare moves between abstract truisms – what Renaissance readers called 'sententiae', brief bits of moral wisdom – and more specific examples, images and concrete objects. It can also help you resist the gravitational pull in the direction of abstraction as you write your analysis. We often associate generalization with analytic distance (with some good reason), which is why, I think, students writing analytic essays often lean towards a far more abstract vocabulary than they might use in conversation. The more abstract the vocabulary, so the reasoning goes, the more intellectual the paper sounds. Certainly abstraction is sometimes appropriate, especially in a thesis statement, and sometimes a bit of academic jargon can capture a complicated argument or perspective in a single phrase. But a predominantly abstract vocabulary runs the serious risk of non-committal vagueness and vapid waffling. Close observation of detail and accurate description can themselves be powerful forms of analysis. As a general rule, your vocabulary will almost always benefit by moving down the abstraction ladder a rung or two, particularly when you are explaining key concepts or conclusions.

Now to the issue of nuance. Have you ever wondered why we have different words for the same thing? The truth is that there are different words for the same thing because they don't designate *exactly* the same thing. Take the words 'sleep', 'slumber', 'nap' and 'snooze'. 'Slumber', a word which survives in nursery rhymes, is a word most of us associate most with children, and it has a more poetic cast than any of the other words; 'sleep', by contrast, belongs to the world of both childhood and adult experience and is more prosaic. 'Nap' and 'snooze' are associated with shorter periods, and both are done during the daytime (one 'slumbers' only at night). Like 'slumber', 'nap' is associated with childhood, though not exclusively so; a 'snooze' is more casual, less planned than a 'nap', and it is also linked to boredom in a way that napping is not. My point is that though these words are certainly synonyms, they refer to slightly different experiences or slightly different ways of viewing the same experience. Those slight but significant distinctions are 'nuances', a word taken from the French word for 'shades of color'. Part of learning to be a skilful painter involves training oneself to perceive subtle gradations of hue, tone and modes of light. An artist who can distinguish pink from magenta from mahogany from scarlet is more likely to portray the world with precision than is one who sees all these shades merely as 'red'. So too it is with language: to create interesting, perceptive writing and communicate with some precision, you should first follow Shakespeare's example by becoming a connoisseur of words, cherishing their distinctive shades of meaning and qualities. It is because Shakespeare is such a master of verbal nuance that he makes us cognizant of shades of meaning that otherwise might escape our notice, which is to say, he stretches the mind's perceptual categories and can say a lot with very little.

To drive this point home, let's look at two examples. The first involves one of Shakespeare's favourite ploys, the use of a single word with multiple meanings or connotations. In the play's second scene, Portia laments her inability to select her own suitors with this sentence: 'I may neither choose who I would, nor refuse who I dislike, so is the will of a living daughter curbed by the will of a dead father' (*MV* 1.2.22–4). The repeated word 'will' sets several different meanings into motion at once: 'will' refers to the document that specifies the terms of the casket test, yet one more example of a bond; 'will' also refers to the authority of Portia's father and Portia's authority as a mature woman. Like 'bond', 'will' can have two contradictory shades of meaning: it can refer to an act of conscious, rational volition, or it can refer to an act of unconsidered impulse, what we might call wilfulness. In the Renaissance, the second sense of 'will' is sometimes linked to carnal desire or lust. This one sentence, actually just one clause of that sentence, suggests at least two different ideas at once. On the one hand, Portia feels as if her choices are being tyrannically controlled – dare we say, bound? – by her father from beyond the grave. This is the sort of patriarchal power over marriage we see in many plays of the period, taken to its logical extreme. On the other hand, the father's motive for that control here is presented to us as virtuous (so says Nerissa in *MV* 1.2.26–7), a distrust of the ease with which his daughter's choice of suitor might be swayed by her 'will' or erotic desire. His distrust is not entirely unwarranted, for Portia's pulse seems to quicken when Nerissa reminds her of Bassanio at scene's end

(*MV* 1.2.110–6) and again when Bassanio arrives in Belmont in *MV* 2.9.98–9 and *MV* 3.2.1–24. In fact, it is possible to argue that Portia ends up with precisely the kind of suitor her father most feared – a gold-digger. The multiple senses of 'will' allow the scene to be played in multiple ways, and the line can reveal more than Portia may intend, particularly if we remember it in the course of later events. It's notable that Nerissa returns to the term 'will' in the final line of 2.9 as the two women go to meet Bassanio. Speaking to Portia, Nerissa says, 'Bassanio, lord, love, if thy will it be' (*MV* 2.9.100). This may be Shakespeare's cue for us to recall this word and the earlier key line in which it appeared. But whether you buy that point or not, this line moves in several directions at once: whose 'will' are we talking about here, Bassanio's or Portia's? What sort of 'will' is in play? And what's the relationship of Portia's and Bassanio's wills to the dead father's 'will' and the test?

My second example suggests how Shakespeare can use words in novel yet precise ways. When Shylock learns that Jessica traded away his turquoise ring for a monkey, he memorably laments, 'I would not have given it for a wilderness of monkeys' (*MV* 3.1.111). A glance at the *Oxford English Dictionary* tells us that a 'troop' or 'tribe' would be the more conventional way to indicate a group of monkeys, though notably neither word is used in this way before the nineteenth century. So why 'wilderness', a word that typically indicates an expanse of uncivilized land uninhabited by human beings? The word carries with it a sense of vast size that may be Shylock's primary meaning. A wilderness is an area where its animal inhabitants are so many they cannot be counted, unlike, say, a 'park' or 'preserve' where animals may be plentiful but not innumerable. Unlike 'forest', the word 'wilderness' suggests a remote land, particularly so for Renaissance audiences thrilled by tales of strange, faraway realms newly open to European exploration, so 'wilderness' enhances the fantastical exoticism of the pet monkey. Indeed, the word 'monkey' only entered English in the early sixteenth century, suggesting that the English were only recently familiar with them (not so 'ape', a word with a much longer pedigree). And 'wilderness' has long been associated with human exile, so it may glance backwards at Shylock's condition as a Jew in Christian Venice – a man suddenly without a family and socially isolated. This is not the first time that Shakespeare uses 'wilderness' as a word for a group of beasts. In *Titus Andronicus*, Titus cautions his son about the rapaciousness of the Roman elite: 'Why, foolish Lucius, dost thou not perceive / That Rome is but a wilderness of tigers?' (*Titus Andronicus* 3.1.53–4). His use of 'wilderness' deploys many of the same senses we see operating in Shylock's line: vast numbers, exoticism, pseudo-civilization, isolation of the speaker. Indeed, this way of using the word seems to be Shakespeare's own invention. My point is that what appears to be an odd word choice on Shakespeare's part, even an error, often becomes extraordinarily apt if you attend to the word's nuances.

As you are analysing Shakespeare's word choices, it's equally important that you attend to nuance and connotation in your own vocabulary, especially so as you are drawing conclusions or making generalizations. Let's say you are writing on Shakespeare's depiction of love in *The Merchant of Venice*: what sort or quality of love do you mean? Infatuation? Passion? Affection? Contentment? Intimacy? Idolization? Matrimonial love? Platonic love? Each of these terms evokes a distinct emotional shading that will prompt you to look for slightly different elements in Shakespeare's dialogue and help you make more subtle distinctions. To take a second example: let's say you are evaluating Bassanio's behaviour in play. How to move beyond the simple binary categories of 'good' and 'bad', 'moral' and 'immoral', or worst of all, 'positive' and 'negative'? What words or phrases might best capture the full complexity of this character's particular ethical orientation (and does he change in the course of events)? Sharpening your analytic vocabulary, being in control of the distinctions and connotations your key terms bring into play, will make you a closer reader, a more critical thinker and a far more interesting and creative writer. If words are the tools of the writer's trade, each shaped to do a slightly different task, it's worth expanding your storehouse of tools and knowing precisely what each one does.

CHAPTER FIVE

Language in Dramatic Context

So far we've examined various forms of language in *The Merchant of Venice* that stretch across scenes – imagery, wordplay, allusion, resonant terms and the like. These play-length patterns of language form thematic threads that hold the fabric of the drama together, giving the story a sense of unity and a set of distinctive concerns. In this chapter we will be looking at how language functions within a single dramatic scene, the basic unit of Shakespeare's playwriting. Characters speak, we will be assuming, not just to make poetic pronouncements but to accomplish specific goals within a particular social situation. Language is one of their means to do things – a form of action. Understanding characters' words, then, requires us to take account of the dramatic context established by the scene and the purposes characters want to accomplish by speaking. What characters say, what their language means, occurs within a history established by the play. Every speech, no matter how short, is a response to what has come before, and every speech anticipates some response to it. If we regard characters' language as their means for pursuing their goals and we situate their words firmly in the give and take of dramatic dialogue and action, we get a much richer sense of Shakespeare's performative sense of language, and we can see more clearly how he achieved the effect of multidimensionality in his plays. We'll be focusing on two key scenes in the play – Bassanio's choice of the lead casket in 3.2 and the trial scene in 4.1 – because in each one strand of the story – the romance plot and the bond plot – reaches its climax. What's more, each scene features a famous speech that serves as a crucial articulation of the play's ideals. We'll have occasion to consider these speeches as thematic statements, but it will become apparent that these speeches make a quite different, more complicated impression when we examine how they function within particular dramatic contexts.

The casket scene (*MV* 3.2)

As they wait impatiently for Lorenzo to elope with Jessica in *MV* 2.6, Salerio and Graziano have a short, seemingly throwaway conversation about the nature of desire. Salerio observes wryly that lovers, like the doves that pull Venus's chariot, zealously 'fly / To seal love's bonds new made', but they are far less eager 'to keep obligéd faith unforfeited' (*MV* 2.6.6–7). Gratiano, warming to this theme, expands upon it with a pile-up of proverbs:

> Who riseth from a feast
> With that keen appetite that he sits down?
> Where is the horse that doth untread again
> His tedious measures with the unbated fire
> That he did pace them first? All things that are
> Are with more spirit chaséd than enjoyed. (*MV* 2.6.8–13)

This psychological principle of courtship – the notion that men lose interest in women once women consent to their desires – is an idea to which Shakespeare often returned. Most memorably, the speaker of his Sonnet 129 suggests that men madly pursue sex, but once they are satisfied, they despise the object of their desire – lust is 'past reason hunted, and no sooner had / Past reason hated' (ll. 6–7). But Gratiano gives this idea a new spin with the image of a merchant ship that starts off its voyage fully outfitted but returns bare and bedraggled, 'beggared by the strumpet wind' (*MV* 2.6.19). This ship illustrates a more general economic principle – risk in search of reward entails the possibility of loss or destruction by 'the strumpet wind', his metaphor for faithless fortune. At first glance the ship might seem to refer to men, sexually and financially depleted by their pursuit of faithless, 'strumpet' women. Perhaps this is even how Graziano intends it. But if that's the case, the metaphor works against his intention, for Graziano identifies the 'scarféd barque' as female ('her native bay', 'doth she return'), suggesting, perhaps not entirely consciously, that the victim of strumpet-like fickleness and infidelity is a woman.

As is so often the case, Shakespeare uses this passage to plant a thematic seed. Women's distrust of men, their awareness of men's willingness to abandon them at the end of courtship, hangs over Portia and Bassanio's relationship throughout the play's last three acts, particularly during the casket scene (*MV* 3.2). Portia's opening speech involves two alternating voices, one fearful of exposing herself emotionally, the other, more forceful voice seeking to control the situation by directing Bassanio's actions. Portia tells Bassanio to 'tarry' (one of her favourite words), anxious that he postpone taking the casket test so she won't risk losing him forever. She even confesses that she wishes to teach him 'how to choose right' (*MV* 3.2.11), though she is forbidden to do so. Yet Portia is also reluctant to confess outright why she wants Bassanio to tarry: 'There's something tells me – but it is not love – / I would not lose you, and, you know yourself, / Hate counsels not in such a quality' (*MV* 3.2.4–6). As we observed in Chapter Three, the convoluted quality of this line, with its vague 'something tells me' and the inserted denial 'it is not love', nicely communicates the struggle between Portia the virtuous, properly silent, passive, chaste maiden, and the assertive Portia, a woman forthright about her desires and intent upon pursuing them. She wants to give herself to Bassanio, and yet she fears the loss of self-possession that might come with that surrender. Shakespeare communicates this conflicted state of mind in a sequence of lines where she oscillates between maintaining ownership over herself and giving herself over in love:

>   Beshrew your eyes,
> They have o'erlooked me and divided me:
> One half of me is yours, the other half yours.
> Mine own I would say: but if mine, then yours,
> And so, all yours. O, these naughty times
> Puts bars between the owners and their rights:
> And so, though yours, not yours. (*MV* 3.2.14–20)

Towards the end of this passage, Portia seems to realize that she does not have the right to give herself to Bassanio because of her father's casket test. That is what bars Bassanio from claiming his right to own her fully, even though Portia suggests that she's given herself over emotionally to him.

The Merchant of Venice demonstrates repeatedly how economic considerations impinge upon all kinds of human relationships, even love. This passage makes clear that as a woman Portia doesn't yet entirely own herself. In the case of her father, she is the prisoner of his casket test, a test designed to root out suitors interested only in her dowry. As she falls in love, however, Portia also recognizes that she will become the property of Bassanio, both emotionally and literally, since her inheritance and her legal rights to property will become her husband's upon their marriage. Little wonder that Portia may feel some reticence about moving from being the property of one man, her father, to another, her prospective husband, particularly given men's penchant for violating a woman's trust after they have, to use a common phrase, 'experienced the goods'. In fact, we might share Portia's concern, given that Bassanio has himself earlier revealed to Antonio that he's pursuing Portia to get out of debt. Like Antonio with his maritime commercial 'ventures', Bassanio is taking a calculated risk – the casket test – in hopes of a spectacular profit, the 'golden fleece' of Portia and her wealth. What will Bassanio do once he's taken full possession of her?

Portia's anxiety about just that prospect underlies the witty exchange between her and Bassanio before he undergoes the casket test. Bassanio begs to take the test, claiming hyperbolically that tarrying has become a kind of torture for him; 'as I am', he says, 'I live upon the rack' (*MV* 3.2.25). Bassanio is deploying a familiar trope from Petrarchan love poetry – the idea that unrequited true love entails suffering. Bassanio wants to communicate that his feeling for her is intense and sincere and that waiting any longer would be torture. But Portia hears something else. The rack was used on traitors to force confessions, and so for Portia Bassanio's metaphor dredges up her fears of male betrayal. 'Confess', she asks him, 'what treason there is mingled with your love' (*MV* 3.2.26–7). Her remark is witty and perhaps teasing, but behind it lies apprehensiveness about men's potential for infidelity. With equal wit Bassanio tries to wipe away the 'ugly treason of mistrust' (*MV* 3.2.28) that hovers over his speedy courtship, but Portia persists in her questioning. In *MV* 3.2.32–3, she returns to his metaphor of the rack yet again. She suggests that Bassanio may be speaking under the compulsion of torture (in this case, the torture of waiting), and so he may be professing love just to end his 'pain'. Eventually Bassanio turns the situation into a mock 'confession' of his love. This exchange of wit makes an important point about Portia and Bassanio's relationship. Even though Portia wrings a confession of love from Bassanio, there's a part of her that remains wary of him, in part because she comes with so rich a dowry, in part because she knows that she will lose ownership of herself – emotionally and financially – when she becomes married. When she sends him to the caskets, she frames the test as one of true love over money: 'If you do love me,' she says, 'you will find me out' (*MV* 3.2.41).

In their deliberations over the caskets Morocco and Aragon concern themselves with issues of outward worth, with Portia as an object of everyone's desire or a sign of a suitor's 'desert' (i.e., aristocratic merit). Bassanio focuses his choice differently, homing in on the issue of 'ornament'. Ornament refers to outward decoration, often fancy or gaudy, that has been added to something but isn't essential to its basic function. Ornament – a gold button, a fancy paint job, an elevated vocabulary – can make something – a coat, a car, an argument – look more valuable or important than it actually is. Though ornament creates a superficial appeal, it is no reliable guide to what's beneath the surface, that thing's true inner nature. Ornament, he argues in his casket speech, is everywhere a principle of deception – in the law where eloquent speeches cover up malicious intents, in religion where Biblical citations support heretical ideas, in war where fierce-looking men are actually cowards, in courtship where women make themselves look fetching with wigs made of corpses' hair. (Bassanio's comment about 'tainted and corrupted' pleas 'seasoned with a gracious voice' 'obscur[ing] the show of evil' may bear upon our perceptions of the trial scene.) Ornament, Bassanio concludes, is 'the seeming truth, which cunning times put on/To entrap the wisest' (*MV* 3.2.100–1), which is to say, it is nothing but an outward seeming, a misleading appearance that can trick even the wisest person into thinking it is the truth. Gold and silver are perfect examples of superficially attractive metals – in fact both were often used in the Renaissance to create ornamental decorations. Lead, by contrast, a dull, unbeautiful metal nevertheless practical for many purposes, gives little outward indication of its great inherent value.

By choosing lead, Bassanio suggests his ability to see past sources of Portia's outward allure – her dowry, her beauty – to her inner value as a virtuous woman, and, what's more, he signals his heroic willingness to risk it all, to 'hazard' his future, on the basis of his perception of her. As if to underline the point, once Bassanio opens the lead casket and finds Portia's portrait within, he praises the painting's capacity to enthral the viewer's eye and 't'entrap the hearts of men', yet he takes care to stress that the portrait is but a 'shadow' of the actual woman, a 'counterfeit' that 'doth limp behind the substance' (*MV* 3.2.115, 122, 128–9). (Whether Bassanio's extravagant praise is itself a kind of verbal ornament that conceals more than it reveals is worth our considering.) Bassanio's choice of lead, in short, would seem to indicate that he has reformed himself. He is no longer the prodigal who vainly pursues honour by spending other people's money. Instead, his 'confession' of love, his ability to see through 'ornament' to the substance beneath and his heroic willingness to risk it all, to 'hazard' his future, for his perception of Portia, all suggest that he has fallen genuinely in love with the woman rather than the heiress. He has become the heroic Alcides that Portia represents him as in her speech (*MV* 3.2.53–61), redeeming her from being sacrificed to monsters from the sea (her various suitors from afar). What earlier might have seemed like a rather sordid, purely financial venture on Bassanio's part has become a beautiful love story.

This is a very tempting way to see this scene, fitting for a comedy. But it is complicated by the dramatic context, what comes immediately before Bassanio's casket speech. This casket scene is different from the other casket scenes in several respects. For one thing, Portia makes clear her preference for Bassanio, and she even entertains the possibility of 'teach[ing] you / How to choose right' (*MV* 3.2.10–11), though she immediately remarks that she is bound by an oath not to. For another, Portia arranges for a song to accompany Bassanio's choice. That song rewards close scrutiny. Its subject is 'fancy', which is to say, romantic or erotic fascination, that spark of immediate attraction between lovers, something preserved in the British use of that word ('she fancies you'). 'Fancy' is related to the word 'fantasy', the Renaissance word for the imagination, insubstantial and potentially deceptive mental images derived from our fallible perceptions. The song asks about the source of romantic 'fancy': does it spring from the heart or from the head, that is, the mind? The second stanza provides the answer. Fancy is 'engendered in the eye', by one's 'gazing' at the beloved (*MV* 3.2.66–7), which is to say, romantic fancy is ginned up by dwelling upon the beloved's beautiful appearance. It's not a matter of the heart so much as of the erotic imagination. And fancy ends up where most crushes so often do – you wake up to reality and say to yourself, 'What did I ever see in that guy?' As the song puts it, 'fancy dies / In the cradle where it lies' (*MV* 3.2.68–9). Fancy, both being born and dying in the cradle of the mind's eye, never matures out of infanthood into something that lasts, a true love of the heart. If the casket test is a test of the suitor's romantic orientation, the song identifies the wrong answer – fleeting 'fancy' based upon appearances – and hints at the correct one – love bred in the heart, one that can see beyond the flesh. Bassanio's first line in his deliberation speech, 'So may the outward shows be least themselves, / The world is still deceived with ornament' (*MV* 3.2.73–4), suggests that he has grasped the principle the song conveys. If this were not enough, the rhyme scheme of the song's first stanza – 'bred', 'head', 'nourishéd' – also points to the correct choice 'lead'. There is some evidence, then, that Portia covertly guides Bassanio to select the right casket – or at the least she gives him a strong nudge in the proper direction. As part of his witty exchange with Portia earlier, Bassanio exclaims, 'O happy torment, when my torturer / Doth teach me answers for deliverance!' (*MV* 3.2.37–8). That line refers to Portia's assurance to Bassanio that he can confess his love and live, but it may also serve as a bit of foreshadowing for us and even perhaps as Bassanio's cue to Portia to toss him a lifeline in the test to come.

None of this establishes beyond a doubt that Bassanio has cheated on the test. His comments about ornament may be sincere, or he may be manipulating Portia by saying what she wants to hear. What Shakespeare introduces is lingering doubt. Bassanio's speech on ethical principles appears in a dramatic context that complicates it without entirely negating the point he makes. Shakespeare also introduces an element of irresolution in Portia and Bassanio's relationship. The issue the casket test was designed to settle – does Portia's suitor *really* love her? – remains open, despite all fairy-tale appearances to the contrary. Portia has gotten the man she desires, perhaps by tilting the table in her favour. But the fact that she offered Bassanio help means her romantic anxieties remain.

When she presents herself to Bassanio after the test, she does so without ornament, with lines that emphasize her emotional vulnerability – 'You see me, Lord Bassanio, where I stand, / Such as I am … the full sum of me / Is sum of something: which to term in gross, / Is an unlessoned girl, unschooled, unpractised' (*MV* 3.2.149–50, 157–9). Peppering her speech are words – 'rich', 'account', 'sum', 'gross', 'converted', 'yours', 'mine' – that remind us of the economic considerations that hover over this marriage. In fact, Portia treats her romantic commitment to Bassanio as a shift in ownership of property and power:

> Myself, and what is mine, to you and yours
> Is now converted. But now, I was the lord
> Of this fair mansion, master of my servants,
> Queen o'er myself; and even now, but now,
> This house, these servants and this same myself,
> Are yours, my lord's. (*MV* 3.2.166–71)

Marrying Bassanio involves Portia losing sovereignty over her money, her household, her very self, becoming vulnerable to the man she desires, but a man who has not yet extinguished all doubt about his professed love.

It's interesting in that context, then, that Portia takes paradoxical control of the situation. Rather than simply being passive, she actively cedes control to Bassanio by presenting him a ring – 'I give them with this ring', she says in a boldly declarative sentence, casting herself as the 'giver'. And she adds conditions to his possession of the ring – 'when you part from, lose or give away, / Let it presage the ruin of your love, / And be my vantage to exclaim on you' (*MV* 3.2.171–4). Portia uses this crucial moment to strike a contract that protects her emotionally if Bassanio turns out to be faithless. As we noticed in Chapter Four, this is an equivalent to Shylock's bond with Antonio: if he fails properly to cherish the ring and by extension her, she has the right to exact the forfeit, the destruction of his gentlemanly reputation. Notably, Bassanio overpromises in his acceptance of her terms – 'when this ring / Parts from this finger, then parts life from hence' (*MV* 3.2.183–4). With the giving of the ring, Portia establishes a second test to replace her father's casket test, this time in the form of a ring-bond that tests the truthfulness and fidelity of Bassanio's love. It allows her to reassert power even as she gives herself over to her new husband, and it reminds us that the question of Bassanio's motives for marrying Portia has not been fully resolved by the caskets, despite the ravishingly romantic poetry of the scene.

The casket scene is yet another example of how in *The Merchant of Venice* mercantile ways of thinking – issues of value, risk, profit, debt and contracts – intertwine with all human relationships, here love between men and women. Because Portia knows she is a commodity on the marriage market, valuable and potentially disposable, she finds it difficult to trust Bassanio, desire him though she does. Like her, we may find ourselves wondering at his professions of love, given our knowledge of his prodigal past and his plan for clearing his debts. The conventions of comedy drive Portia and Bassanio towards the happy ending of a love match (and Shakespeare gives us one), but the potential for Bassanio forfeiting Portia's trust continues to hover over the couple even after Bassanio receives her ring. The letter from Antonio, arriving only a moment afterward, signals a return of all the ugly financial dealings this beautiful love story has briefly swept aside. The letter forces Bassanio to confess his actual financial state to his new bride and his debt to Antonio. When Portia tells him to pay the bond many times over and be done with it, her casual command makes clear that even though she has given herself and her property to Bassanio, she continues to wield primary power in their relationship. Antonio's plight sweeps away the romantic veil from our eyes, in other words, and pushes economic values once again to the fore.

The trial scene (*MV* 4.1)

If certain moments in *The Merchant of Venice* open the possibility of our seeing Christians and Jews as sharing a common humanity, the trial scene forcefully reasserts a stark, unbridgeable difference between the two groups. One way it does so is through the language characters use to refer to Shylock. In some cases, metaphors from earlier in the play are reframed. Earlier, with their images of skin pricks and incisions (*MV* 2.1.6, 3.1.58) Morocco and Shylock presented blood as common to all races and creeds. It is a metaphor for an essential humanity which all people share, no matter their superficial differences. In the trial scene, blood and bleeding comes to mark the insurmountable difference between Jew and Christian. Out of mercy Portia asks Shylock to provide a surgeon 'to stop [Antonio's] wounds, lest he do bleed to death' (*MV* 4.1.256), but Shylock is unwilling to do so because "tis not in the bond' (*MV* 4.1.258). Antonio's bleeding thereby becomes a sign of Shylock's Jewish *inhumanity*, his cruel legalistic adherence to the letter of the bond and refusal of fellow feeling for Antonio, in contrast to Portia's Christian call for mercy.[1] Other kinds of anti-Semitic language return to be intensified at the trial. In the next chapter, we will observe how Gratiano picks up the image of Jew as dog from earlier in the play when he refers to Shylock as a wolf (*MV* 4.1.127–37). References to the Jew as devil, heard in Lancelet's opening monologue (*MV* 2.2.1–28) and again in Salanio's sneers at Shylock (*MV* 3.1.19–20, 71), are now heard from Bassanio (*MV* 4.1.213, 283) and become his preferred epithet for Shylock in the trial scene.

And new images for Shylock emerge as well. Especially prominent is his Jewish hardness of heart, imaged in a variety of ways. When the Duke first speaks of Shylock in the trial scene, he calls him 'a *stony* adversary' (*MV* 4.1.3, emphasis added). Antonio develops this idea when he speaks of the impossibility of moving Shylock to mercy: 'You may as well do anything most hard / As seek to soften that, than which what's harder – / His Jewish heart' (*MV* 4.1.77–9). And the heart as stone lies behind Gratiano's wordplay as he watches Shylock sharpen his knife: 'Not on thy sole, but on thy soul, harsh Jew, / Thou mak'st thy knife keen' (*MV* 4.1.122–3). His grim pun turns on the notion of a whetstone, used for honing cutting tools, to which Gratiano likens Shylock's rock-hard spirit. Gratiano highlights that hard-heartedness by rhetorically asking, 'can no prayers pierce thee?' (*MV* 4.1.125), a question that may remind us obliquely and ironically of Shylock's 'if you prick us, do we not bleed?' (*MV* 3.1.58). These references to Shylock's impenetrably hard heart mark him as, in the words of the Duke, 'an *inhuman* wretch, uncapable of pity, void and empty / From any dram of mercy' (*MV* 4.1.4–5, emphasis added). From a Christian perspective Shylock's rigorous fidelity to his bond, underwritten by his 'oath to heaven' (*MV* 4.1.224) and a Jewish adherence to the law, makes him irremediably Other, less than human and thus needful to be purged. When the Duke begs Shylock to reconsider, he groups him with other uncivilized, inhumane peoples with 'brassy bosoms and rough hearts of flint', those 'stubborn Turks, and Tartars never trained / To offices of tender courtesy' (*MV* 4.1.30–2). The stress upon Shylock's hard-heartedness suggests that his refusal of mercy is not a matter of principle for Shylock but the result of his profound defect of spirit. His Jewishness becomes something perversely wilful, a choice for which Shylock can be held responsible, and it thus repeats what many Christians regarded as the primal crime of the Jews, their refusal of mercy to Christ in gospel stories of the crucifixion.

Most prominent are references to Shylock simply as 'the Jew' or simply 'Jew'. Earlier in the play these kinds of references are more typical of Lancelet and Salanio, but in the trial scene they escalate considerably, particularly after Portia passes sentence. In fact, though Portia knows Shylock's name, she uses it only twice, both times to ask him to show mercy. Otherwise, she calls him 'Jew', for a total of nine times. By contrast, before Portia pronounces sentence she refers to Antonio only as 'the merchant', perhaps in an effort to project legal objectivity and balance. After sentencing, however, she begins to refer to Antonio by his name, and she never again uses the name Shylock. For the Duke, Antonio, Gratiano and Portia, calling Shylock 'the Jew' reduces him to a type standing in for all Jews. He becomes not an aggrieved individual but the mythic, murderous foe of the Christian community. The increasingly abusive deployment of the word 'Jew' also keeps before us the prejudices that run throughout the proceedings, despite the fact that the Duke and Portia labour to appear impartial. Tellingly, the Duke ends his plea to Shylock for mercy with the line, 'We all expect a gentle answer, Jew!' (*MV* 4.1.33). We noted earlier that line dangles before Shylock the possibility of being 'gentle/gentile', an honorary Christian aristocrat. Yet that final word 'Jew' reminds Shylock of his alien status within Christian Venice. As Portia's address to Shylock in her 'quality of mercy' speech turns from the king's to God's mercy, she too uses the word 'Jew' to remind him of his exclusion from divine grace and the Christian community:

> Therefore, Jew,
> Though justice be thy plea, consider this:
> That in the course of justice none of us
> Should see salvation. We do pray for mercy,
> And that same prayer doth teach us all to render
> The deeds of mercy. (*MV* 4.1.193–8)

Her use of 'we' and 'us' might seem at first glance to refer to all humankind, but in fact these pronouns refer only to Christians. Portia's 'we', like the word 'Jew', is another mark of Shylock's exclusion. As the trial scene proceeds, the tone attached to the word 'Jew' becomes more savage. It becomes the anti-Semitic equivalent of the n-word particularly as it appears in Gratiano's triumphal quips, a tone which Portia increasingly comes to echo, culminating with her devastating question, 'art thou contented, Jew?' (*MV* 4.1.389). 'Jew' is the verbal means for putting Shylock in his 'proper' place – denigrated, isolated, alien, at the mercy of the Christians.

Also widening the gulf between Jews and Christians in this scene is intensification of Antonio's status as an exemplar of Christian virtue. Antonio's willingness to take on Bassanio's financial sins and suffer mortal consequences already has resonances with Christ's willing assumption of humankind's mortal debt to God for its sins. As early as *MV* 3.3, when Antonio is taken off to jail, he speaks in terms that for Shakespeare's audience would obliquely recall Christ's supreme sacrifice: 'Pray God Bassanio come / To see me pay his debt' (*MV* 3.3.35–6). Antonio returns to this theme in the trial scene, but what is new is Antonio's Christ-like forbearance. 'I do oppose', he tells the Duke, 'My patience to [Shylock's] fury, and am armed / To suffer with a quietness of spirit / The very tyranny and rage of his' (*MV* 4.1.9–12). This formulation stresses a fundamental difference in temperament between Christian and Jew, though Antonio's words have the ring of classical stoicism as much as of Christian patience. Antonio's heroic 'patience' continues when he speaks of himself as 'the tainted wether of the flock, / Meetest for death' (*MV* 4.1.113–14), humbly accepting his death by presenting himself as a kind of Agnus Dei, a sacrificial lamb of God. His parting words stress that he is willingly dying for Bassanio's sake – 'grieve not that I am fall'n to this for you', 'he repents not that he pays your debt' (*MV* 4.1.262, 275) – in language that cannot help but evoke Christ and amplify our pity for his plight.

Antonio's words, we shouldn't fail to notice, also require from Bassanio to be a witness to and evangelist for his devotion: 'Say how I loved you, speak me fair in death, / And, when the tale is told, bid her be judge / Whether Bassanio had not once a love' (*MV* 4.1.271–3). This is language familiar to Shakespearean readers from his tragedies – as they die both Hamlet and Othello ask onlookers to tell their stories aright – and this language may even prime the audience to expect Antonio's tragic end. But more important, it is here that Antonio identifies his motive all along as love, something beyond friendship. The word 'love' certainly accords with Jesus's sacrificial love for humanity. But it has other, more earthly connotations as well, a suggestion of queer desire that might explain Antonio's melancholy at Bassanio's parting, his sense of being tainted, his fatalism at the prospect of growing old, his use of the forfeit to see Bassanio one last time and confess his feelings. In fact, Antonio's adoption of a Christlike stature in this scene may work to redeem those queer feelings, aligning them with self-sacrificial Christian virtue.

The play's most direct articulation of the difference between Christian and Jew can be found in Portia's 'quality of mercy' speech. There Portia lays out the key elements of a Christian conception of mercy: it is 'not strained', that is, not constrained, required or forced, but a freely offered gift; by blessing both 'him that gives and him that takes' (*MV* 4.1.183) mercy stands outside the zero-sum logic of trade; while justice involves following the letter of the law, mercy answers to the higher calling of the spirit and the heart's emotions; mercy springs not from a lack of power but is paradoxically the highest form of power, 'an attribute to God himself' (*MV* 4.1.191), and most importantly, salvation depends entirely upon God's mercy, not on adherence to earthly justice, fidelity to oaths or obedience to rabbinical law. Alluding to Paul's discussion of salvation in *Romans*, Portia presents mercy as the primary trait distinguishing Christian from Jew, underlining the point with the now familiar 'gentle/gentile' wordplay: mercy, she says, is 'the gentle rain from heaven' (*MV* 4.1.181). Throughout the speech runs an implicit critique of the Jewish principles that support Shylock's case: strict adherence to the letter of the law, a heartless fixation with punishment, a desire for power and superiority, the sacred nature of an oath or 'covenant'. There is an irony at work in Portia's critique of Jewish principle, because, as Graham Holderness notes in a discussion of this famous speech, she draws upon both Jewish and Christian ethical traditions, 'synthesizing the values of Judaism and Christianity into a common ethical language'.[2] Nevertheless, Portia's central claim, that 'in the course of justice none of us / Should see salvation' (*MV* 4.1.195–6), has a deeply Pauline ring to it. The clear implication is that Shylock, by pursuing his Jewish sense of justice, is seeking his own damnation. In retrospect, we may see this as foreshadowing – Shylock is unwittingly constructing the terms of his own legal defeat.

As much as Portia's speech anatomizes a central Christian virtue in highly idealized terms, it is also part of the legal case she is developing against Shylock, even though it may not look like that. Her suggestion that Shylock consider mercy, like several other suggestions she makes, is designed to ferret out Shylock's essential values, just as the casket test is designed to reveal the values of her suitors and, like the tests of Morocco and Aragon, to make their values the means of their undoing. To Portia's description of mercy Shylock offers this blunt riposte: 'My deeds upon my head, I crave the law' (*MV* 4.1.202). His reply names the method by which Portia will defeat him – his deeds in court will come back to haunt him – but it also absolves Portia of any guilt for her rough treatment of him later in the scene. Shylock's line is reminiscent of the Archbishop of Canterbury's reply to King Henry V when the king asks him about justifying war against France. To urge the king into battle Canterbury answers, 'The sin upon my head, dread sovereign' (*Henry V* 1.2.97), shifting the blame from the king to himself. Both lines echo the words of the Jewish crowd in the Bible who, as Pilate washes his hands, calls for Christ's crucifixion: 'His blood be on us, and on our children' (Matthew 27.25). So too with Shylock, though he doesn't realize the full consequence of his words as he says them.

There is, then, a dual quality to much of Portia's interplay with Shylock before she turns on him, reminiscent of the two Portias we examined in Chapter Three. On the one hand, though she recognizes that the bond between Shylock and Antonio is legally binding, Portia repeatedly returns to the theme of mercy, urging Shylock to accept Bassanio's triple payment (*MV* 4.1.223, 229–30) and asking him to hire a surgeon to staunch Antonio's wounds (*MV* 4.1.253–4). On the other hand, these moments provide Portia with bases for the case she will soon build against Shylock. His refusal of Bassanio's payment establishes that 'he hath refused [money] in the open court', supporting Portia's judgement that 'he shall have merely justice and his bond' (*MV* 4.1.334–5); Shylock's rejection of a surgeon for Antonio establishes that he, an alien, has sought the life of a citizen and so justifies Portia's taking of his goods and placing his life at the Duke's mercy (*MV* 4.1.344–52). To put this another way, it's important to see Portia both as the voice of Christian virtue, patiently coaxing Shylock to show mercy, and as a cunning prosecutor, teasing out Shylock's convictions so she can use them in her judgement.

And that judgement poses a considerable challenge for audiences. Certainly there are reasons to approve of Portia's actions. Shylock's unwavering insistence upon his bond, a bond which Portia concedes is legally enforceable, poses a very real threat to Antonio's life. After all, we see Shylock sharpening his knife in open court. Because Shylock tricked Antonio into the deadly bargain by presenting it as a 'merry bond', Portia's tricking of Shylock into legal jeopardy may seem like poetic justice. If we think of Shylock as a version of the ogre from folk tradition who tricks the hero into a dangerous oath or commitment, Portia serves as the plucky companion who finds a loophole to free the hero. And considered within the context of Christian myth, Shylock's designs upon the Christlike Antonio resemble the Jews' designs upon Jesus in the gospel. This time around Portia has the opportunity to thwart a replay of the most terrible event in history. Literally and symbolically, then, the audience is primed to applaud Portia's defeat of Shylock, particularly since Shylock, by demanding the law, authors the means of his comeuppance. And it offers the added aesthetic pleasure of being witty and deliciously ironic – and also surprising, since on a first read we may not see it coming. In fact, it has the quality of a sardonic joke at Shylock's expense, though one with real consequences. Plus Portia is distanced from blame. In his letter to the Duke, Bellario claims that he and Portia 'turned o'er many books together; he is furnished with my opinion' (*MV* 4.1.154–5). This suggests that Portia may simply be executing Bellario's legal judgement, as the character Balthasar and not as herself. This is all to say that we have multiple reasons to think Portia's verdict as virtuous, justified and dramatically satisfying. And her judgement involves not just the defeat of a single upstart Jew. It is the occasion for forcefully and decisively reasserting Christian rule over Venice and for stressing the cardinal place of mercy in that rule. Shylock's defeat marks the defeat of Jewish principles and the triumph of Christian ideals.

And yet, and yet … Shakespeare also includes much in Shylock's sentence and Portia's conduct that should give us pause. For all the references to moral and even physiological differences between Christian and Jew, in her handling of this court case, Portia comes to seem remarkably like Shylock. She outsmarts him by relying on Shylock's own Jewish principles, strict adherence to the letter of the law. Just as Shylock does with Antonio, she uses trickery to ensnare Shylock. Like Shylock sharpening the knife, throughout her sentencing Portia relies on the power of cruel theatrics, epitomized by her repeated word 'tarry'. She orchestrates the proceedings so that Shylock thinks matters are settled, only again and again to pull the rug out from under him. Far in excess of simply denying Shylock a legal victory, Portia subjects him to escalating public humiliation – denying him the triple payment, then his principal, then stripping him of his goods, potentially his life and, Antonio adds, eventually his faith. The fact that the Duke and Antonio join Portia in offering rough justice makes this a coordinated, communal effort, and it raises the possibility of collusion. The judgement is framed as mercy – for conspiring against a citizen's life, Shylock's life 'lies in the mercy / Of the Duke only', and so Portia tells Shylock to fall to his knees and plead for clemency: 'Down, therefore, and beg mercy of the Duke' (*MV* 4.1.351–2, 359). In showing mercy to Shylock by reducing confiscation of half his wealth to a 'fine' (*MV* 4.1.368), the Duke stresses 'Thou shalt see the difference of our spirit', that is, the essential distinction between Christian and Jew. But he uses the opportunity to make Shylock display 'humbleness'. As Shylock notes in his anguished reply, it is a perverse form of mercy that pardons his execution only to plunge him into abject poverty: 'Nay, you take my life and all, pardon not that. / You take my house when you do take the prop / That doth sustain my house. You take my life / When you do take the means whereby I live' (*MV* 4.1.370–3).

Antonio's 'merciful' alternative to the Duke's proposal is even more humiliating. Antonio proposes to take half of Shylock's wealth 'in use' and upon Shylock's death to give it to 'the gentleman / That lately stole his daughter' (*MV* 4.1.379–81). What's more, he will force Shylock to give up his faith which, in effect, will put Shylock out of the usury business. With its echoes of 'usury' Antonio's phrase 'in use', meaning both 'held in trust' but also 'lent for profit', is another indication of how the Christians have eroded the distinction between Christian and Jew in their effort to defeat Shylock. Given the escalating humiliations involved with the Christian exercise of 'mercy', Portia's question 'art thou contented, Jew? What does thou say?' (*MV* 4.1.389) has the force of a threat towards Shylock – if he did not consent, what new humiliation might follow? Shylock's answer, 'I am content' (*MV* 4.1.390), is, as is often the case with short simple lines in Shakespeare's writing, packed with emotion. Its brevity eloquently communicates Shylock's fearful desire that he not precipitate more humiliation, the falling away of his resistance to the Christians, and the awful weight of Venetian power upon his capitulation.

As Shylock exits, he hints that he may be leaving to die – 'I am not well' (*MV* 4.1.392) – and indeed he never appears again in the play. We may be reminded of the extraordinary penalty exacted by the casket test, what is in effect a death sentence for one's family line, since unsuccessful suitors cannot woo or marry and so cannot father legitimate heirs. In Shylock's case, the court's sentence has the same effect: all elements of Shylock's Jewish legacy are cut off. He is forced to renounce his faith, and his daughter and his wealth fall into the hands of Lorenzo, a Christian. Like Morocco and Aragon, he may be alive after failing, but his line is snuffed out. In short, the exercise of Christian mercy in Shylock's trial hardly matches up with the idealized vision in Portia's famous speech. Instead in practice it seems motivated by the desire to catch Shylock 'on the hip'. This is a judgement imbued with religious and racial discrimination and a will to power. Christian mercy ought to turn upon the model of Christ, the son of God who willingly took on humankind's sins and paid their debt – death – so that humanity might be saved; it involves sacrificing a scapegoat for the good of the group. The 'mercy' offered to Shylock reveals a much darker side of Christian behaviour, the extent to which 'merciful' scapegoating is a way to exterminate the Other and perpetuate an elite's power and hypocrisy. In practice, this form of mercy blurs the very difference between Christian and Jew that the trial seeks to establish.

As many writers have observed, comedy often concerns painful matters, the sufferings of characters or ourselves. Part of what separates comedy from tragedy is our emotional distance from that pain. If a clown slips on a banana peel, we laugh because the clown's outlandish costume and make-up assure us his suffering isn't real; if someone close to us slips on a banana peel, however, we rush to see if they are all right, fearing they might be hurt. The same event can be comic or tragic, depending upon how our empathy is engaged. And we are capable too of complex responses: we may delight in seeing an enemy slip on a banana peel, though our response may change if we see him bleeding from the fall.

Because *The Merchant of Venice* is identified as a comedy, it is important to contemplate how the trial scene fits that designation, if it does at all. Where does our empathy lie in this scene? How is it directed and manipulated from moment to moment? Do we empathize with Antonio, presented to us as a Christlike victim of Shylock's machinations but who we know has tormented Shylock in the past? Do we empathize with Shylock, whose fixation with his bond makes him seem cruel but who has suffered at the hands of the Christians? When Shylock is sentenced, do we remain distant from him and regard his fall with glee? Do our sympathies shift from Antonio to Shylock in the course of the trial as Shylock's humiliations mount and Antonio uses the opportunity to rob him of his faith? Are we perhaps caught up short by our initial empathy for Antonio when he shows Shylock such rough mercy at scene's end? Or does Shakespeare encourage a distance from both characters that short-circuits any simple comic response? How does Shakespeare's language direct our developing sympathies throughout this painful scene? My point in dwelling on the question of empathy and distance is to remind you that analysing Shakespeare's language involves more than charting patterns of word choice or unpacking imagery. It also entails attending to the purchase those words make on our emotions and moral sensibilities. This is not to say that you must accept how the text directs your sympathies and judgements. It is to say that recognizing how Shakespeare's words engage our hearts as well as our heads will allow you to respond to the script with greater nuance, power and sensitivity.

Writing matters – context

What does the phrase 'you're killing me' mean? How about 'I'm tired'? Anyone reading this book will understand the dictionary meaning of the words in these phrases, but the meaning of these passages is unclear. Is 'you're killing me' the cry of a murder victim or praise from someone delighted at your joke-telling skills? Does 'I'm tired' mean 'I want to sleep,' 'I don't want to have sex,' 'I am filled with existential angst,' 'I've just completed my workout' or something else? What these mundane phrases show is an essential quality of all language – the dependence of meaning upon context.

The Russian theorist Mikhail Bakhtin suggests that language is fundamentally dialogic, by which he means that we always speak in a particular context of communication in response to prior speech and in anticipation of future responses to what we say. Our words and phrases take on particular casts of meaning depending upon the specific context in which we use them, the tone we impart to them and the purposes for which we utter them. The same phrase – like 'you're killing me' – can mean entirely different things in different conversations. Though dictionaries are helpful, what they offer us are generalized definitions of words, not the particular shades of meaning we impart to language when we use it in a specific speaking situation. If we are to understand the meaning of a word or phrase fully, we need to consider in what context and to what purposes it is being used.

In this chapter, we examined two of the most famous speeches in *The Merchant of Venice*, Bassanio's discussion on 'ornament' and Portia's oration on 'the quality of mercy'. As we have seen, both eloquently lay out two of the key ideals of Christian thought – the ability to see beyond appearances to an essential spirit or truth and the capacity to show mercy. But we miss something important if we consider these speeches only in isolation. Both speeches are part of ongoing dialogue and action, and their full meaning depends upon how they function as parts of conversational exchanges. What this chapter emphasizes is that characters speak not just to express ideas or feelings. They also speak in response to one another, and they use language to accomplish certain goals: to agree or ally themselves with someone, to refute or refuse someone else's ideas, to wound or woo, to project a certain image (even to oneself!) or to destroy someone else's, to exert power or to submit to it, to provoke a particular response from another character. The full meaning of Shakespeare's language emerges from both the words' dictionary meanings and the purposes to which they are put, even if those purposes misfire or fail. The word 'Jew', for instance, denotes a member of a specific religion, but we miss its full significance in the trial scene if we fail to recognize how the Venetians use that word to belittle Shylock. To understand a passage fully we need to ask not only 'what does the speaker mean?' but also 'why is she saying this? What is she trying to do by using these words?'

Analysing language in dramatic action requires us to remind ourselves of what has come before. What exchanges led up to the passage at hand? What was at issue between the characters in those exchanges? Since there are often several matters in play, you need to identify which particular one is relevant for the passage you're analysing. This is why whenever you are citing a substantial passage of dialogue, you need to identify the salient dramatic context for your quotation so that your reader knows how to interpret what you're citing. It's less helpful to your reader to say 'in the fourth act, Bassanio begins to use the term "devil" to refer to Shylock' than to say 'as his friend comes under threat from Shylock in the trial scene, Bassanio begins to use the term "devil" to refer to Shylock'. The latter formulation introduces a crucial bit of dramatic context for understanding how and why Bassanio uses that word. The longer your analysis, the more context you'll need to supply. Some other elements to consider: who is the passage directed to? Who else might be listening? What was said immediately before that prompted the speaker to respond in this way? Is the speaker using terms or images that have been used earlier in the play, and if so, what new spin is she putting on them?

Most important is to think about the purpose of the passage, the goal that the speaker seeks to accomplish by saying these words. Is the speaker seeking to resolve the dramatic conflict, to intensify it, to subtly change its nature, to open up a new issue or reopen an old one? Sometimes a character will reorient the meaning or intent of another's words (as is the case with 'rack' and 'confess' with Bassanio and Portia). Sometimes a character will use a word or phrase that signifies more than he knows or intends (such is the case with Shylock's 'my deeds upon my head', the full meaning of which only comes into view later in the scene). And sometimes a character's language will fail to achieve the purpose he intends (such is the case with Lancelet and Old Giobbe's inflated vocabulary, which seeks to elevate their status). How we construe a character's purpose in speaking changes the meaning of that speech. If we think of Portia speaking about 'the quality of mercy' to move Shylock to release Antonio from his bond, her speech looks quite idealistic, even naive; if we think of her as trying to provoke a response from Shylock with which she can entrap him, her speech looks quite Machiavellian. We might note that in both of these cases we are conceiving of Portia's speech as forward-as well as backward-looking – she speaks in order to elicit a particular future response from Shylock. Thinking of characters as responding back and forth to the particular situation and to each other as they pursue their developing, often conflicting aims makes us more insightful interpreters of their words. And thinking of dialogue as a moment-by-moment, back-and-forth dynamic of verbal tactics rather than a static sequence of statements restores to us as readers the exciting experience of Shakespeare's plays *as drama*.

CHAPTER SIX

The Language of Racial and Ethnic Humour

One of the more uncomfortable elements of *The Merchant of Venice* is its frequent recourse to anti-Semitic humour. *Titus Andronicus* and *Othello* take up racist discourse, and several other Shakespeare plays include passages that turn upon ethnic stereotyping – *Henry V* 3.2.54–142 is a famous example, as is the mockery of French and Welsh accents in *The Merry Wives of Windsor*. There are also isolated examples of anti-Semitism, as in Benedick's quip in *Much Ado about Nothing* about falling for Beatrice: 'If I do not take pity of her, I am a villain; if I do not love her I am a Jew' (*Much Ado about Nothing*, 2.3.252–3). But it is only in *The Merchant of Venice* that Shakespeare makes anti-Semitism so sustained a source for humour and couples it with jokes about ethnicity, nationality and race. To be sure, the play does include passages in which we are encouraged to sympathize with Shylock and Jessica, and perhaps even Morocco. But those passages seem to sort oddly with other passages where our laughter – often derisive laughter – comes at the expense of Jews, Moors, Spaniards and others. How then to understand the play's approach to verbal humour, particularly since so much of that humour is rooted in stereotyping of outsiders, what we have come to call 'Othering'? By making othering funny, does this kind of humour encourage us to accept anti-Semitism and racism? Are these jokes one of the means by which the play perpetuates bigotry? Should we understand this sort of humour only as an element of characterization, as evidence of the prejudices of those characters who make such jokes? Do these jokes reveal the spiritual corruption of the play's Christian characters? And does the play provide moments which resist the humour of stereotyping? This chapter will explore how the play's humour operates on our perceptions and so becomes a serious issue itself.[1]

Portia

Let's begin with Portia. We are first introduced to Portia in her conversation with Nerissa about the burden of the casket test. Like girls a-gossip, Portia evaluates her various suitors with devastatingly sardonic wit. Each of the various suitors is identified by his national origin, and each is reduced to a caricature that corresponds to the ethnic stereotypes of the day: the prince of Naples, for example, is so much the horseman that Portia surmises 'my lady his mother played false with a smith' (*MV* 1.3.41–2), suggesting that he is the bastard child of one who deals daily with horses, a blacksmith (and so no nobleman); the French lord is so obsessed with all manner of courtly pursuits – posing in stately fashion, horsemanship, dancing, fencing – that he seems to Portia 'every man in no man' (*MV* 1.3.57), with the implication that he is effete and unmasculine; the Scottish lord is quick to fight and especially antagonistic to his English neighbour; and the German Duke of Saxony's nephew likes his wine so well that when drunk he 'is little better than a beast' (*MV* 1.3.84, with a pun on 'beast/best') and whom Portia suggests she can trick with 'a deep glass of Rhenish wine on the contrary casket' (*MV* 1.3.90–1).

This is a noteworthy passage for several reasons. First, the Portia whom we glimpse here does not seem to fit the paragon of 'wondrous virtues' (*MV* 1.1.163) described by Bassanio in the play's opening scene. Here instead is a woman who, though she must abide by the terms of the casket test, nonetheless exercises a kind of rhetorical power over her prospective suitors, subjecting them to withering criticism. With her comment about setting a glass of wine on the wrong casket, she even hints playfully that she might be willing to manipulate the casket test to her advantage. This 'mean girl' Portia is yet another example of the two Portias that we noticed in Chapter Three. Second, this passage has the feel of a comic routine, detachable from the plot of the play. In fact Shakespeare had crafted a quite similar comic set piece for an earlier play, *The Comedy of*

Errors. There in 3.2 Dromio of Syracuse describes the body of the fat kitchen wench Nell in terms of various national and ethnic stereotypes – her buttocks like the soft, smelly bogs of Ireland, her hard hand like the barren highlands of Scotland, her hot breath like the weather of Spain.

This scene suggests that Portia is comfortable with thinking in these terms. Her snarky commentary offers her a form of consoling superiority in a situation that otherwise she does not control. But the passage is also seductive for the viewer because Portia's thinking in stereotypes is veiled with humour. This comedy routine, the first really funny passage in the play, coaxes us into going along with, even embracing the sentiments Portia expresses. It is an example of what theorist Louis Althusser calls 'interpellation', a process of subtle coercion. Althusser suggests that certain situations and certain forms of address (what he calls 'hailing') carve out a position for us to occupy that we are then encouraged to adopt, often against our will or against our self-interests. It's why we feel a tinge of nervousness and guilt when a policeman says 'hey you!' The words of the policeman, his 'hail', assume that the addressee is a criminal, so even though you know you are innocent, you tend to adopt the position of a guilty person within the situation.[2]

Portia's ethnic humour works in much the same way. Her mocking characterizations coax you into laughing along with her, but if you do, you have been interpellated into consenting to the stereotypes she is using. Racist humour often has this structure: it uses wit and laughter to coax the listener into affirming the racist content of the joke. Anyone who's heard a racist joke and felt uncomfortable knows how this works. The pull to laugh along is very strong, even though 'laughing along' means you are also according with the racist caricatures on which the joke depends. In this case, Portia also includes an Englishman among the suitors she mocks, making the familiar complaint that the boorish English take what little style they have from Continental fashions. To be sure, this is a calculated joke at the expense of Shakespeare's original audience, one that they probably enjoyed, but the joke has the effect of immunizing Portia – and perhaps Shakespeare – against the charge that she is being crudely ethnocentric. It establishes Portia, in other words, as an equal opportunity mocker, and so it gives us permission to go along with the sentiments expressed and join in the laugh because she is mocking us too.[3]

Interpellation aside, this passage is not especially worrisome because the ethnic humour is fairly mild. But the stereotyped thinking it models prepares us for other comic encounters with Portia's suitors that are potentially more troubling. One is the encounter with Morocco which Shakespeare stretches over two scenes. Until relatively recently Morocco has been usually played as a comic character, a warrior-general whose military bravado is way over the top, a Moor who doesn't seem to understand the humility proper to European courtly behaviour. His heroic boasts that he will vanquish his rivals with his Turkish scimitar or take the cubs from a ferocious she-bear are outdated exaggerations, and as we saw in our discussion of allusions, he seems to get his reference to Hercules wrong. In some performances, he comically brandishes his sword to underline his boasts. But we should not fail to notice that, comic if he may be, Morocco opens with a serious issue – the matter of his dark skin. The Quarto specifies that Morocco is a 'tawny Moor', that is to say, a brown skin Muslim rather than dark 'blackamoor', but it also specifies that Morocco be clad 'all in white', a traditional colour of North African robes but also a colour which by contrast accentuates Morocco's skin colour. Elizabethans equated dark skin with ugliness and servility, so right out of the gate Morocco asks Portia not to reject him simply on the basis of 'my complexion' (*MV* 2.1.1).[4] According to racial theories of Shakespeare's day, his black skin was the result of his African nation's proximity to the sun, so Morocco tries to recast his skin colour metaphorically as the mark of a royal house, as if he were wearing a dark, impeccably smart uniform, what he calls 'the shadowed livery of the burnished sun' (*MV* 2.1.2). Even so, Morocco, anticipating being rejected for his appearance, makes a remarkable appeal for Portia's affection on the basis of his shared humanity with white people (those 'northward born', *MV* 2.1.4). That shared humanity, he claims, springs from the common element of red blood beneath all people's skin, and he thereby offers to 'make incision for your love / To prove whose blood is reddest, his [Morocco's white rival] or mine' (*MV* 2.1.6–7). This appeal to shared humanity from a man who is racially and religiously different from the Christians, an appeal grounded in the human body, anticipates Shylock's famous 'Hath not a Jew eyes' speech, which pursues a similar line of argument, and it returns us to the question of what 'blood' signifies in the play.

We already have some evidence that Morocco's concerns about racism are well founded. At the end of her earlier conversation with Nerissa when she learns of Morocco's approach, Portia comments, 'If he have the condition of a saint and the complexion of a devil, I had rather he should shrive me than wive me' (*MV* 1.3.124–6). The verbal contrasts of 'condition' and 'complexion', 'saint' and 'devil', 'shrive' and 'wive' give this quip a jokey quality, but the sentiment is baldly racist: even if this man with the appearance of a devil (the devil was sometimes portrayed as black) were as virtuous as a saint, I'd rather be dead than marry him. We need to see this brutal private remark as part and parcel of Portia's ethnic humour throughout the scene – ethnic and racial stereotypes seem endemic to her thinking. Portia's public answer to Morocco's comments regarding racism, then, is surprisingly polite but nevertheless equivocal. At first she claims that 'in terms of choice I am not solely led / By nice direction of a maiden's eyes' (*MV* 2.1.13–14). The word 'solely' does a lot of work in that sentence, since it leaves in place the possibility that she is partly or even mostly led by what she sees. The second reply is even more tricky: 'Yourself, renowned prince, then stood as fair / As any comer I have looked on yet / For my affection' (*MV* 2.1.20–2). This response seems gracious and complimentary enough, but if we recall the contemptuous regard Portia had for her other suitors, this is exceedingly faint praise. (One is reminded of the backhanded praise the Duke gives Othello in the Senate scene, spoken to Othello's father-in-law: 'If virtue no delighted beauty lack / Your son-in-law is far more fair than black' [*Othello* 1.3.290–1]. The highest compliment he can offer is that Othello, because of his virtue, can be an honorary white man.) With knowledge of her earlier comments about suitors, we know what Morocco doesn't, that Portia is offering a clever non-denial denial of prejudice. Indeed, would an audience knowingly smile, perhaps even laugh at her reply? And if so, how are we being interpellated by Portia's wit?

Of course, it is entirely possible to play Morocco as dignified in bearing and formal in his rhetoric and to play Portia as honourable and virtuous in her treatment of him. In fact, a number of commentators have suggested that the word 'complexion' does not refer to skin colour or appearance at all but rather has the meaning of 'temperament, nature, inner character', referring to the particular mix of bodily fluids or 'humours' that, according to the reigning Renaissance theory of character, shape an individual's personality.

This was the word's primary definition of the word in Shakespeare's day, and plainly it is what 'complexion' means in Salanio's nasty joke about Jessica's abandonment of Shylock: 'And Shylock, for his part, knew the bird was fledge, and then it is the complexion of them all to leave the dam' (*MV* 3.1.26–8). I suppose it is possible to read Morocco's concern about his 'complexion' in terms of a worry about his personality. That interpretation, however, seems to deny the more obvious meaning of the word, and, more important, it seems motivated by editors' desire to purge Portia of an unpleasant, decidedly unvirtuous component of her character.

The word 'complexion' comes back with brutal force from Portia after Morocco fails the casket test. Upon opening the gold casket, Morocco exclaims, 'O, hell! What have we here?' (*MV* 2.7.62). This line, a sure laugh in performance, suddenly bursts his grand pretences, and the deflation continues with his reading of the singsong, single-rhymed verse on the casket's scroll, and in particular the stinging lines 'Had you been as wise as bold' and 'Fare you well, your suit is cold' (*MV* 2.7.70, 73). Morocco underlines his humiliation by reminding us not just of his pledge never to woo another woman if he failed but also of his loss of the sun's livery about which he'd earlier boasted – 'Cold indeed, and labour lost, / Then farewell, heat, and welcome frost' (*MV* 2.7.74–5). After he beats a hasty exit, Portia gives the rhetorical *coup de grace*: 'A gentle riddance. Draw the curtains, go. / Let all of his complexion choose me so' (*MV* 2.7.78–9). This couplet turns upon wordplay with two important words, 'gentle' and 'complexion'. 'Gentle' means both 'noble, genteel' and 'kind, nonviolent' – Portia is emphasizing her own nobility in getting rid of a man she sees as socially inferior, and she has defeated this battle-hardened warrior without herself resorting to force. There may even be a hint of the meaning 'gentile' here too, the sense being that Portia, a Christian or 'gentile', has rid herself of a non-believer. 'Complexion' should remind us of the controversy over skin colour with which the Morocco scenes began, and Portia now uses the same word to make a racist quip at Morocco's expense. But that word now collapses the sense of skin colour and the sense of personality into one. With his wrong choice Morocco has demonstrated the link between his race and a defect of character, which Portia underlines with a bit of wordplay. At this moment the casket test becomes at once a test of racial or ethnic appropriateness and proper moral and aristocratic bearing. Those who fail it are in effect ethnically cleansed, for they are barred from wooing and thus from bearing legitimate heirs to carry on their legacy. Their potential family lines, their 'races', die with them. As Portia with her witty couplet dances on Morocco's grave, she lumps him in with all of the other ethnic types she has rejected – all men of inferior 'complexion'.

The Morocco scenes establish a pattern of Portia triumphing over racial or ethnic Others by setting up tests for them that they are bound to fail. It's important for the effect of these scenes that each participant's own words be the means for their own destruction. Their own self-revealed 'complexion' works to confirm the stereotype and leave Portia blameless and justified in her contempt. That is certainly the case with Aragon, whose inflated sense of aristocratic merit leads him to think that the inscription 'Whoso chooseth me shall get as much as he deserves' refers to his great worthiness for Portia. 'I will assume desert', he says, calling for the key to the silver casket, 'And instantly unlock my fortunes here' (*MV* 2.9.50–1). Of course, the casket's inscription actually means something quite different and for him deeply ironic – by choosing me you will get exactly what you deserve, the fate of being publicly self-exposed as a fool by the 'portrait of a blinking idiot', a fate most spectators can see coming well before it happens. By his choice Aragon reveals that he is but a fool 'Silvered o'er' (*MV* 2.9.68), that is, a silver-plated aristocrat rather than a genuine one. It matters here that early on Portia tells him, 'To these injunctions everyone doth swear / *That comes to hazard for my worthless self*' (*MV* 2.9.16–17, emphasis added). With that line she lays out very clearly the central principles of the casket test and with it the correct answer for those with the ears and wit to hear it. Portia's comment renders herself blameless for Aragon's wrong answer and all the more justified in the disdain she – and the audience – feels for him. Later, when after choosing Aragon complains that 'are my deserts no better?' (*MV* 2.9.59), Portia stresses that 'To offend and to judge are distinct offices / And of opposed natures' (*MV* 2.9.60–1), underlining that she has done nothing so impolite as to publicly offend Aragon: any offence he has brought on himself.

It matters too that Aragon is Spanish, an ethnic foe of the English particularly after the failed Spanish Armada of 1588. Aragon is yet another in the parade of stereotyped ethnic and national suitors whom Portia mocked in *MV* 1.2, except that in this case the casket test – and Portia's clever orchestration of it – does the mocking for her. For its comic effect it helps that Aragon himself, like Morocco before him, comes to accept his status as a stereotypically arrogant aristocratic Spanish fool, declaring in the end that 'With one fool's head I came to woo / But I go away with two' (*MV* 2.9.74–5).[5] Even so, the fact that he dwells upon his wounded Spanish pride would be especially delicious for the English audience of Shakespeare's day. After Aragon's exit, Portia repeats the pattern established with Morocco's exit, offering a sardonic parting line of triumph: 'Thus hath the candle singed the moth. / O these deliberate fools! When they do choose, / They have the wisdom by their wit to lose' (*MV* 2.9.78–80). The witty passage hammers home the point that Morocco has done himself in. The metaphor of the candle and moth suggests that Morocco was irresistibly attracted to a false sense of honour that ultimately ruins him; fools like Morocco and Aragon are 'deliberate' in the sense of using their powers of deliberation foolishly and also in the sense of being deliberately, intentionally and not accidentally, stupid; these men's 'wisdom' leads them paradoxically to choose foolishly. The verbal humour here once again invites us to share Portia's sense of triumph over this aristocratic ninny, though the ethnic nature of Portia's triumph – though certainly in play – is less explicitly marked than with Morocco. (Notably, most modern performances are more willing to present Aragon as a Hispanic caricature than Morocco as a Moorish caricature, an indication of the relative cultural acceptability of the two stereotypes for contemporary audiences.)

We've examined patterns of racial and ethnic humour in these scenes for two reasons. First, we should not shy away from the problems posed by these passages for our image of Portia, who is too often portrayed as unproblematically virtuous, divorced from the ugly anti-Semitism that characterizes the Venetian characters. Portia participates in ethnic and racist thinking too, though it's masked by humour and irony and strategies of displacement. And that sort of humour has the effect of drawing the viewer into that mode of thinking, of giving us permission to laugh at the Other. Second, the pattern established by the scenes with Morocco and Aragon – in which the potentially threatening Other is tricked into providing the means for his own destruction – is at the very heart of the trial scene, though that scene is played for far more earnestness than are the Morocco and Aragon scenes. Do these scenes allow us to see Shylock's comeuppance in more comic terms than we might otherwise see it? Or are we caught up short by Portia's triumph over Shylock, finally brought face to face with the nasty aspects of ethnic stereotyping we laughed at earlier?

Lancelet Giobbe

Lancelet Giobbe serves a function familiar from many Renaissance comedies, that of the clown, a rustic, often dim-witted, who provides comic counterpoint for the main plot with a series of largely detachable routines. These routines involve such matters as mangling learned vocabulary, indulging in comic bravado, satirizing various established social targets (like lawyers, courtiers, tailors, assertive women, cuckolds and the like) and being the butt of slapstick violence. Lancelet also exhibits the traits of another stock comic character, the *dolosus servus* or crafty servant, which Shakespeare would have known from Latin comedy. Unlike the rustic clown, the crafty servant is typically much smarter than he might first appear. He is able to use his considerable verbal facility to pursue his own goals and make fun of his master, all while pretending to be properly servile. Typically he strikes a special relationship with the audience, stepping outside the dramatic world to speak with us directly in soliloquies and asides. Under the veil of wit this figure can speak truth to power, supplying a working-class perspective on the social world of the play, a form of wisdom from below. And the crafty servant is often how the comic protagonist gets the better of the blocking figure, often a father who stands in the way of the protagonist's fulfilling his desire, often marriage to the father's daughter.

Many of Lancelet's little set pieces are variations on these comic commonplaces. He tricks his blind father into thinking he is dead just for the fun of 'rais[ing] the waters' (*MV* 2.2.44), that is, getting him to cry, but when he tries to reverse course he is hoist by his own petard, for he struggles to get old Giobbe to believe it is really him and that he is very much alive. This routine (*MV* 2.2.29–105) gives us a taste of Lancelet's penchant for fun at the expense of authority, something we see again in his interactions with Shylock (*MV* 2.5) and Lorenzo (*MV* 3.5). His begging of a position from Bassanio (*MV* 2.2.106–46) becomes a tag-team routine in which father and son make a mockery of the conventions of polite address with their malapropisms and constant interruption of each other. The target in the scene is clearly not Bassanio but the uncouth manners and mentality of the Giobbes. These routines offer parodies of discourses of authority – Biblical allusion and religious language, Latinate vocabulary, the long-winded rhetoric of obeisance – but the mockery tends to be accidental, the product of ignorance rather than genuine, intentional subversion.

The final sequence of this scene (*MV* 2.2.147–58), Lancelet's triumphal rant upon his good fortune, is a fine example of comic bravado. Lancelet's reading of his own palm does a comic turn on the play's theme of fortune and hazarding: whereas Bassanio presents his relation to fate as a matter of his own agency, of actively taking a risk in hopes of reward, Lancelet presents that relation as a matter of fixed destiny, inscribed by Fortune in the lines on his hand. The prize for both men are wives – for Bassanio Portia, for Lancelet a preposterous 'eleven widows and nine maids' (*MV* 2.2.152–3). Lancelet's name, meaning 'little knife', highlights his equivocal nature in the play. He has some of the cutting wit we expect of a crafty servant, but in his case that wit is rather limited in scope and effect; his bragging about his future sexual exploits is undercut by the phallic implications of the name 'little knife'. And the echo of the name 'Lancelot', Arthur's famously righteous knight, provides an ironic chivalric context for Lancelet's decidedly unheroic behaviour, particularly since, like Lancelot, he is undone by illicit sex (*MV* 3.5.34–9).

Despite his seemingly conventional nature as the play's clown and crafty servant, we should notice that much of Lancelet's humour is blatantly anti-Semitic, misogynistic and racist, and unapologetically so. Indeed, he is introduced to us with a long comic routine in which he considers whether to break his bond of service to Shylock, what would under normal circumstances be considered a crime or sin. The temptation to leave service was not uncommon – in *1 Henry IV* 2.4.40–7 Prince Hal nudges a boy drawer to consider leaving his service to a tapster – but in Lancelet's opening speech (*MV* 2.2.1–28) he frames the issue in terms of rival moral demands. He plays out a scene familiar from morality drama: the choice between salvation and damnation, allegorized as a choice between the good angel (his 'conscience') and the fiend.[6] Onto this familiar scene Lancelet maps the notion that as a Jew Shylock is himself a kind of devil. This is the first moment in the play where this anti-Semitic commonplace has been presented so baldly, though Antonio refers to it earlier when in an aside he speaks of the devil citing scripture (*MV* 1.3.94–8). Lancelet makes this commonplace the centrepiece of an extended anti-Semitic joke: he would rather follow the fiend's counsel to run away, committing a potentially mortal sin, than follow his conscience and remain with his Jewish master Shylock, whom he presents as the greater devil. This is comic chop-logic, that is, an obviously flawed argument used to justify an otherwise indefensible or foregone conclusion, and the parodic allusion to morality drama contributes to the fun. But, as is the case with Portia's ethnic and racist humour, Lancelet's comedy routine nudges us to embrace – or at least accept – the joke's anti-Semitic premise.

The difference here has to do with the directness of Lancelet's prejudices. The bourgeois characters in the play – with the notable exception of the boisterous fool Gratiano in the trial scene – tend to express their religious and social prejudices less openly, in private, among themselves, cloaked in legalism or moral rectitude. (Another exception is Salerio and Salerino's mockery of Shylock's loss of 'daughter and ducats' in *MV* 2.8, though this mockery is shared only between the two men.) Throughout the play Lancelet's anti-Semitism seems unguarded, funny because he unwittingly violates the unspoken prohibitions against expressing such sentiment so openly. That is not to say that his prejudice is not broadly shared. When Lancelet gets his service from Bassanio, he tells his new employer, 'the old proverb is very well parted between my master Shylock and you, sir: you have the grace of God, sir, and he hath enough' (*MV* 2.2.140–2). The 'old proverb' Lancelet alludes to is 'the grace of God is enough',[7] meaning that God's forgiveness, available only to Christians, is wealth enough. In Lancelet's version, Shylock has wealth enough, but Bassanio, who refers to himself as 'so poor a gentleman', has Christian grace, the far more valuable possession. What's notable is Bassanio's response to Lancelet's little anti-Semitic quip: 'Thou speak'st it well' (*MV* 2.2.143). It's possible that Bassanio speaks this line with a touch of embarrassment or quick dismissal, but it nevertheless reveals his own rarely expressed prejudice, one widely held among the Christians. Lancelet, as the play's resident rube, too unsophisticated to master polite discourse, says outright what others are reluctant to say in public and so he gives comic voice to an anti-Semitism that is cloaked in a wittiness and foolery that encourages us to laugh along.

What makes Lancelet's anti-Semitism all the more striking is his close relationship with Jessica. What the two share are servile status in Shylock's household, a status made abundantly clear in *MV* 2.5 by Shylock's shabby, overprotective treatment of his daughter. Lancelet's antics, Jessica suggests, have provided the two a measure of covert insubordination and shared merriment in an otherwise relentlessly dreary home. Their tearful parting in *MV* 2.3 suggests an affection akin to that shown by Antonio at Bassanio's parting in *MV* 2.8, and upon his leaving Lancelet becomes the means by which Lorenzo can outwit Shylock and steal Jessica, serving as their crucial go-between. The special bond between Lancelet and Jessica, then, sits rather uneasily with his explicit anti-Semitism. At their parting Lancelet tries to address the contradiction in his tender epithets 'most beautiful pagan, most sweet Jew' (*MV* 2.3.10–11) by imagining that Jessica is in fact Christian by birth after all, albeit a bastard birth: 'If a Christian do not play the knave and get thee, I am much deceived' (*MV* 2.3.11–12). Lancelet's desire to make Jessica a Christian accords with Jessica's own loathing of her heritage and her desire to convert, though she intends to make the change by marrying into the faith: 'I shall end this strife, / Become a Christian, and thy [Lorenzo's] loving wife' (*MV* 2.3.20–1).

Yet after Jessica marries Lorenzo, it is Lancelet who insists that she cannot evade the curse of her Jewish blood:

> Yes, truly, for, look you, the sins of the father are to be laid upon the children; therefore, I promise you, I fear you. I was always plain with you, and so now I speak my agitation of the matter. Therefore be of good cheer, for, truly, I think you are damned. (*MV* 3.5.1–5)

This becomes an occasion for a reprise of the Christian bastard joke Lancelet earlier plied, though, he concedes, that would mean that she were 'damned both by father and by mother' (*MV* 3.5.13–14). When Jessica asserts that 'I shall be saved by my husband; he hath made me a Christian!' (*MV* 3.5.17–18), Lancelet suggests that her conversion will undermine the integrity of the Christian tribe: 'Truly, the more to blame he; we were Christians enow before, e'en as many as could well live one by another' (*MV* 3.5.19–21). His joke about the making of Christians raising the price of pork touches on a familiar complaint about accommodating aliens – that they put a squeeze on already limited resources. The tone of this routine is open to interpretation: is Lancelet in earnest, speaking 'truly' as he says he is? If so, should we see him as clownishly wrong-headed about Jessica's spiritual fate or as a voice for the uncomfortable truth, clumsily expressed though it may be? Or is this a bit of merry banter meant to entertain Jessica, a throwback to Lancelet's amusing antics in Shylock's house? Is it even perhaps a parody of anti-Semitism? In any case, Lancelet's affectionate alliance with Jessica seeks to soften some of the ugliness of the anti-Semitism he presents, even as he gives such sentiments a voice in the play. Their relationship suggests that his certainty about the spiritual fate of the Jews, their congenital devilishness, is not a matter of some blanket hatred of Jews. It is another means by which Shakespeare makes anti-Semitism seem compatible with comedy.

The responses to Lancelet's final anti-Semitic routine are interesting to consider. Though Jessica declares that 'Lancelet and I are out' (*MV* 3.5.28–9) and reports their exchange to Lorenzo, it is not clear what her attitude is. Whether she is amused and wants to share the joke with her husband, or she is upset to learn that she may not be assimilable into the Christian community, Shakespeare leaves up to the actor playing Jessica. We should notice nevertheless that after Lancelet leaves, Lorenzo asks, 'How cheer'st thou, Jessica?' (*MV* 3.5.63), hinting that she has fallen into melancholy. There also seems some hint of tension between the newlyweds as they leave for dinner (*MV* 3.5.76–83), a tension that may be more developed when we see them again at the start of Act 5. Many modern performances suggest that Lancelet plants a seed of doubt and regret in Jessica's mind about her plan to become a Christian, something that grows into a realization that she will always remain a Jewish outsider.

Lorenzo's direct riposte to Lancelet in 3.5 is to reveal that he has gotten a Moorish woman pregnant. His implicit argument is that Lancelet is a hypocrite to complain that Lorenzo has sullied the Christian community when Lancelet has done so himself by fathering a cross-racial child. Lancelet responds with a bevy of 'Moor/more' puns: 'It is much that the Moor should be more than reason; but if she be less than an honest woman, she is indeed more than I took her for' (*MV* 3.5.37–9). Lancelet uses his verbal facility to make light of his sin, suggesting that the Moor is 'less than an honest woman' and so he is not to blame for her downfall. This bit of wordplay is intended to divert attention from the issue at hand, and indeed, all mention of the Moorish woman disappears after this moment. Though Lorenzo complains 'how every fool can play upon the word' (MV 3.5.40), he soon veers off into banter with Lancelet about dinner preparations. Even so, we should not fail to notice that Lancelet's joke turns upon a racist assumption – that the woman is by her nature as a Moor disreputable and promiscuous. The sheer verbal wit of his reply coaxes us to laugh along with that premise, and any sense that our laughter may be troubling may be eased by all of Lancelet's goofy, innocuous wordplay that follows – we're just punning around.

What purpose does this comic sequence serve? Beyond the obvious fun of wit and jokes, one purpose has to do with the trial scene that follows, the play's climactic moment where the conflict between Jew and Christian comes to a head. Lancelet's jokes give voice to anti-Semitic thinking just as we are about to enter the courtroom. They suggest that the distinction between Jew and Christian is rooted in differences of birth and blood and that the Christian community cannot accommodate difference of this sort without undermining or even destroying itself. This perspective works in tandem with the extravagant praise of Portia's Christian virtue that Jessica offers towards the end of the scene (MV 3.5.66–76). Taken together, Lancelet's anti-Jewish humour and Jessica's praise of Portia's righteousness establish an interpretive orientation in which Shylock is demonized as a Jewish threat and Portia, an agent of Christian righteousness, is justified in her treatment of him.

This is not to say that we *must* accept this perspective as the trial proceeds. For one thing, we might remember that Lancelet in his rustic ignorance often misuses Christian discourse. That is to say, he is hardly a reliable source on matters of race and theology, though he does often voice attitudes that other Christians harbour but rarely state openly. Similarly, we have already seen that some of Portia's actions do not quite match up with her public image as a paragon of virtue. It's debatable whether we should accept the assessment of Portia's virtue from Jessica, who arguably is prone to over-idealizing the Christians. For another thing, we always have the opportunity to 'read against the grain', that is, to interpret the scene from a different, much more critical perspective. Indeed, it is possible that Shakespeare primes us with an attitude in one scene that he tests against the characters' actions in the next scene so that we find it wanting. Nevertheless, Lancelet's jokes and Jessica's praise of Portia seek to shape our perceptions of the trial scene that follows, and recognizing that they do so is to take a step towards responding actively and critically, not passively, to the perspective they purvey.

Shylock

Shylock may seem a strange figure to include in a discussion of racial and ethnic humour. For one thing, he is often the butt of anti-Semitic joking – and of anti-Semitic discourse in general – throughout the play. For another, Shylock is presented as an enemy of humour, a killjoy whose spirit of dour penuriousness, separation from the Christian community and vengefulness towards Antonio runs directly counter to the image of open-handed generosity, mirth, mercy and festive inclusion the Christian characters seek to project. Shylock occupies the role of the refuser of festivities, that traditional character type who churlishly rejects the larger community and its traditional pleasures. When Bassanio invites Shylock to join him, Antonio and other Christians in a banquet to seal their deal, Shylock pointedly refuses, citing his adherence to Jewish dietary law as a reason 'not [to] eat with you, drink with you nor pray with you' (*MV* 1.3.33–4). Shylock's disgust at the smell of pork points to not just a religious objection but also a visceral distaste at the prospect of Christian merriment. Later, when he learns from Lancelet that the Christians will be engaging in 'masques', that is, Venetian street carnival, he orders Jessica to seal up 'my sober house' against the sights and sounds of the community's festivities. His line 'stop my house's ears – I mean my casements' (*MV* 2.5.33), with its confusion between Shylock's house and his body, reveals how much Shylock wants to wall himself off from all signs of Christian mirth. His own daughter remarks that her father's stinginess and opposition to frivolity have made the family home a 'hell' (*MV* 2.3.2). Shylock's refusal of festivity springs in part from his adherence to orthodox Jewish practice, something which Shakespeare's contemporary audiences would likely have seen as analogous to the strict practices of the Puritans, and this quality of his character anticipates his later insistence upon adhering rigorously to law in the trial scene.

And yet even though Shylock sets himself in opposition to Christian mirth and allies himself with strict moral law, he exhibits moments of considerable wit and humour, moments likely to be missed if we overemphasize his role as the refuser of festivity. Shylock's flashes of humour are often mordant and barbed.[8] Those qualities, rooted in the experience of anti-Semitic oppression, take aim at self-important or overbearing figures of authority he cannot otherwise resist overtly, and they distinguish Shylock from other targets of prejudice in the play like Morocco and Aragon. These qualities are especially apparent in Shylock's opening scene, where he uses tactics of delay and passive aggression to needle his condescending Christian foes. There is something comic, for example, in Shylock's repeated non-committal 'well's in answer to Bassanio's request for a loan. Shylock relishes that Antonio, so high-mindedly scornful of usurers, must come to him for a loan, so he drags out the decision as a way of reminding Bassanio and Antonio who holds power in this situation. Similarly passive-aggressive is Shylock's seemingly innocent comment that 'Antonio is a good man' (*MV* 1.3.12). Bassanio suspects some irony in Shylock's delivery, but Shylock insists that the word 'good' refers only to Antonio's financial sufficiency. Even so, the word seems to aim subtly at Antonio's reputation for moral rectitude. What's more, Shylock insists that he means Antonio is financially 'good' only after reciting a long list of hazards that threaten his sufficiency, even including a little pun on 'pirates'. There is also a comic anti-Christian barb embedded in Shylock's comments about pork at *MV* 1.3.30–1, where he reminds Bassanio that Christ himself exorcised devils out of possessed men and conjured them into pigs that Christians so eagerly eat. Buried here is a reference to the scapegoat, the creature onto which a community's sins are projected so that they can be expelled, a role Shylock himself will soon be forced to play at the trial. At the moment, however, Shylock is using this trenchant remark to anticipate and deflect his being demonized by the Christians, since they, unlike him, willingly ingest the devil in the form of roast pork. In fact, throughout this scene Shylock uses comic quips to deflect Christian contempt for him. When Antonio criticizes Shylock's tale of Jacob's sheep, asking him 'was this inserted to make interest good? / Or is your gold and silver ewes and rams?' (*MV* 1.3.90–1), Shylock replies with an evasive yet pointed gibe about his own business acumen: 'I cannot tell, I make it breed as fast' (*MV* 1.3.92). And when Antonio responds with a diatribe about 'what a goodly outside falsehood hath' (*MV* 1.3.98), Shylock doesn't reply directly but turns the conversation back to the loan, reminding us of Antonio's previous moral objection to usury and not too subtly suggesting that Antonio too has merely a 'goodly outside'.

Shylock's comic skill at wittily fending off Christian contempt for the Jews and even turning it back on the Christians can be seen clearly in the play's many dog references. Shylock repeatedly complains in *MV* 1.3 that Antonio was prone to call him a 'dog' or a 'cur'. The epithet cuts in several directions at once. It gives metaphorical specificity to the idea that Shylock is bestial, not of the human race, 'un-kind'. The word 'dog' here refers not to a beloved pet or hunting hound but rather the sorts of feral dogs that plagued ancient and early modern cities, indiscriminate scavengers, uncivilized pests to be despised. Indeed, Shylock makes the connection when he says that Antonio would 'foot me as you spurn a stranger cur / Over your threshold' (*MV* 1.3.114–15), kicking him from his door like a homeless, begging dog. The insult has a Biblical pedigree, for especially in the Old Testament (and the ancient world more generally), dogs were among the proverbially unclean, despicably servile beasts. The phrase 'cut-throat dog' adds ravenousness, untrustworthiness and murderousness to the picture. It is possible that the insult even evokes, through the dog's pack nature, Antonio's contempt for the tribal quality of Jews in Venice and also the nomadic, diasporic nature of the Jews like feral dogs without a place to call their proper home. Though Shylock calls him out for this slur, Antonio, far from chastened, declares that 'I am as like to call thee so again' (*MV* 1.3.125), one of several indications that his zealously 'Christian' antipathy to Shylock has a disturbingly racist quality.

The epithet 'dog' clearly bothers Shylock, for he mentions it repeatedly in his accusatory speech in *MV* 1.3, coupling it with Antonio's spitting upon his 'Jewish gaberdine', his overcoat. It is interesting, then, to watch how Shylock responds to this attribution, for he embraces the insult 'dog' so he can use it to his own argumentative advantage. Shylock's sly question, 'What should I say to you? Should I not say / "Hath a dog money? Is it possible / A cur can lend three thousand ducats?"' (*MV* 1.3.116–18), points up Antonio's hypocrisy in coming to him for a loan when he had heretofore so loathed Shylock and his usury. Shylock then mocks Antonio's expectation that he should simply ignobly kowtow to the Christian's request after such mistreatment. Shall I, Shylock asks, say 'You call'd me dog; and for these courtesies / I'll lend you thus much moneys'? (*MV* 1.3.123–4). The echo of 'cur' in the word 'courtesies' provides a punning reminder of just how uncourteous Antonio's behaviour is and highlights the savage sarcasm of the passage. Later, when Shylock encounters Antonio with the Jailer, he reminds Antonio of his scurrilous epithet and once again makes a nasty quip of it: 'Thou call'dst me dog before thou hadst a cause; / But, since I am a dog, beware my fangs' (*MV* 3.3.6–7). Shylock's rhetorical strategy here is to turn the stereotype of the rapacious, beastly dog projected onto him back upon the Christians so that the insult justifies Shylock's vengeful behaviour and exposes Christian hypocrisy. This strategy is also one we can see at work in the 'merry bond' he proposes to Antonio. This 'merry' nature of the bond has long raised questions for scholars and readers. Does Shylock really intend this bond as 'merry', never really meaning to impose the forfeit? Does the bond shift from 'merry' to 'earnest' only after Shylock feels himself to be betrayed by the Christians? Or does Shylock present the bond as 'merry' in order to trick Antonio into a dangerous bargain he intends from the start to enforce? Either way, there seems something parodic about the terms of the bond: Shylock amplifies the Christian stereotype of the rapacious usurer to the point of absurdity and so turns it into a joke, making it as ridiculous as a dog that loans money.

Antonio is not the only Christian of the play to use the words 'dog' or 'cur' to refer to Shylock. When he mocks Shylock's lamentations for the loss of his daughter and his ducats, Salanio connects his cries with a dog's howls, laughing at what 'the dog Jew did utter in the streets' (*MV* 2.8.14). Shylock's refusal to show Antonio mercy with the Jailer prompts Salanio to call him 'the most impenetrable cur / That ever kept with men' (*MV* 3.3.18–19). In the trial scene the 'dog' insult returns with special force. There Antonio, echoing a famous proverb, speaks of Shylock as a bloodthirsty wolf who has targeted a lamb and will not be moved by pleas of mercy (*MV* 4.1.72–3). That analogy, we should notice, identifies Antonio with the innocent sacrificial lamb and through that to Christ ('the lamb of God').

It is Gratiano, in one of his many unfiltered moments, who offers the most developed version of the dog insult, in his frustration at Shylock's refusal of mercy:

> O, be thou damned, inexecrable dog,
> And for thy life let justice be accused!
> Thou almost mak'st me waver in my faith,
> To hold opinion with Pythagoras
> That souls of animals infuse themselves
> Into the trunks of men. Thy currish spirit
> Governed a wolf, who, hanged for human slaughter,
> Even from the gallows did his fell soul fleet,
> And whilst thou layest in thy unhallowed dam,
> Infused itself in thee; for thy desires
> Are wolvish, bloody, starved and ravenous. (*MV* 4.1.127–37)

Gratiano here develops the common analogy between usurers and ravenous wolves, but he makes the equivalence literal rather than just figurative. He is referring to metempsychosis, the doctrine of the pagan philosopher Pythagoras that the souls of the dying migrate into the unborn children of the living. Shylock's 'currish spirit', he claims, is really the soul of a dog, a wolf who turned to killing humans, and upon being destroyed for it, was 'infused' in Shylock's body when he was still in his mother's womb. Implied here is the idea that Shylock's vulnerability to such transfer of souls springs from his mother being 'unhallowed', that is, unprotected by Christian baptism because she is a Jew. The word Gratiano chooses to refer to Shylock's mother, 'dam', echoes the word 'damned' in the speech's opening line. Gratiano thereby links Shylock's 'wolvish' nature to his Jewish birth and blood.

In this case Shylock does not respond with a 'dog' quip, preferring to brush Gratiano's remarks aside and rest upon the strength of his bond, though there may be a 'cur' pun buried in his dismissive retort, 'Repair thy wit, good youth, or it will fall / To *cure*less ruin' (*MV* 4.1.140–1). In the end, Shylock's sardonic humour is not enough to resist the power of his Christian enemies. Even so, through his wit Shylock exerts some degree of rhetorical agency in circumstances that frame him either as devilish villain or powerless victim. His wily quips provide us with a different perspective from which to view the dominant Christian anti-Semitism, perhaps a space from which we can resist the interpellation of racist and ethnic humour.

Writing matters – asking analytic questions

In the preceding discussion I've left a significant figure for you to consider: Gratiano, Bassanio's boisterous, fun-loving sidekick. I invite you to consider what Gratiano contributes to the humour of *The Merchant of Venice*. Early in the play, in response to Antonio's declaration that 'every man must play a part, / And mine a sad one', Gratiano grandly proclaims his intention to 'play the fool' (*MV* 1.1.78–9). In the speech that follows, he draws on the familiar Renaissance contrast between melancholy and merriment, with Antonio serving as the embodiment of 'sadness' and Gratiano the embodiment of mirth. What particular spin does Gratiano give to this familiar contrast? How does he characterize melancholy, and why does he prefer mirth to melancholy? What particular images and terms does Gratiano use to frame this contrast? Does Gratiano actively embrace the benefits of mirthfulness, or does he just reject melancholy (which aren't exactly the same thing)? What motives might Gratiano have for saying what he does? Is he, for example, trying to get Bassanio to reject Antonio as his best friend in favour of him? As the first moment in this comedy where the issue of humour is discussed, what impression of mirthfulness does this passage establish?

It's striking that after Gratiano leaves in this opening scene, Bassanio and Antonio talk about him behind his back. Though Gratiano is supposed to be his friend, Bassanio observes that 'Gratiano speaks an infinite deal of nothing, more than any man in all Venice' (*MV* 1.1.114–15), as if he were embarrassed by his speech about playing the fool and his insistence upon talking. These comments suggest a resemblance between Gratiano the fool and Lancelet the clown, both figures of mirth who apparently don't know how to keep their mouths shut on sensitive matters. Later when Gratiano begs to join Bassanio on his voyage to Belmont, Bassanio cautions him 'to allay with some cold drops of modesty / Thy skipping spirit' (*MV* 2.2.178–9). Clearly Gratiano's mirthful chattiness is not entirely compatible with the gentlemanly demeanour Bassanio wants to project. Are there moments when Gratiano says too much? (Notice, for example, the conversation he has with Salarino as the two wait for Lorenzo under Shylock's penthouse at *MV* 2.6.1–21, a conversation which Salarino hushes up when Lorenzo approaches. Note too that he speaks of Portia as the golden fleece in her presence at *MV* 3.2.240.) Does Gratiano, like Lancelet, sometimes express what other Venetians think but are too circumspect to express openly, or are his witty comments his opinions and his alone? If Gratiano is something of a loose cannon, why do the Venetian merchants keep him around? What might the concern about Gratiano's merry talkativeness tell us about Venetian codes of verbal decorum?

One distinctive element in Gratiano's fooling, something not especially prominent in Lancelet's, is sexual jokes or jokes at women's expense. One small example can be found when he exits in *MV* 1.1, yammering on about the virtues of chattiness: 'silence is only commendable / In a neat's tongue dried and a maid not vendible' (*MV* 1.1.111–12). Gratiano's 'maid not vendible' quip refers to a woman, like Katherine Minola in *The Taming of the Shrew*, whose assertive tongue has rendered her unappealing as a marriage partner. The word 'vendible' – meaning saleable – with its connotations of commodification is a far cry from the high-minded discourse of love that Bassanio uses to speak of Portia. It's illuminating to trace this persistent thread through Gratiano's jokes. Are his sexist quips similar or different from the ethnic and racist quips of Portia and Lancelet, and in what ways? The racist discourse which Lancelet articulates certainly informs how we view the bond plotline of the play; does the sexist discourse of Gratiano bear upon how we understand the romance plotline, and if so, how?

In the trial scene, Gratiano calls Shylock a wolvish dog, mocks his praise of Portia as a 'second Daniel' and even calls for him to be hanged rather than shown mercy. Suddenly Gratiano becomes the nasty voice of anti-Semitic sentiment and Christian triumphalism, something we've not earlier heard from him. What might be the relationship, if any at all, between Gratiano's sexism and his vocal anti-Semitism in this scene? And what might his words contribute to the overall meaning of the trial scene? Is, for example, Gratiano an onstage surrogate for the offstage audience, coaxing us to join him in despising Shylock? Or does he make explicit for us the unstated bigotry behind Portia's, Antonio's and the Duke's legal manoeuvres in the trial? Do we have any evidence of how the other Christians react to Gratiano's words in the trial scene?

The art of literary criticism rests upon learning to craft good questions about the material you've assembled, questions that help you develop an analysis. So you may find it useful to look back at the kinds of questions I've asked above. In each of the paragraphs above, I've first isolated one element of Gratiano's nature – his self-proclaimed status as a fool, his penchant for talkativeness, his joking about sex and women. I prompted you to gather further evidence of these elements. Then I asked these sorts of questions:

- *Definition questions*: These questions help you sharpen your understanding of key ideas or actions. I asked, for example, about how Gratiano understood 'play[ing] the fool' (and avoiding the opposite, playing the 'sad one'). Paying close attention to his images and metaphors in his opening speech is one way to answer that question.

- *Comparison-contrast questions*: These questions help you explore how different characters or concepts might be related to one another. For instance, I asked you to compare and contrast Gratiano and Lancelet as a way of sharpening our understanding of Gratiano's role as the 'fool' in the play. I also asked you to compare and contrast his sexism throughout the play to his anti-Semitism in the trial scene.

- *Dramatic context questions*: These questions encourage you to consider a character's words and the motives behind them within the developing action of the play. I asked you to consider, for example, what Gratiano might want to accomplish by insisting upon playing the fool, and what motives might lie behind Bassanio's discomfort with his talkativeness.

- *Audience effect questions*: These questions prompt you to think through how a character's words or actions might shape our perception of certain aspects of the story. I asked, for example, about how Gratiano's anti-Semitic taunts of Shylock might affect our understanding of the trial scene.

This list certainly doesn't exhaust the kinds of questions we might ask about Gratiano. One might, for example, ask questions about historical context (how might Gratiano's quips about women fit [or not] with attitudes towards women in Shakespeare's day?) or questions about performance (what tone might be appropriate for delivering Gratiano's 'play the fool' speech?). Asking these kinds of analytic questions will help you develop a more refined, complex understanding of the play's language.

CHAPTER SEVEN

The Language of Comedy

Comedy and humour are not the same thing, though they have a certain kinship to one another. Decrying the impoverished state of comedy on the Renaissance English stage, Sir Philip Sidney, one of the great literary lights of Shakespeare's day, distinguishes between the laughter that springs from humour and the 'delight' that springs from comedy:

> Our comedians think there is no delight without laughter; which is very wrong, for though laughter may come with delight, yet cometh it not of delight, as though delight should be the cause of laughter; but well may one thing breed other together. Nay, rather in themselves they have, as it were, a kind of contrariety: for delight we scarcely do but in things that have a conveniency to ourselves or to the general nature: laughter almost ever cometh of things most disproportioned to ourselves and nature. Delight hath a joy in it, either permanent or present. Laughter hath only a scornful tickling.[1]

Sidney's diatribe has its source in early modern theories of humour and comedy. Humour, he argues, has its roots in exaggeration and incongruity; we laugh at what is outsize, out of its proper place, unsuitable for the situation, what Sidney calls 'disproportioned'. Humour involves a violation of some social or natural norm but one that is not threatening enough to have the potential for tragedy. Comedy, by contrast, involves delight, even joy in the portrayal of some social or natural ideal, what Sidney calls 'a conveniency to ourselves or to the general nature', 'conveniency' being a now archaic word for what is harmonious or advantageous. A comic plot, then, should properly work towards establishing such an ideal – or at least the promise of it – in its resolution. A bit of verbal humour or silly business might accompany a comic resolution, but humour is not required for one, nor does the delight that comes from our witnessing a comic ending originate in humour: 'though laughter may come *with* delight, yet cometh it not *of* delight' (my emphasis). The ultimate focus of comedy, Sidney explains, is not 'upon scornful matters as stirreth laughter only, but mixed with it, that delightful teaching which is the end of poesy',[2] 'poesy' being Sidney's word for literature. For Sidney, comedy's high ambition is ultimately to instruct us in moral and social ideals, to provide us a fictional world exhibiting things and people in harmony, proper order, 'conveniency', a world purged of those elements that might disrupt or threaten it, an ideal order in which we instinctively find joy.

Undoubtedly Sidney's vision of the difference between humour and comedy is informed by a class bias. He is disturbed by the extent to which 'clowns' have displaced aristocrats and kings in English plays, and he worries that writers of comedy cater too easily to audience demands for cheap laughs, what Sidney regards as the lowest common denominator of response. And Sidney has a puritanical streak that Shakespeare did not share. Even so, his distinction between humour and comedy is one typical of the age. In the last chapter we looked closely at various styles of verbal humour and how they participate in the ethnic, religious and racial tensions in the play. In this chapter we will turn to the question of comic resolution, exploring the 'ring episode' and references to music as ways of looking more closely at the 'ideal' world established by the defeat of Shylock.

Rings

The fourth act of *The Merchant of Venice* addresses heavy matters suitable for tragedy – economics and religion, life and death. Purged, it would seem, is the play's great threat to social harmony, Shylock. The final scene of the play returns us to the realm of Belmont, the world of romantic comedy and the courtship that set the bond plotline in motion. As we noted in Chapter Five, the uncertainties of the courtship plot were seemingly resolved when Bassanio chose the lead casket. With that choice he exhibited the proper values as Portia's suitor (not being deceived by the outward trappings of wealth, being willing to 'hazard' for Portia's hand) and afterwards he pledged himself to her by accepting the ring. Superficially this looks like a fairy-tale marriage, though Antonio's letter delays the proper consummation and communal celebration of the union. But Bassanio reopens the question of the marriage bond's status when at the trial scene he declares he would give up everything, including his relationship with Portia, to save Antonio from Shylock's clutches. As is typical, Gratiano follows suit and in terms more crass than his suave compatriot – he would wish his wife dead so that she could beg for Antonio's life in heaven.

The tone and terms of Bassanio's declaration reward a closer look:

> Antonio, I am married to a wife
> Which is as dear to me as life itself;
> But life itself, my wife and all the world
> Are not with me esteemed above thy life:
> I would lose all, ay, sacrifice them all
> Here to this devil, to deliver you. (*MV* 4.1.278–83)

On its surface, this declaration might seem exceptionally noble, particularly since Bassanio uses religious vocabulary ('sacrifice', 'devil', 'deliver you'). He presents his offer as Christlike martyrdom, a willingness to suffer death himself to rescue another from damnation. Here Bassanio picks up Antonio's martyrdom discourse, the way he frames himself as a willing scapegoat for the Christian community. But for Bassanio to include Portia in the list of what he would willingly sacrifice is troubling, and he adds that it is Antonio, not his new wife, whom he 'esteems' above all else. The word 'esteemed' – here meaning 'valued' as well as 'held in high regard' – tips us off that this is another test of Bassanio's core values, and he has, at least in Portia's eyes, failed it. Though he regards Portia as 'dear', the word 'dear' means not only 'beloved' but also 'expensive', and that second meaning may subtly remind us of the financial circumstances that moved Bassanio to pursue her. Bassanio's tone is also worth considering. Is this an impulsive act, egged on by Antonio's guilt-tripping, a hyperbole prompted by the emotional heat of the moment? Or does this point to some deeper, more profound bond on Bassanio's part, one perhaps that Bassanio himself didn't realize but which Antonio's potential death has clarified for him? How to gauge the intensity or truth of this declaration, which is much more direct than his rather formal declaration of love for Portia in the casket scene? Given the anxiety and vulnerability Portia expresses in the casket scene, and the fact that she engages in a little surveillance on her husband, it is understandable that Bassanio's declaration, however intended, might reopen the question of how fully committed he is to her.

The business with the rings in *MV* 4.1 and 4.2, then, returns us to the test of values we saw in the casket scene, only this time the test is under Portia's control, not her dead father's. When Portia (as Balthasar) asks for Bassanio's ring, she seeks to determine how Bassanio understands the meaning of the ring: does he value it merely for its material worth, or does he understand its symbolic value as the sign of his bond to her? She is also testing which bond means the most to her new husband – his marital commitment to his wife, his friendship (and perhaps more) with Antonio, or devotion to his own personal honour and wealth. Portia has already heard an answer in the trial scene – Bassanio has declared publicly that he esteems Antonio's life the highest – so her request for the ring can help her determine precisely how sincere Bassanio was in making such a statement.

At first Bassanio passes the test. He politely refuses Portia's/Balthasar's request for the ring, struggling between remaining true to his offer of any tribute to the clerk and maintaining faithfulness to his marriage vow. With his comment 'there's more depends on this than on the value' (*MV* 4.1.430) Bassanio seems to recognize that the ring's worth lies not in its financial price but in its symbolic value. He goes on to declare, 'Good sir, this ring was given me by my wife, / And when she put it on, she made me vow / That I should neither sell, nor give, nor lose it' (*MV* 4.1.437–9). With that, Bassanio seems to have passed with flying colours. Even so, we may hear a hint of legalism in Bassanio's reply, the sense that he refuses to give away the ring because Portia made him make a vow, rather than because he himself invested the ring with special emotional worth as a token of love.

We might compare Bassanio's comment about his ring to Shylock's comment when he learns from Tubal that Jessica traded his wife Leah's ring for a monkey: 'Out upon her! Thou torturest me, Tubal. It was my turquoise: I had it of Leah when I was a bachelor. I would not have given it for a wilderness of monkeys' (*MV* 3.1.109–11). Even though Shylock is often presented elsewhere in that scene as being excessively focused on his loss of money when Jessica elopes, he is deeply emotionally attached to his wife's ring, a symbol of their long loving relationship. This is one of Shylock's great humanizing moments, a moment where he shows he values more than just money. Jessica's callous disregard for the ring's symbolic value, particularly since she trades it for a frivolous pet like a monkey, wounds Shylock and seems to redouble his determination to take revenge upon the Christians who have so corrupted his daughter. Bassanio's talk of the ring reveals no such deep attachment. This may be why he succumbs rather quickly to Antonio's reprimand after Portia/Balthasar leaves: 'My Lord Bassanio, let him have the ring. / Let his deservings and my love withal / Be valued 'gainst your wife's commandment' (*MV* 4.1.445–7). The word 'valued' reminds us yet again that this is a test of relative values, and Antonio frames the choice in a telling way: Bassanio's bonds with the clerk and Antonio are ones of 'deserving' (merit, gratitude) and 'love', whereas Bassanio's bond with his wife is merely one of legalistic 'commandment'. The text gives no indication that Bassanio dawdles in choosing. Seemingly immediately, he bids Gratiano give the ring to the clerk and ask him to join the two for a celebratory supper, in an effort to draw the clerk into Bassanio and Antonio's homosocial company.

In the play's final scene Portia responds to Bassanio's broken bond by exacting a comic revenge, a response that echoes Shylock's revenge upon Antonio. And her revenge raises once again the tricky question of tone. Comedy as a genre demands that the play eventually establish an image of a moral or social ideal, in this case the mutual accord of heterosexual love, but as we saw in the trial scene, the pursuit of revenge – both by Shylock and the Christians – puts us in the realm of tragedy or, at the least, of forced reform, hardly the stuff of comic 'delight'. In this case, Bassanio has not committed any real infidelity (nor has, for that matter, Portia, despite her talk about laying with the doctor). So is the tone playful? Or is

Portia genuinely angry about Bassanio surrendering the ring? Does the text offer clues?

Undoubtedly Portia makes Bassanio squirm. At first, he tries to extricate himself from the situation by mansplaining:

> Sweet Portia,
> If you did know to whom I gave the ring,
> If you did know for whom I gave the ring,
> And would conceive for what I gave the ring,
> And how unwillingly I left the ring,
> When nought would be accepted but the ring,
> You would abate the strength of your displeasure! (*MV* 5.1.192–8)

This is a textbook example of two rhetorical figures: first, and immediately perceptible, the rhetorical figure *epiphora*, the repetition of the same word ('the ring') at the end of several phrases or sentences; and second, and perhaps more subtle, is the passage's deployment of *anaphora*, the repetition of the same word or phrase ('if you did know') at the beginning of phrases or sentences ('if you did know' becomes absent but understood after line 194 because of the parallelism). Both figures are typically used for emphasis, and taken together they communicate Bassanio's vehemence. Portia, however, is having nothing of it. She disarms Bassanio's rhetorical strategy by imitating it:

> If you had known the virtue of the ring,
> Or half her worthiness that gave the ring,
> Or your own honour to contain the ring,
> You would not then have parted with the ring. (*MV* 5.1.199–202)

Thwarted in this strategy, Bassanio tries to swear his way out of trouble:

> Portia, forgive me this enforced wrong,
> And in the hearing of these many friends
> I swear to thee, even by thine own fair eyes
> Wherein I see myself – (*MV* 5.1.240–3)

This passage picks up Bassanio's discussion of Portia's beautiful eyes (*MV* 3.2.115–18, 123–6), the romantic arabesque he offers when he sees Portia's portrait in the casket scene. Indeed, it is as if he were returning – out of desperation or insincerity? – to what worked on Portia's affections before in hopes of getting himself out of the doghouse. It doesn't help that he stresses he's offering this vow in front of 'these many friends', since he also declared his devotion to Antonio in open court before witnesses. Portia picks up on his potential insincerity and recasts the eye metaphor to her advantage.

> Mark you but that!
> In both my eyes he doubly sees himself,
> In each eye one. Swear by your double self,
> And there's an oath of credit! (*MV* 5.1.243–6)

Bassanio, she says, should see a reflected image of himself in each of her eyes and see himself as a double self, with 'double' also meaning 'deceptive, duplicitous'. Portia's appropriation of Bassanio's metaphor is subtly complex. She is saying that if he looks at her eyes, not only will he recognize his own duplicity but he will also see that Portia knows his duplicity about the marriage vow. With the phrase 'oath of credit', a phrase she clearly means sarcastically, she lands on another of the play's many economic terms. An 'oath of credit' is another term for the kind of financial bond Antonio drew up with Shylock, a vow to pay a debt. 'Credit' here means 'reputation for truthfulness', with the implication that Portia knows exactly how little Bassanio's vows of devotion actually mean. But 'credit' also refers to a loan rather than a direct payment of debt. The implication is that Bassanio isn't really paying the love he owes to Portia himself with his heart but is financing it by remaining in debt to another (Antonio).

Portia's last remark prompts Antonio to speak and provide a resolution for what is now a rising romantic crisis. For there to be a harmonious heterosexual marriage, Bassanio needs to pass from an arena of life in which male-male bonds are central (the business world of Venice) to an arena of life in which those bonds are subordinated to male–female bonds (the romantic world of Belmont). Bassanio has brought Antonio, his benefactor from Venice, into the world of Belmont, another sign that he has not fully made this passage from homosocial to heterosexual relations, so it becomes necessary to renegotiate Antonio's place in Portia and Bassanio's relationship. And that happens when Antonio takes blame for the loss of Bassanio's ring and pledges to subordinate himself to their marriage:

> ANTONIO
>   I once did lend my body for his wealth,
>   Which, but for him that had your husband's ring,
>   Had quite miscarried. I dare be bound again:
>   My soul upon the forfeit, that your lord
>   Will never more break faith advisedly.
> PORTIA
>   Then you shall be his surety. Give him this,
>   And bid him keep it better than the other. (*MV* 5.1.249–55)

It's important to see that Antonio is not so much rejected from the emerging social harmony as he is incorporated in it. The logic of the play's happy ending is not 'either-or', that is, either male–male bonds or male–female bonds, so much as 'both-and', a male–female relationship reconceived so that it can accommodate properly subordinated male–male relationships. This subordination happens through a second bond, in which Antonio's new place in Bassanio's life is to guarantee his marital fidelity. The stakes of this new bond are considerably higher than Antonio's bond with Shylock. There the forfeit was a pound of flesh, but here the forfeit is Antonio's very soul. Portia engineers this scene so that it is Antonio who delivers the marriage ring to Bassanio, an echo of Portia's giving the ring to Bassanio in the casket scene. Once potentially a rival to Bassanio and Portia's marriage, Antonio now becomes the vehicle, both rhetorically and materially, of the couple's (re)bonding. And for Antonio's willingness to underwrite this new venture Portia gives Antonio an unforeseen reward, a nearly magical *quid pro quo*: news of his saved fleet. Antonio may not end up with Bassanio, but he gets the considerable consolation prize of restoration of his wealth and his status as a mighty merchant.

Hovering in the background of this final sequence are issues of children and cuckoldry. The dominant order of English Renaissance society depended upon heterosexuality, for ideally heterosexual coupling produced male heirs, the means by which property within families would be passed down from generation to generation. It's telling that as soon as Gratiano becomes betrothed to Nerissa in the casket scene, he starts betting which couple will first produce a son:

GRATIANO
    We'll play with them the first boy for a thousand ducats.
NERISSA
    What, and stake down?
GRATIANO
    No, we shall ne'er win at that sport and stake down.
    (MV 3.2.213–16)

The joke turns on 'stake down'. Nerissa, taken aback by the size of Gratiano's bet, is concerned that he might have to ante-up beforehand; Gratiano, ever the jokester, construes 'stake down' in phallic terms, the gag being that he can't win the bet with his 'stake down', that is, with a limp penis. This joke makes clear what is expected of heterosexual marriage: male heirs and with them, the preservation through time of the reigning social and economic order through primogeniture, the practice of passing property down through the eldest son. This may point to why same-sex relationships, especially between men, pose a potential problem and why in this play Antonio's place in the final social order emerging at play's end must be addressed. Same-sex relationships, satisfying though they might be, cannot produce children, and so men of social stature, no matter what their sexual orientation might be, were expected eventually to marry and father sons to inherit the family's accumulated wealth. For early modern Renaissance comedies, then, the harmonious social order a comic ending creates necessarily depends upon heterosexual unions and the possibility of progeny they provide. Antonio and his intense same-sex bond with Bassanio potentially threatens Portia and Bassanio's heterosexual marriage, as Bassanio's pledge to Antonio in the trial scene and his giving away of the ring demonstrates. So Portia cleverly redirects Antonio's attachment to Bassanio, putting it through his oath into the service of the new couple's heterosexual fidelity.

Interestingly enough, the play's comic ending turns upon the possibility of infidelity and cuckoldry. For English Renaissance playwrights, cuckoldry is a go-to source of humour. Patriarchy dictated that a man control his wife's sexuality, lest she by dalliance with other men create bastard children, rival claimants to the family inheritance. A man sexually betrayed by his wife was an object of comic derision, to be laughed at as impotent or insufficiently assertive. It's noteworthy, then, that Portia and Nerissa frame the giving away of their rings as a matter of sexual infidelity on the men's part; even more, because their husbands say they gave rings to men, the women vow to cuckold them with those men in revenge. Portia puts it very plainly: 'I will become as liberal as you; / I'll not deny him anything I have, / No, not my body, nor my husband's bed' (*MV* 5.1.226–8). We might hear in Portia's vow of sexual revenge a distant, comic echo of Shylock's logic in his 'hath not a Jew eyes' speech – 'If you wrong us shall we not revenge? If we are like you in the rest, we will resemble you in that' (*MV* 3.1.60–1). More to the point, the possibility of cuckoldry – which especially horrifies Gratiano (*MV* 5.1.263–5) – is a way for the women to take back power in their marriages, to remind their husbands of their potential sexual agency and so their capacity to ruin the men's reputations. This line of thinking may help explain why Shakespeare ends the play with this quip from Gratiano: 'Well, while I live, I'll fear no other thing / So sore as keeping safe Nerissa's ring' (*MV* 5.1.304–5). This bawdy joke – which depends upon the slang meaning of 'ring' (that is, 'vagina') – may seem to modern audiences as gratuitous and inappropriate, but it makes an important connection between the great value of the ring as marker of the marriage bond and Nerissa's power (and value) as a sexual partner in marriage. Gratiano's joke verifies that he (and by implication Bassanio too) is now far more vigilant of and attentive to his wife as a sexual partner. He has been definitively reoriented from male–male relationships to a male–female relationship. As the play presents this change, it is a happy circumstance for the wives that their men are now focused on keeping their 'rings' safe from other men, but the lived reality of women living under patriarchal surveillance of their sexuality was of course quite different. Gratiano's final joke, then, serves a second purpose: it coaxes us with a laugh to see this ending as happy rather than, in the next frame out, potentially troubling.

The heterosexual thrust of this ending (sorry, couldn't resist) doesn't eliminate every single trace of queer desire. Once it becomes clear that Portia and Nerissa played the doctor and clerk and that their comments about the doctor and clerk laying with them were just a joke, Bassanio and Gratiano engage in banter about lying with male partners. To Portia Bassanio says jokingly, 'Sweet doctor, you shall be my bedfellow. / When I am absent, then lie with my wife!' (*MV* 5.1.284–5); right before delivering his 'ring' joke, Gratiano declares that 'were the day come, I should wish it dark / Till I were couching with the doctor's clerk!' (*MV* 5.1.304–5). Once again, the logic of desire operating in this comic ending is not 'either-or' so much as 'both-and', so long as heterosexuality emerges as the dominant, explicitly ratified mode of desire. With the revelation about Portia and Nerissa's disguise, it is as if these two husbands get the best of both sexual worlds with their wives. Now the tantalizing hint of homosexuality that was part of Bassanio's relationship with Antonio is part of the erotic fantasy, perhaps enlivening the couple's desire and thus Bassanio's faithfulness. And we mustn't forget that the actors playing the women's roles are indeed male, fuelling our perception that what had been a conflict between male–male and male–female desire has now been resolved. Nerissa reminds us of the boy beneath her character's costume when she answers Gratiano's question, 'Were you the clerk that is to make me cuckold?' (*MV* 5.1.281). 'Ay', she replies, 'but the clerk that never means to do it', adding pointedly 'Unless he live until he be a man' (*MV* 5.1.282–3). Of course, the (cross-dressed) boy actor saying these lines will indeed live to be a man and have the appropriate male 'means' for cuckolding Gratiano, so Nerissa's promise never to do it is comically equivocal and erotically ambiguous. Perhaps this is yet another reason that the play ends on a joke that draws our attention to Nerissa's ring: after all the erotic playfulness and ambiguity at work in this section of the scene, the joke establishes definitively that heterosexual desire, that engine of social stability in Renaissance comedy, is now in the zenith.

One person is not explicitly included in this final socio-erotic order: Jessica. What to make of that? To address that question, we will need to attend to music.

Music

Comedy involves, we have been suggesting, the restoration of harmony after a period of confusion, strife, discomfort, even genuine (if temporary) suffering. The return of social order, the appearance of an ideal, is often marked in Renaissance comedy by those potent symbols of social comity: marriage and a communal feast. That said, the harmony that emerges at the end of Shakespeare's comedy isn't ideologically neutral. Comic endings involve different individual elements finding the place in a cooperative, 'proper' relation with one another, and those 'proper' relations are in the service of quite specific social ideals, among them a 'proper' relationship between men and women, servants and masters, and social insiders and outsiders, and a 'proper' subordination of vice to virtue, loss to gain. Musical composers know that our experience of harmony relies upon a larger system of tonality into which individual notes of a melody seem to fit naturally. They also know that there are many different sorts of tonality, into which certain notes fit quite differently in relation to others. Even as we recognize that a plotline leads to a comic resolution, we ought also to recognize the way in which it conceives of comic harmony, the particular system of relationships and values it endorses and the particular persons it privileges.

Music is an apt metaphor for the harmonious vision comedy leads to, so it is appropriate music becomes a central part of *The Merchant of Venice*'s final scene. Music plays as Portia and Nerissa return to Belmont from the trial scene, and Lorenzo discusses it at length in two substantial speeches. Strictly speaking, music is not essential to the plot's resolution, so why would Shakespeare include it? In the Renaissance music is affiliated with social and natural harmony. According to traditional cosmological theory, the turning of the cosmic spheres in the heavens generated music that could be heard in the celestial realm. Earthly music is but a pale reflection of that celestial harmony, but a reflection of it nevertheless, a taste of an ideal concord that lay beyond the experience of mortals. Comedy, then, had a natural affiliation with music, for it too offered a taste of that harmonious ideal.

In the final scene musical references work in several ways at once. Music underlines that the purgation of Shylock in the trial scene has led to harmony in Belmont and a happy resolution of the bond plotline, while helping to mitigate any potential perception that Shylock's treatment was cruel, unjust, even tragic, patently un-ideal. And music serves as aural foreshadowing of the lovers' eventual amity, establishing the proper tone for the resolution of the romance plotline. But music is also a means for Shakespeare to reflect upon the kind of comic harmony *The Merchant of Venice* offers, to fine-tune our perception of that comic harmony, to draw attention to whom that final harmonious vision includes and whom it does not.

This heavenly conception of music is at the surface of Lorenzo's speech to Jessica concerning the music that sounds upon Portia and Nerissa's arrival:

> How sweet the moonlight sleeps upon this bank!
> Here will we sit and let the sounds of music
> Creep in our ears. Soft stillness and the night
> Become the touches of sweet harmony.
> Sit, Jessica. Look how the floor of heaven
> Is thick inlaid with patens of bright gold.
> There's not the smallest orb which thou behold'st
> But in his motion like an angel sings,
> Still choiring to the young-eyed cherubins.
> Such harmony is in immortal souls,
> But, whilst this muddy vesture of decay
> Doth grossly close it in, we cannot hear it.
>   [*Enter Musicians*]
> Come, ho, and wake Diana with a hymn,
> With sweetest touches pierce your mistress' ear,
> And draw her home with music. (*MV* 5.1.54–68)

This mellifluous passage, itself a bit of word music, captures nicely the link between musical harmony and the eternal harmony of the spheres. Lorenzo's description of the 'sweet' music combines an image of exquisite visual beauty – the starry night as a gold-adorned 'floor of heaven' – with an image of great tenderness – the heavenly spheres singing to childlike angels. Notably Lorenzo dwells upon the gap between earthly and heavenly music. Following Plato's theory that mortals can only imperfectly comprehend the realm of the Ideal, Lorenzo stresses that humans cannot hear the eternal harmony of heavenly folk, even though we are naturally drawn to the earthly music that imitates it. The passing reference to Diana, virginal goddess of the hunt, would seem to align Portia with Diana's fierce defence of women's independence and dignity, an interesting use of classical allusion to lend a heroic quality to Portia as she returns victorious from the trial scene and prepares to do battle with her husband about the ring.

The reference to Diana, also goddess of the moon, accords with the passage's many references to moonlight. This scene, as every other scene in this play, would have been played in daylight, so we need to be told that the scene is at night, with dawn arriving only with Portia's final lines. But moonlight has symbolic resonance here as well. The moon conventionally marked the dividing line between the heavenly realm and the earth, where life was subject to fallibility, change and death. The references to moonlight position us, then, all the more firmly in the realm of mortal imperfection. We are able to see the exquisite beauty of heaven from afar, but like the music of the spheres we cannot directly experience it. So too, Shakespeare seems to signal, is the nature of this comedy. This final scene in the never-neverland of Belmont offers us a tantalizing taste of an ideal in the form of a comic resolution, a world in which threats to social order – Shylock's legalism, Bassanio's wavering commitment to Portia, the painful reality of Antonio's lost ships – have been eliminated, and those gathered there come to share amity, plenty and joy. But these references seem to remind us, what made this resolution possible – the destruction of Shylock – remains troubling, laced with hypocrisy and vengefulness as cruel as the crime it punished. Even as we may admire the charming moonlit world of Belmont, we remain aware of how far it falls short of heavenly ideals. Perfection remains, it would seem, ever out of reach.

Shakespeare underlines our distance from the heavenly ideal when upon their arrival Portia and Nerissa discuss the candlelight they can glimpse far off in her manor house window:

PORTIA
    That light we see is burning in my hall.
    How far that little candle throws his beams!
    So shines a good deed in a naughty world.
NERISSA
    When the moon shone we did not see the candle!
PORTIA
    So doth the greater glory dim the less.
    A substitute shines brightly as a king

> Until a king be by, and then his state
> Empties itself, as doth an inland brook
> Into the main of waters. Music, hark! (*MV* 5.1.89–97)

Once again, Shakespeare offers a complex perspective with his metaphors. On the one hand, the shining candle, like a moral act, throws a small ray of light into a world otherwise engulfed in darkness. On the other hand, that small ray pales in comparison to 'the greater glory' of the moon, a heavenly body (and the moon pales in comparison to an even greater heavenly body it reflects, the sun). Though Portia's actions may be framed as 'good deeds' that lead to comic harmony, Shakespeare makes sure that we see them as imperfect substitutes when set next to the real celestial thing. Music and moonlight, then, make versions of the same point.

Lorenzo's second speech about music is prompted by Jessica's plaintive observation, 'I am never merry when I hear sweet music' (*MV* 5.1.69), a comment that may bear upon the perception of distance from an ideal harmony we've been exploring. We will return presently to the hint of melancholy in Jessica's comment, but we should first note that Lorenzo's reply adds several new elements to the discussion of musical harmony:

> The reason is your spirits are attentive.
> For do but note a wild and wanton herd,
> Or race, of youthful and unhandled colts
> Fetching mad bounds, bellowing and neighing loud,
> Which is the hot condition of their blood;
> If they but hear, perchance, a trumpet sound,
> Or any air of music touch their ears,
> You shall perceive them make a mutual stand,
> Their savage eyes turned to a modest gaze
> By the sweet power of music. Therefore the poet
> Did feign that Orpheus drew trees, stones and floods,
> Since naught so stockish, hard and full of rage,
> But music for the time doth change his nature.
> The man that hath no music in himself,
> Nor is not moved with concord of sweet sounds,
> Is fit for treasons, stratagems and spoils;
> The motions of his spirit are dull as night

And his affections dark as Erebus.
Let no such man be trusted. Mark the music. (*MV* 5.1.70–88)

Lorenzo stresses the extraordinary capacity of music to captivate the listener and civilize the spirit. His extended example is of a herd of young, unbroken horses who, upon hearing music, are seemingly tamed in an instant – 'their savage eyes turned to a modest gaze / By the sweet power of music'. The allusion to Orpheus, the mythic classical musician who could charm even rocks and trees with his song, extends the point from beasts even to non-sentient beings and inanimate objects. In fact, it might extend even to conquering death, for the most famous of stories attached to Orpheus concerned his rescuing his wife Eurydice from Hades, the ruler of Hell. Orpheus was not only a musician but also a poet, and so the irresistible effect of musical harmony is by extension related to the effect of comic harmony has on its audiences. As Lorenzo formulates the matter, music and poetry are manifestations of the very force of civilization.

Lorenzo's reference to something 'hard and full of rage' cannot help but recall Shylock, whose heart's rock-hard stoniness, you will recall, Antonio, the Duke, Bassanio and Gratiano all associate with his Jewishness. You may also remember that Shylock has a particular antipathy to music. When Lancelet lets drop that there may be masquerades in Venice on the night Shylock is to visit Antonio, Shylock, horrified, closes off his house and his daughter from the communal melodies on the street:

What, are there masques? Hear you me, Jessica,
Lock up my doors, and when you hear the drum
And the vile squeaking of the wry-necked fife,
Clamber not you up to the casement ... (*MV* 2.5.27–30)

This speech ties Shylock's refusal of music to several other qualities – his miserly protection of his house and daughter; his contempt for Christians; his standoffishness from Venetian public culture; and most of all, his rejection of merriment, that quality most associated with comedy. The implication is that Shylock's hatred of music is endemic to the Jewish character. As a Jewish refuser of music, Shylock cannot be assimilated to the harmonious comic resolution that emerges at the end of the play – he can only be purged, never accommodated. In fact, to return us to Lorenzo's speech, Shylock's hatred of music places him outside all of creation and marks him as fundamentally unnatural, 'un-kind', uncivilizable, inhuman. Humankind, beasts, even stones and trees have an affinity for music, observes Lorenzo, but the man who is unmoved by music 'has no music in himself', which is to say, he is almost without a soul, and he is constitutionally incapable of participating in the harmony of the cosmic order. Such a man is the quintessential outsider, an irredeemable malcontent, 'fit for treasons, stratagems, and spoils'. 'The motions of his spirit' are allied with moonlight's opposite, the dark night over which rules the god Erebus, the son of Chaos. And, Lorenzo implies, such a man is Shylock.

What then of Jessica, to whom Lorenzo offers this long speech? What prompts Lorenzo's musings on music is her confession that 'I am never merry when I hear sweet music' (*MV* 5.1.69), a line we might see as aligning her with her father and with Jewish antipathy to merriment. We should notice that Jessica is describing how she *always* responds to sweet music, rather than just to this particular song or situation. What in her nature causes such a reaction? Does Jessica, like her father, habitually fail to respond to music's harmony because she, like her father, is a Jew? Does this moment bear upon Jessica's evident desire to become a Christian through marriage to Lorenzo and through him to become a member of the Belmontian community?

Much turns on the puzzling word 'attentive' in Lorenzo's reply: 'The reason is your spirits are attentive' (*MV* 5.1.70). 'Attentive' here would seem to mean 'intent, heedful, observant'. The *Oxford English Dictionary* offers those very definitions of the word and cites this line from *The Merchant of Venice* as an example. In his edition of the play, John Drakakis proposes the somewhat less favourable definition 'preoccupied'.[3] So what does Lorenzo mean? Is he suggesting that Jessica's soul and intellect are already civilized, focused on the proper spiritual matters, and so she already has achieved the state of harmony to which music might otherwise move her? This is certainly possible, but Lorenzo is quite adamant later in the speech the person who 'is not moved with concord of sweet sounds' – and it would seem Jessica is such a person – cannot be trusted or redeemed. Is he suggesting that Jessica is otherwise preoccupied (with what?), and so music is not able to work its usual magic? This is also possible, but the image of colts suddenly turning from their preoccupation with frolicking to listen the sound of music would seem to contradict that sense of the line. Is Lorenzo trying to teach Jessica how to respond to music, in effect telling her not to be so 'attentive' and let music have its effect upon her? If that's the case, he's contradicting his central point about the universally and naturally compelling power of sweet sounds. Myself, I'm not entirely sure what Lorenzo means with this crucial line – perhaps you have some ideas.

What is certain, however, is Jessica falls utterly silent after his speech. The script does not indicate her exit, so apparently she remains on stage throughout the final scene. What is she doing as the comic harmony emerges in Belmont? What does her silent presence indicate? Does it suggest that she remains an outsider, just as her father was ever the outsider in Venice, unmoved by the music that so charms everyone else? Does this dawn upon her as Lorenzo describes the kind of 'man who hath no music in himself'? Is her silence motivated by guilt at leaving her father or disillusionment at her realization that as a Jew she can never fully become a Christian? Or does Jessica, listening to music after Lorenzo's speech, demonstrate to him (and to us) silently that her spirits have indeed been moved? Jessica's evident melancholy despite the merry music may recall for us Antonio's sadness in the opening scene, both of which are left unexplained. As we have seen Antonio is given a place in the harmonious order that ends the play, and he even gets a magical financial restoration. Jessica's place in that order, however, is far less secure. The discordant grace note of melancholy, something that begins the play and returns at its end, reminds us yet again that the ideal of harmony comedy offers is imperfect, not the whole story of humankind. Though issues of financial and marital disorder may have been resolved, Jessica, heir to Shylock, may silently but palpably point to the limits of comic resolution in this play, to the sad question of a shared humanity, as yet unresolved.

Writing matters – conclusions

It is a common misconception that conclusions involve recapping all over again the points you've just made. That sort of summary is certainly appropriate for a speech, where listeners might miss a key point or need to have the argument assembled for them to follow it on the fly. This may be why, by the way, Shakespeare often uses two metaphors or images where he might use one – if a theatregoer misses one, she can pick up the same idea in the next. Summarizing one's points may also be appropriate for a long piece of writing like a book, where the reader can't be expected to complete the entire work in one sitting. To be sure, readers expect you to restate the thesis in an essay's final paragraph – freshly reworded, of course! – to remind them of the overarching argument you've made. But for a short essay a recapitulation of each supporting point is unnecessary and, more importantly, tedious to read.

What then is the purpose of a conclusion? Essays typically move from a broad claim (thesis) to specifics (evidence). In the conclusion, you offer the reader a new, broad perspective on the claim you've just supported. It provides a chance for you to reflect upon that argument, to consider its larger significance or implications, to offer qualifications or limit your scope. In a concluding paragraph you no longer have the burden of presenting textual support for your argument, as you do in the essay's main body. Instead the conclusion is a space for considering the implications of a thesis you can now regard as sufficiently established. Shakespeare sometimes adopts a similar structure in his plays – that's definitely the case with *The Merchant of Venice*. The main plot is substantially completed by the end of the fourth act so that the fifth act becomes a place to tie up loose ends and point towards the larger implications of the play's resolution.

Hanging over the conclusion is the bedevilling but essential question, 'so what?', a question any good essay will need to engage. The strategy of most scholarly essays is to address broad issues by examining quite specific topics. Since that's the case, the conclusion becomes the occasion where you connect the specific topic to some more general concern likely to interest your reader, one that justifies spending time and effort on what otherwise might seem like minutiae. Say, for example, you are writing about the state of Lorenzo and Jessica's marriage at the end of *The Merchant of Venice*, focusing on the 'in such a night' exchange they share at the start of the final scene. You argue that despite the romantic moonlit setting this initially playful conversation between the lovers morphs into something tense and unhappy. This, you claim, indicates the general direction of Lorenzo and Jessica's romance, from mutual infatuation (what is called 'fancy' in *MV* 3.2.63) to a strained relationship. (It's possible to argue the opposite, that the tone remains playful throughout this exchange. Otherwise, your claim would not really be a thesis.) So what conclusion might you write to such an essay? What is the more general implication of your argument? What larger issues might it help address? Granted that your claim is true ... so what?

Like most theses, this argument allows for many possible answers to the question 'so what?' You might, for example, suggest that the deteriorating state of Lorenzo and Jessica's marriage brings into focus Shakespeare's interest in the fragility of romantic bonds, an interest that might coax us to rethink the image of Shakespeare as a poet of love. Or you might suggest that this moment is an important clue to the complicated tone of the play's final scene, something scholars and performers have long discussed. Or you might observe that Lorenzo and Jessica's souring marriage suggests even with Shylock's defeat in Act 4, the problem of relations between Christians and Jews remains a live, perhaps unresolvable issue to the end. Or you might claim that this one conversation demonstrates a dynamic of romantic psychology, the ease with which a Freudian slip – in this case the word 'steal' – can reveal far more than a lover intends and so destroy mutual trust. In all these cases, your concluding paragraph can home in one of these answers and so tease out some larger implication of your paper's central claim.

Try creating several different answers to the question 'so what?' for your own essay's thesis. Once you're done, choose one to pursue in your concluding paragraph. Every thesis suggests multiple answers to the question 'so what?', so pursue the one you think is most important or interesting. If you include them all, your conclusion is likely to read like a laundry list rather than a paragraph. This is another case where less is more. And resist the temptation to choose an implication that is exceedingly broad, such as 'Lorenzo and Jessica's deteriorating marriage tells us much about the nature of love'. If the topic of your concluding paragraph is too broad, it will be difficult for your discussion not to be seen as unrefined, obvious or, worst of all, clichéd. Think of an angle that will give your readers a pay-off in insight, something they might not have thought of on their own. That is, after all, what readers really want from a conclusion.

CHAPTER EIGHT

Language through Time: Adaptations and Performance

Performances and adaptations of *The Merchant of Venice*, indeed of any Shakespeare play, often involve making some change to Shakespeare's language. Directors and adaptors make cuts (almost no stage or film performance includes the entirety of Shakespeare's script); they add passages like prologues or epilogues; they rearrange the dialogue; they modernize the language, whether it's the occasional arcane word or the entirety of the play; they change the context of the language by situating it in a different place or era than Shakespeare specified; in a few cases they even jettison Shakespeare's language entirely, performing the play in silent form, though perhaps some spectators familiar with their Shakespeare can supply the dialogue from memory. Knowing this raises some questions. Should we feel obligated to be faithful to Shakespeare's language? If so, is it possible to perform his plays without somehow altering the meaning of Shakespeare's language? (The romantic essayist Charles Lamb famously claimed that *King Lear* could not be acted because no performance could ever measure up to the grandeur of the play's language.) And what exactly counts as being faithful to Shakespeare's language? Even if I speak all the dialogue of *The Merchant of Venice* just as Shakespeare wrote it, will his words be understood as Shakespeare intended them? Do the words 'bond', 'will' and 'hazard' have the same resonances for contemporary playgoers as they had for Shakespeare's early modern audiences? Might substituting a modern word for Shakespeare's choice actually be more faithful to Shakespeare's intended meaning? So if I want to be utterly faithful to Shakespeare's language, paradoxically aren't there times when I should change that language in order to accomplish that goal?

This raises another question: if performances and adaptations inevitably alter Shakespeare's language in some way, why study them at all? Shouldn't we be studying Shakespeare's language itself, the very essence of his achievement, free of the contaminations of latter-day actors, directors and adaptors? These questions are hotly debated, and I will be suggesting several answers in the course of this chapter. But I will begin with this claim: by observing how directors and adaptors have changed Shakespeare's language, we can remind ourselves that Shakespeare is himself choosing from alternatives as he writes. The Shakespearean text comes to us imbued with an almost scriptural authority, as if it were written on marble tablets and handed down from on high. But if you can see the Shakespearean text as the result of a series of very human choices, if you start to ask 'Why did Shakespeare do it or say it this way and not another?', his work becomes far more alive, less an object of worship than an intriguing record of his formidable mind at work.

A recent Australian performance of *The Merchant of Venice* by the Bell Shakespeare company ended with a tearful Jessica falling to her knees, crying 'What have I done?' Lorenzo, distressed and comforting, tore up the bond promising the couple Shylock's fortune, and as the lights slowly came up Portia proclaimed, 'It is almost morning' (*MV* 5.1.295), a line that became more hopeful when repositioned to the play's end. This ending, director Anne-Louise Sarks's solution to the problem of performing the play in the modern age, raised some hackles among Shakespeare purists. Yes, this is not what Shakespeare wrote, but it powerfully raises the question: why did Shakespeare *choose* to end *The Merchant of Venice* as he did? Why did he choose to have Jessica fall silent? Why did he choose to end the play on a bawdy joke from a secondary character? Why did he choose to set the final scene at night, and why did he choose to have Portia say 'it is almost morning' in his version? Beside the value of the Bell Shakespeare performance in itself, which one critic found 'electrifying' and 'profoundly affecting',[1] one value of 'unfaithful' performance is that it sends us back to Shakespeare's script with a fresh eye, better able to see his script as but one path of the many paths he might have taken. In this chapter, we will be exploring from several angles how performance, adaptation and recontextualization can reshape our perceptions of what Shakespeare's language in *The Merchant of Venice* might mean. This is a huge topic, enough for a book of its own, so we'll be addressing only a few examples in an effort to illustrate some interpretive principles.

Print editions

It may seem strange to begin a chapter on performances and adaptations of *The Merchant of Venice* with a section on the play's first printed texts. After all, aren't they the most reliable records we have of Shakespeare's language? In what way are they adaptations and not the thing itself? To understand the challenge printed texts pose, it's important for us to understand a bit about Shakespeare's writing practices. Shakespeare didn't himself produce any printed plays. What Shakespeare did produce was a handwritten script which a skilled scribe would have made a clean copy of. That manuscript, known as the 'fair copy', was jealously guarded by the company performing the play. Only later would that copy or some transcript of a performance be taken to the print shop (probably not by Shakespeare himself), where it would be set by compositors and made into books. In some cases, compositors worked from an earlier printed versions of a play with changes of various sorts added in by hand. Most compositors tried to be reasonably diligent in setting the copy they received, but some were sloppy or made mistakes. And evidence suggests that some of the texts they were working from were defective or difficult for the compositors to understand. What's crucial to recognize is that there are myriad intervening hands between Shakespeare's handwritten draft and the printed page. None of Shakespeare's handwritten manuscripts survive, so the printed texts of Shakespeare texts that come down to us are versions of the copies the Renaissance printer received, versions that include various mistakes, elements of reformatting and revision. And often those versions added features typical of a book aimed at readers but not included in a manuscript of dialogue aimed at actors – stage directions, consistent speech prefixes, italics and punctuation, act and scene divisions, prefatory material, page formatting. In short, producing a print edition involved adapting what the printer received from the playhouse to the conventions of a book in the day. Without a doubt the early print editions are crucially important pieces of evidence from the period, the closest thing we have to 'the thing itself', but they are not exactly the thing itself, a point I'll be addressing in the remarks below.

Like about half of Shakespeare's plays, *The Merchant of Venice* first comes down to us in two print editions. The play first appeared in quarto, a booklet-sized format printers used for single plays and pamphlets, the rough equivalent of a modern trade paperback. It is called a 'quarto' because four pages were printed on a single side of a standard sheet of paper. That sheet was then folded into quarters (hence 'quarto'), and pages cut and assembled with other folded-and-cut pages to form a book. The first quarto of *The Merchant of Venice* was printed by Thomas Heyes in 1600, eight years after the play premiered onstage. A second quarto, largely a reprint of the first quarto with small changes, was printed by J. Roberts in 1619, though apparently for copyright reasons the title page says 1600. The next major early edition of *The Merchant of Venice* appeared in the First Folio, the first complete collection of Shakespeare's plays in print, published in 1623. The folio format was much larger than the quarto format. Folios used only two pages per side of a standard sheet, and so folios were far more expensive to produce. This format was reserved for big, important works – collections of plays, classical writing, extended treatments of theology or politics, Biblical translation, compendious histories – the kind of book you'd keep on your shelf for generations. A rough equivalent of the folio might be a hardback coffee table book. After the First Folio (as it came to be called), there were subsequent folio editions in 1632, 1664 and 1685. *The Merchant of Venice* appears in all four folio editions, and there was an additional quarto edition of the play in 1637. To a remarkable extent, the early editions of *The Merchant of Venice* agree in most respects, though we'll examine some differences below.

Let's begin with the play's title. Interestingly the title of *The Merchant of Venice* changes as it travels from edition to edition. In the first quarto version (1600), the title on the front page reads

'The most excellent Historie of the *Merchant of Venice*. With the extreame crueltie of *Shylocke* the Iewe toward the sayd Merchant, in cutting a iust pound of his flesh: and the obtayning of Portia by the choyse of three chests'. It's an intriguing title for several reasons. Notice, for example, that the title divides up the plot into its three main threads – the tale of Antonio ('history' in Renaissance English means 'story', either grounded in fact or fanciful), the tale of Shylock (with emphasis on potential tragedy), and the tale of Portia and Bassanio (though Bassanio's name is not mentioned). This play would seem to offer it all: history with an exotic setting, tragedy, romantic comedy. Note too that Shylock is specified as a 'Jew', and the phrasing hints that in this play we just might see an especially grisly onstage murder. It's possible that the title intended to capitalize upon memories of Christopher Marlowe's *The Jew of Malta*, which featured just such lurid acts of 'extreame crueltie' by a diabolical Jew, or maybe it sought simply to exploit anti-Semitic myths about bloodthirsty Jews. This was the title for the play for all the early quarto editions, though there are some minor variations in the second quarto's title from 1619. Instead, of a 'most excellent Historie', the 1619 title trumpets an 'EXCELLENT history'; instead of 'chests', we get 'caskets'. When we turn to the first page of dialogue in both the quarto editions, the title is slightly different – both read 'The comicall History of the Mer*chant of Venice*'. The potential for tragedy we noted earlier disappears (since 'comicall' suggests a happy ending), and Antonio is placed at the centre of the plot. These two significantly different titles frame the play in quite different ways and may serve different purposes. The jacked-up title on the front page ('most excellent', 'extreame crueltie') seeks to catch a potential buyer's eye, whereas the title on the opening page of dialogue establishes the proper generic expectations ('comicall') for the work that follows.

The First Folio text (1623) has a much simpler title, the one that has become conventional for the play: *The Merchant of Venice*. That title first appears in the 'Catalogue of the several Comedies, Histories, and Tragedies Contained in This Volume' among the comedies. The catalogue certainly sets generic expectations for the reader, but it also groups *Merchant* with plays like *A Midsummer Night's Dream* and *As You Like It* which appear before and after it in the list, plays whose approach to comedy, most critics would agree, is very different from that in *Merchant*. On the first page of dialogue one sees simply *The Merchant of Venice*, with no indication of the genre at all and no mention of a Jew as the villain. That bare title puts the focus squarely on Antonio, the setting and the theme of mercantilism. All of the subsequent folio editions (in 1632, 1664 and 1685) follow the lead of the First Folio in titling the play.

Why do these admittedly subtle differences in all these titles matter? First, they remind us that books use titles to shape our particular responses to the works that follow them. In this case, the quarto and folio titles are prompting different responses. Crudely put, the quartos tend to stress the entertainment value of *The Merchant of Venice*, perhaps in an effort to get a reader to buy a single edition of the play. It's quite possible that the quarto is directed to someone who has seen the play onstage and wants to relive the experience by reading it. The folio version encourages a different kind of reading experience, a bit more deliberative and critical, more distant from the theatrical experience. We are encouraged to read this play in the context of Shakespeare's entire output. Second, these differences in titles remind us that different print formats have different conventions and that putting Shakespeare's play in a particular format is in reality a matter of adapting that play. We have become so used to encountering Shakespeare's plays in print that it's difficult for us to think of the 'real' Shakespeare as anything other than the print editions. In reality, however, most Renaissance consumers of *The Merchant of Venice* would have encountered the play as a live performance. The print editions appeared only afterwards, adaptations aimed at a much smaller reading market.

Stage directions are one feature of print editions that spectators would be largely unaware of. Those directions add in for the reader what would simply be part of the viewing experience for the spectator. Most early modern print editions of plays are sparse with their stage directions, so it's illuminating to see what is included in editions of *The Merchant of Venice*. For Morocco's entrance, for example, the first quarto reads, 'Enter *Morochus* a tawnie Moore all in white, and three or foure followers accordingly, with *Portia, Nerissa*, and their traine'. There's much to be gleaned here: we learn that Morocco is a 'tawny' (that is to say, a light-skinned) Moor, a fact significant for all the talk about 'complexion', and that he is dressed in 'all in white', perhaps in a *thawb*, the traditional long white tunic of Arab men, visually marking Morocco as Muslim. Morocco has a significant retinue, more than Bassanio has, for when Bassanio first encounters Lancelet, the stage direction specifies that he enter 'with a follower or two'. The focus on the 'trains' of Morocco and Portia, a focus we see again with the stage directions for Morocco's later entrance and for Aragon's entrance, suggests that these moments involve some manner of aristocratic pageantry. The folio stage direction tends to confirm that hypothesis: it adds a flourish of cornets to the direction. The cornet is an instrument associated with the entrance of important figures. (Speaking generally, the folio edition does more to specify the play's music than does the quarto.) When Portia enters the trial in disguise, the stage direction for both quarto and folio reads, '*Enter Portia* for *Balthazer*' (the folio spells it *Balthazar*). For spectators, this direction is unnecessary – they can see that Portia is in disguise – but for the reader this is a potential point of confusion, since the dialogue thereafter still marks the law clerk's lines as Portia's. That is, this direction is aimed at readers, who must be reminded of what spectators simply see. Readers get a reminder of the name of Portia's alter ego, Balthasar, but spectators get to hear that name only once, in the letter that the Duke reads.

Speech prefixes, those designations in the script of who is saying what line of dialogue, are also a feature of print editions that spectators would not be aware of. Only a newbie actor would ever speak them out loud. Speech prefixes are particularly interesting in early editions of *The Merchant of Venice*. The quarto editions specify that Lancelet's opening speech, for example, be spoken by *Clowne* (*Clo.* in the Folio), not by 'Lancelet'. Indeed, *Clowne* is Lancelet's prefix throughout the play, with the one exception of his exchange with his father, where he is designated as *Lancelet* (*Lan.* in the Folio). This designation also extends to stage directions associated with Lancelet: '*Enter the Clowne alone*', '*Enter Jessica and the Clowne*' and the like. This frames Lancelet less as an individualized personality and more like a stock comic character. At the very least, it keeps his rural unsophistication ever before us as we read. The same tension between individualization and type characterization extends to Shylock. At some times in both quarto and folio, his speech prefix is *Shy.*; at other times he is designated as *Jew*. We see the same oscillation in stage directions: '*Enter Bassanio with Shylocke the Jew*', '*Enter Jew, and his man that was the Clowne*', '*Enter Shylocke*', '*Enter the Jew, and Solanio, and Anthonio, and the Jaylor*', '*Enter Shylocke*'. In Shylock's case, there seems to be no clear rationale governing when the early editions specify *Shylock* or *Jew*. Many commentators have argued that 'Jew' indicates what Shakespeare himself wrote in his original manuscript before he settled on the name for this character. In any case, the easy slippage between 'Shylock' and 'Jew' suggests that the character was at some level intended as a generic Jewish villain, even though we modern readers tend to see Shylock as highly individualized. The slippage between these two designations also fits with the way in which characters within the play flip from using Shylock's name to calling him 'Jew' and back again as the occasion suits them.

One last feature of early print editions needs our attention, a feature at the very heart of editorial practice. Sometimes editors encounter a word or phrase that doesn't make sense or is deeply ambiguous. We can find such a case in Lorenzo's discussion of the night-time sky in the play's final scene. Here's how that passage appears in the first quarto:

> sit *Jessica*, looke how the floore of heaven
> is thickly inlayd with pattens of bright gold …

Except for capital letters, this passage runs the same in the First Folio. So what are 'pattens'? A glance at the *Oxford English Dictionary* reveals that the word refers to thick-soled slip-on shoes. That makes no sense. The second quarto reads 'pattents', referring to documents conferring some right or privilege, an equally untenable alternative. This is what editors call a 'crux', meaning a point where the received text makes no sense and it is not clear what the author originally wrote. Is this an error for 'patterns', which would make sense? That's how the line reads in the Second, Third and Fourth Folios, and many editors have accepted that change, even though these folios are later editions produced well after Shakespeare's death. The great eighteenth-century Shakespeare editor Edmond Malone suggested that Lorenzo is referring to 'patines', that is, patinas, burnished surfaces, a suggestion that makes sense for the meaning of the passage and tries to be faithful to the first quarto edition, the text produced in Shakespeare's lifetime. It's also possible that Lorenzo means 'paten', the plate upon which the Host is laid in the Catholic mass. Such plates were often made of silver or gold and ornately decorated, and that word would certainly enhance the religious connotation of 'heaven' in the previous line. But a floor inlaid with patens would be a strange image indeed, for holy objects of this sort would never be used in that way.

This is admittedly a minor example, but it reminds us that to produce a readable text editors must figure out ways to resolve such cruxes. One must either print the nonsensical 'pattens' (which will only frustrate readers) or replace it with something more comprehensible, close but not exactly the same as the text that's come down to us – 'patterns', 'patines', 'patens' or something else. The differences between these alternatives may be subtle, but they can be significant for one's understanding of Lorenzo's speech. 'Patterns' puts emphasis on the intricate workmanship and purposefulness of God, 'patines' stresses heaven's timeworn beauty, and 'patens' heightens the sense of holiness and suggests a more specifically Catholic context.[2] (You may want to look at a second crux, the 'rage/page' crux at *MV* 2.1.35, a crux with consequences for how we understand Morocco's grasp of classical mythology.) What this means is that any modern text of *The Merchant of Venice* you might read comes to you filled with such decisions made by editors. At least in part every text of the play has always already been interpreted for you, even before you start reading. This isn't necessarily something to be lamented because no matter how you encounter your Shakespeare, in print, on stage, on the screen, such intervening decisions are always being made by editors, performers, directors, actors, cinematographers. All are versions or adaptations of *Merchant* in one way or another. The point is to be aware of that fact and to be cognizant of interpretive consequences such editorial decisions introduce.

Performance

The Merchant of Venice has had a long stage history, far too long to cover in any detail in this short section.[3] Two elements of Elizabethan stage practice might concern us as students of Shakespeare's language. The first concerns how Shylock looks. Circumstantial evidence suggests that Shakespeare's Shylock may have been played with a red wig and beard, a choice that would link Shylock to Christ's betrayer Judas Iscariot, who was conventionally depicted with a red beard.[4] When the famous actor Edmund Kean played the role in a black wig in 1814, it was such a novel choice that it prompted concern from his fellow actors. Long-standing stage tradition also has it that stage Jews were played with a false hook nose, as was the stock figure of Pantalone, the greedy, meddling, aristocratic old fool of *commedia dell'arte*. Shylock mentions his 'Jewish gaberdine' (*MV* 1.3.108), a loose cloak or mantle with long hanging sleeves, so it's likely too that he wore a costume that marked him as a Jew, visually different from the other Venetians. These visual details establish Shylock as a conventional Jewish villain, and so this would be the primary context within which Shakespeare's audiences would understand Shylock's words.

Passages eliciting their sympathy – such as the 'hath not a Jew eyes' speech – would be all the more startling given how he appears and so might have jammed the codes of Renaissance anti-Semitism. After Henry Irving's performance of the part in the late nineteenth century, a performance that established a tragic conception of Shylock, most – though certainly not all – twentieth- and twenty-first-century performances ditched the red wig and beard of earlier performances in favour of other indications of Shylock's ethnic and religious identity. The gaberdine still appears occasionally, particularly in traditional productions (perhaps because it is mentioned in Shakespeare's text), but now the yarmulke, payot (the long side-curls of Orthodox Jewish men), the tallit katan (the Jewish prayer shawl) or even just a thick beard identifies Shylock as Jewish, different from his peers. The effect is to distance Shylock's words from anti-Semitic caricature and connect them with authentic Jewish experience. In Jonathan Miller's 1970 production of the play set in a Victorian Venice, for example, Laurence Olivier's Shylock wears a yarmulke under his top hat, a sign of his ambition to assimilate; when he learns of Jessica's betrayal from Tubal and vows to revenge, he dons a prayer shawl to indicate his newfound solidarity with his fellow Jews. Henry Goodman's Shylock, in Trevor Nunn's 2001 production set in 1930s Venice, proudly wore a yarmulke and tallit katan throughout the production, suggesting parallels between his experience of anti-Semitism and that of Jews in Germany during the same period. And Al Pacino in Michael Radford's 2004 period film of the play wears a red cap for outdoor scenes to identify him as a Jew, a historically accurate touch. When we briefly see Pacino's Shylock after the trial scene, he no longer wears the cap, a sign that he has converted, but he is also pointedly left outside and alone, underlining that even as a convert he remains ostracized. And there are a number of modern productions – particularly those set in the business world – where Shylock's difference is hardly marked at all. Such was the case with Peter Zadek's 1988 production of the play (in German) for the Burgtheater in Vienna. Gert Voss's stolid Shylock was dressed in smart modern business attire throughout, and the only indication of his difference from the characters was to be found in the text, not in his appearance. Here the effect was to universalize and modernize, rather than to localize, Shylock's experience of prejudice, to highlight the humanity Shylock shares with his antagonists.

These details of costuming remind us of an important difference between reading Shakespeare's text and encountering it as a theatregoer. When we read, we freely imagine the character who speaks the lines. Indeed, the lines themselves shape how we construct that speaker in our mind's eye, though of course that construct springs in part from various prior literary myths and our cultural experiences. In the theatre, by contrast, we encounter Shakespeare's lines in the context of a concrete character created for us by the actor, costume designer and director. We understand the same lines in different ways, depending upon the performance of them. And one of the theatre's most powerful tools for shaping our understanding of character response is costuming.

This insight extends to a second issue of Renaissance staging, cross-dressing. Standard practice on the early modern English stage was for boys to play the women's parts. In the context of this performance convention, the cross-dressing of Portia, Nerissa and Jessica, the first of several instances of women cross-dressed as men in Shakespeare's comedies, takes on an added layer of meaning. Jessica's shame at cross-dressing as a male torchbearer, for example, reflects one of the religious objections to theatre in Shakespeare's day, that it undermined gender stability and carried with it a sense of sinfulness:

> I am glad 'tis night you do not look on me
> For I am much ashamed of my exchange.
> But love is blind, and lovers cannot see
> The pretty follies that themselves commit,
> For, if they could, Cupid himself would blush
> To see me thus transformed to a boy. (*MV* 2.6.35–40)

It's appropriate that Jessica should voice this sentiment, given that the prohibition against cross-dressing was based upon Jewish Deuteronomic codes (see Deuteronomy 22.5), laws that Jessica, as a Jewish woman, would be expected to follow. The overarching witty irony is that when Jessica speaks of being 'transformed to a boy', the actor playing Jessica is already a boy. Her reference, then, to the blush of Cupid, the tiny boy-god of sexual passion, hints at another reputed effect of cross-dressing – that it encourages homoerotic, even pederastic desire. The same sorts of issues hover over Portia and Nerissa's cross-dressing. When Portia announces her intention to impersonate a man, she piles up jokes about pretending to be 'accomplished / With what we lack' (*MV* 3.4.61–2), that is, a penis, an organ which, of course, the boy playing Portia is already 'accomplished with'. Portia's comments about how she will perform masculinity are all the funnier and ironic because we know a male actor is speaking them. Nerissa's question about cross-dressing, 'why, shall we turn to men?' (*MV* 3.4.78), is understood by Portia in sexual terms because cross-dressing brings sexuality, particularly homosexuality, into play. In Chapter Seven we discussed how cross-dressing brings into play very complex issues of sexuality in the final reconciliation between husbands and wives. Nerissa and Bassanio's quips (*MV* 5.1.281–5) depend upon the pansexual quality of desire set in motion by cross-dressing. Many modern critics have suggested that Portia's cross-dressing gives her access to a masculine realm of experience she would otherwise be excluded from, and as a result she becomes more independent and self-assertive. There is much to be said for this reading, but it seems much more plausible in a modern performance context when women play the female parts and the homoerotic comic subtext is thereby muted.

So far we've addressed conventions of Renaissance performance that we have good reason to think Shakespeare himself might have addressed. In the text of *The Merchant of Venice* itself, however, outside a handful of stage directions and those few actions clearly implied by the text (for example, Nerissa's giving of Shylock's deed of gift in *MV* 5.1.291–2), Shakespeare's script gives us few explicit directions for how to perform the dialogue. *The Merchant of Venice* is what performance critics call an 'open' script, which is to say, it tends not to specify how the play ought to be performed. (A 'closed' script, by contrast, provides the author's directions for how lines should be performed and scenes should be blocked;

some closed scripts even include information about the characters' offstage lives. The scripts of George Bernard Shaw are a good example.) The apparently open nature of Shakespeare's script raises an interesting interpretive problem. When we read the text, we may be only minimally aware of features of the spoken word like intonation, speed of delivery, rhythm, phrasing and vocal pitch. But when we hear the text spoken – and this was how Renaissance audiences typically first encountered their Shakespeare – we hear it with particular intonational choices that emphasize one word over another, at a particular speed that can communicate either enthusiasm or torpor, in particular arrangements of rhythm and pauses that highlight one emotion or idea over others, with a particular vocal quality that can express quite specific information about the speaker's age, class, gender, race or history. Even if you were to speak Shakespeare's dialogue in a monotone at a constantly moderate speed, you can't help but give the text an interpretive spin. Performed that way, you would be emptying out the passion behind Shylock's 'hath not a Jew eyes' speech and so changing its meaning. There is no such thing, in other words, as a neutral delivery. To speak the text aloud is inescapably to interpret the text. This may be why readers of *The Merchant of Venice* often find hearing a performance is such a revelation: speaking the words aloud gives a particular interpretive shape to the dialogue that is clarifying.

This prompts a question: might Shakespeare's script somehow regulate its own vocal performance? Does the written text provide direction for how to speak the lines? This has been the argument of a number of directors (John Barton and Cicely Barton of the Royal Shakespeare Company key among them). They see the placement of punctuation, small variations of iambic pentameter, the use of alliteration or parallel phrasing, or the endings of poetic lines as consistent clues about Shakespeare's intentions regarding the dialogue's performance. Without doubt Shakespeare, a master craftsman of verse, provides some indications of emphasis and speed of delivery in his poetic lines. But we should also remember that the printed texts that come down to us are directed at readers, not actors. We do not know if the punctuation of *The Merchant of Venice*, for example, consistently conforms to Shakespeare's preferences, and, in fact punctuation is one of those elements routinely adjusted by modern editors. What we do know is that Shakespeare's scripts are written for performance, and imagining how his lines might be spoken is crucial to the work of interpretation.

To illustrate the problem, let's look at the question of accent. Though the accents of Shakespeare's characters are not specified by the text of *The Merchant of Venice*, they can have a huge impact upon our perception of the characters' identities and the meaning of their speech. In many modern performances of the play, though by no means all, Shylock is given a 'Jewish' accent, typically the accent of Ashkenazic Jews who fled the pogroms of Eastern Europe in the early twentieth century. That is the case, for example, with Emrys James's Shylock for Terry Hands's 1971 production for the Royal Shakespeare Company (RSC), Warren Mitchell's Shylock for the 1980 BBC Time-Life television production of the play, Anthony Sher's Shylock for Bill Alexander's 1987 production for the RSC, Henry Goodman's Shylock for Trevor Nunn's 2001 production at the National Theatre, and Trevor Peacock's Shylock for the Arkangel audio production in 2005. One can even detect traces of this accent in Al Pacino's clipped delivery in Michael Radford's 2004 film adaptation. This 'Jewish' accent, like the gaberdine, yarmulke and prayer shawl in other productions, immediately marks Shylock as ethnically different from other characters, and since his accent cannot be as easily donned and doffed as costuming can, it marks Shylock as indelibly different, incapable of reform.

Some productions have shown an awareness of the potential thematic complexity of accent. In Jonathan Miller's 1970 production for the National Theatre, for example, Laurence Olivier as Shylock spoke with a muted, slightly mannered accent, that of a man toning down his inherited speech patterns in an effort to conform to polite Victorian society; Patrick Stewart's Shylock for John Barton's 1978 production for the RSC spoke in an over-enunciated accent to suggest that he was a non-native speaker. The question of Jewish assimilation was, in these performances, built into the very quality of Shylock's voice.

Other unscripted accents have also become regular features of modern performances. Directors now routinely assign accents to Morocco and Aragon (African in the case of Morocco, Spanish in the case of Aragon) to bump up the comedy of their scenes, but their accents also mark them as 'foreign' and help establish a pattern of expelling the contaminating alien that is repeated with Shylock in the trial scene. Using accent for comic purposes has also become a way of reinvigorating Lancelet Giobbe's rather dated jokes. In the Arkangel audio performance of the play, for example, David Tennant gives his exuberant Lancelet a very broad Scots accent that immediately distinguishes him in class and nationality from the Venetian Christians, all of whom speak with posh British accents and buttoned-up decorum.

This discussion of accents helps us make two interlocking points. Though Shakespeare specifies none of the accents of the characters, it is impossible to speak the Shakespeare text without bringing accent into play, for the simple reason that we all speak English with an accent. And an accent positions a character for the spectator in particular ways, in a specific social class, nationality, ethnicity, age group, gender, sexuality or history, even if the actor speaks Shakespeare's words exactly as written. Shakespeare doesn't specify the accents of his characters, yet a performer must make a choice of accent for the play to be performed, and that choice has consequences for how we understand Shakespeare's lines. In many recent British productions of *The Merchant of Venice*, Gratiano speaks with a working-class or non-Oxbridge accent, framing him as the uncouth, even crass sidekick of the far more polished Bassanio. But what if Gratiano spoke with the posh accent of a gentleman? Such a choice might change the tenor of his bawdy jokes – they then become a sign of his sense of aristocratic privilege. How might such a posh accent change the meaning of his taunts at Shylock in the trial scene? Would Gratiano then be seen as voicing the ugly anti-Semitism of the entire elite class, rather than just uttering his own working-class prejudices?

And what of Jessica's accent? Most modern productions give her an accent matching that of Portia and Nerissa, suggesting by the very sound of her voice that she is naturally allied with the Christians, already culturally assimilated. But what if Jessica, like her father, spoke with a strong Jewish accent? How might it change her concern about becoming a Christian if she is indelibly marked as Jewish each time she speaks? Imagine a production in which, during the 'in such a night' sequence, Lorenzo mocked Jessica's Jewish accent with his final reply to her. What might such a choice say about Jewish–Christian relations in the final scene, about Jessica's ambition for her marriage and Lorenzo's motives for marrying her, about the possibility for her escaping her father and his legacy? Might such a choice provide a reason for why Jessica falls silent soon after? Not a word of Shakespeare's text need be changed, and yet such a choice would change the meaning of Shakespeare's language profoundly.

Such is the power of performance: the very same sequence of Shakespearean words can mean very different things depending upon how actors situate their characters with costuming and diction. Certainly we ought to attend to performance details specified by Shakespeare's script, stage directions both explicit and implied. But in watching the play in performance we need also to attend to those performance choices actors and directors have made that tease out new resonances and emphases in Shakespeare's text, sometimes even in tension with the text, for through those choices performers keep *The Merchant of Venice* relevant to modern sensibilities and issues. As we watch a performance, we must remind ourselves that we are always watching a process of adaptation at work, even when performers are utterly faithful to Shakespeare's language.

Adaptations

Adapting a Shakespeare play involves recasting all or some of Shakespeare's text to make it suitable for a context different than the one for which Shakespeare wrote – a different time period, a different language, a different culture, a different medium, a different set of social mores or political commitments. Adaptation can take many forms – translation, modernization, rewriting, transposition to a new setting, resequencing of the plot, elimination or addition of characters, or some combination of these techniques. Since I'm concerned in this book with Shakespeare's language, this section will focus on recontextualization, that is, the technique of placing Shakespeare's words in a new context. Unlike other forms of adaptation, recontextualization doesn't entail rewriting of Shakespeare's text. Rather, simply setting Shakespeare's words in some new context encourages us to interpret those words in a new way, while still seemingly remaining faithful to the Shakespearean original.

Allusions to *The Merchant of Venice* take advantage of the power of recontextualization. Shylock's 'hath not a Jew eyes' speech has, for example, become a touchstone in several films addressing the Holocaust. In *To Be or Not to Be* (1942), a Jewish member of a troupe of Polish actors uses the speech to voice resistance against the occupying Nazi army (and to give himself the starring role he's long desired). In *The Pianist* (2002), the camera, surveying the harrowing circumstances of Polish Jews rounded up for transport to concentration camps, settles on a man reading *The Merchant of Venice*; asked about it, the man launches into the speech, ending with the line, 'shall we not revenge?', a line that in context underlines the horrifying powerlessness of the victims of the Holocaust, their inability to resist or revenge. *Schindler's List* (1993) features only a single line from the speech. The line is uttered by the homicidal Nazi officer Amon Goeth as he tries to seduce his Jewish housekeeper Helen – 'Are these the eyes of a rat? Hath not a Jew eyes?' The allusion offers some insight into the psychology of anti-Semitism. Shylock's line suggests the possibility of Goeth seeing Jews as human beings, but almost as soon as he says the line he revolts against that possibility, blaming the housekeeper for his lapse and beating her brutally. In all these cases, Shylock's speech is linked to Nazi-era anti-Semitism in subtly different ways, though of course Shakespeare could not have anticipated the horrors of the Holocaust.

And this is not the only resonance the speech might have. Walter Scott references it twice in *Ivanhoe*, his 1820 novel of post-Crusades England. *Ivanhoe* addresses, among much else, the history of English anti-Semitism, going back to its medieval manifestations and its relationship to the formation of England as a unified nation. Shylock's speech appears first in the novel's dedicatory epistle and again as the epigraph of chapter 5, where Scott introduces the Jewish moneylender Isaac of York, an object of both medieval Christian persecution and enlightened acceptance. Scott uses the reference to highlight his sympathetic treatment of this Jewish figure, though some critics have complained that Scott's revisionism doesn't go nearly far enough. Another, quite different example can be found in 'Out of Sight, Out of Mind', an episode of the TV series *Buffy the Vampire Slayer* (season 1, episode 11, broadcast 19 May 1997), where Shylock's speech is the subject of a classroom scene that opens the show. This episode focuses on the destructive effects of ostracism in high school culture, so Shylock's speech in this context is not concerned with anti-Semitism at all. Rather, it serves as a general plea for accepting those who have been socially spurned or ignored, a moral baseline for the main plot of the episode. These examples illustrate a basic principle of adaptational technique: setting a passage in a new context can tease from it new resonances, some far afield from its original meaning. This principle governs, for example, the now common practice of shifting performances of Shakespeare's plays to new settings, of situating *The Merchant of Venice* in, say, the modern business world, a move which highlights the economic issues of the play.

I want to consider here two plays that use recontextualization in a more thoroughgoing way in order to confront the issue with which this book began, the difficulty of staging *The Merchant of Venice* after the Second World War. Both plays use a play-within-a-play structure, transporting substantial passages of Shakespeare's dialogue, often entire scenes or sequences of scenes, to new locales in order to make Shakespeare's language address directly modern anti-Semitism and the Holocaust. Our first example is Julia Pascal's *The Shylock Play* (2008), set in the Jewish Ghetto neighbourhood of modern Venice. There Sarah, a Polish Holocaust survivor on holiday, waits for a walking tour to begin. After relating her family's harrowing travails during the Second World War to her guide Valentina (Sarah pretended to be Catholic to escape the Nazis), Sarah encounters actors rehearsing *The Merchant of Venice* in the street. This setup allows for interaction between the fictional present of Shakespeare's play, the history of anti-Semitism embodied by the Ghetto's history and by Sarah's past, and the modern present where the history of Jewish persecution risks being turned into a tourist attraction.

As the rehearsal proceeds, sometimes in Shakespeare's language, occasionally in modern English, Sarah is drawn into the performance and tries to intervene. She identifies particularly with Jessica. This Jessica is openly resentful of her suffocating if doting father Shylock, and she longs to escape him and her Jewish legacy, even dying her hair blonde. Sarah, trying to change the trajectory of Shakespeare's play, pleads with Jessica not to abandon her father for the unfaithful Lorenzo but to no avail. Jessica renounces her faith onstage before an Inquisitor, in a scene intercut with Bassanio's wooing of Portia. The ironic juxtaposition undercuts the romantic tone of the courtship scene, highlights Bassanio's hypocrisy (Pascal cuts his speech about 'ornament') and foreshadows the inability of Jessica to assimilate in later scenes. One of the play's key issues is the renunciation of

Judaism as a way of surviving patriarchal or anti-Semitic oppression. What Jessica discovers, as Sarah had before her, is that this strategy leads ultimately to rejection by the Christian community, loss of identity and deep regret.

In Pascal's play, the trial scene is played just as Shakespeare wrote it, but its being set in the Venetian Ghetto – and the responses of Sarah as she watches – focus attention on the place of this iconic scene in the history of Jewish oppression. Though Shylock is bowed, he is not entirely conquered. When Portia asks him, 'Art thou contented, Jew?', the stage directions specify that he 'bursts into outrageous laughter at the absurdity of his situation', replying 'I am "content"' (the marks of irony are Pascal's).[5] Pascal's handling of the final scene of *Merchant* deliberately undermines the comic ending Shakespeare engineers for his plot in potent ways. Pascal specifies that the opening exchange between Lorenzo and Jessica be played with 'deep tension ... as if they are emerging from a row' (86), as it becomes apparent to Jessica that she will never be accepted within the Christian community. Pascal further undercuts Shakespeare's 'happy ending' by directing the actors to perform the remainder of the final scene at double speed, turning the celebration of comic resolution into a farce. The play's true climax is instead Shylock's forced conversion, played onstage with great cruelty at the end, even as Shylock tries to resist by reciting the Shema, a central prayer in morning and evening services and traditionally the last words of a devout believer. The tragedies of Jessica and Shylock are that both conversions destroy their faith but neither allows them to assimilate. And it is the same for Sarah, who tells us early in the play that 'I loved the Church. It didn't love me' (19), and for her father, who defined himself as a Pole rather than a Jew but nevertheless was taken to Treblinka. When Valentina returns to begin her rote tour of the Ghetto, we have a new appreciation of the long-standing plight of the Jews – hated for their faith, denied membership in Christian or secular society when they convert. The very place where Valentina and Sarah stand, the Ghetto, illustrates the terrible exclusion to which the Jews have long been subjected. And we can also see how Shakespeare's script is part of the ongoing plight of the Jews.

Our second example, Tibor Egervari's *The Merchant of Venice in Auschwitz* (1998), is also concerned with the place of the play in the history of anti-Semitism, but it takes a different interpretive tack. His play imagines a performance of the play at the Auschwitz concentration camp, a performance forced upon the prisoners by a sadistic Nazi commandant. In this production, the Jewish prisoners play, strangely enough, the Christian Venetians, gypsy prisoners play Portia and Nerissa, the commandant and his henchman play Shylock and Tubal, and a thuggish *kapo* plays Lancelet Giobbe. Jessica is played by a professional actress who has foolishly travelled to Auschwitz to take the part, unaware that it is a concentration camp. This wilfully perverse casting allows Egervari to explore two themes. First, the commandant uses the hypocrisy of the Venetian Christians and the Belmontese to expose the hypocrisy of those non-Aryans who think they can avoid the consequences of anti-Semitism or deny solidarity with their fellows through privilege, wealth or stealth. Second, and more important, Egervari uses the setting to amplify the anti-Semitic elements of Shakespeare's text. The commandant plays Shylock as a grotesque Jewish caricature, the bogeyman of Nazi propaganda. Berating the actors with appallingly bigoted rants, the commandant periodically interrupts the performance to force his cast to be more stereotypically Jewish, compelling them to speak in a 'Jewish accent' or to draw upon their 'crimes' as Jews in their acting. What's more, he forces them to recite passages from *Mein Kampf*, the tales of *Baal Shem-Tov*, and the Torah, and to tell self-humiliating Jewish jokes.

In this context, Shakespeare's script becomes yet one more way for the commandant to subjugate his prisoners, for he forces them to perpetuate the very stereotype that oppresses them. As the commandant says to the actress playing Jessica, 'It is our duty to unveil the true face of this enemy race which the Führer has defined as a moral plague worse than the black plague of early times'.[6] Performance of *The Merchant of Venice* becomes his means for that unveiling. In the trial scene, for example, the commandant plays Shylock as a Hasidic Jew, and Portia is played as an SS officer. Portia's 'quality of mercy' speech is, so specifies Egervari, to be delivered in 'Hitler's manner, gestures and all' (64) in an effort to convert her articulation of Christian principles into a face-to-face Nazi indictment of the sly, malevolent Jew. The irony is that as much as the commandant hates Jews, he is utterly obsessed with them. His notion of Jewishness, it becomes distressingly clear, is his own creation, necessary to justify his own identity, and he is performing *The Merchant of Venice* to confirm and propagate that stereotype. Such is the logic of his playing Shylock.

Yet it is an interesting effect of the play-within-the-play that we come to sense a gap between the commandant's intent and what Shakespeare's script actually says. Yes, some of Shakespeare's dialogue is anti-Semitic and the concentration camp context heightens those qualities, but other passages push in a different direction. Since many of Shakespeare's scenes from *The Merchant of Venice* are performed in their entirety, we can experience the full complexity of his language, even though the situation threatens to reduce Shakespeare's play to a Nazi screed. What we come to see is that *The Merchant of Venice* offers some small spaces for resistance to the anti-Semitism the play has been made to serve. For all of Portia's Nazi performance of the 'quality of mercy' speech, the words don't quite fit what they are being forced to mean. It's even possible to see her performance as a parody of Hitler rather than an anti-Semitic appropriation of this famous passage.

Yet another space for resistance opens up at the climax of the trial scene, when the commandant as Shylock accidentally drops his knife. Seizing the opportunity, the actors kill him, after which they are mercilessly shot one by one by Tubal. This sequence follows Shakespeare's play in one sense and deviates from it in another. This killing of the commandant takes to its logical conclusion Shylock's defeat in Shakespeare's play, where stripped of his money, legacy and faith, Shylock exits not feeling well, the suggestion being that he soon will die. Yet killing the commandant also involves resisting the anti-Semitism of the trial scene. Whereas in Shakespeare's version of the trial the anti-Semites exterminate the Jew, here the Jews – in their roles as the Christians – exterminate the anti-Semite and with him the virulent caricature of the Jew he uses Shakespeare to create. This is, no doubt, a pyrrhic victory. The Nazi Tubal is the last man standing, fondling Portia's ring, a horrifying version of Gratiano's closing quip about 'keeping safe Nerissa's ring' (*MV* 5.1.307). But this too engages with the caricature of the Jew that Egervari targets in this play, a caricature that arguably Shakespeare himself partly reinforces. With his handling of the ring Tubal exemplifies the very brutish, rapacious greed at the heart of the stereotypical Jew – only now it becomes an attribute of the Nazis. Egervari's play addresses head on the pernicious purposes to which *The Merchant of Venice* has been put, particularly during the Nazi regime. It is clear-eyed about the play's perpetuation of stereotypes while hinting at ways in which it resists wholesale appropriation by the anti-Semitic cause.

Pascal's and Egervari's plays illustrate how by manipulating context an adaptor can recast the meaning of Shakespeare's language, even when the adaptor leaves Shakespeare's text relatively intact. This is yet another reminder of a theme that's run throughout this book – context profoundly shapes the meaning of Shakespeare's language. To close this discussion, let's look briefly at the opposite phenomenon – adaptations of *The Merchant of Venice* that do without Shakespeare's language. When the play first entered the realm of the movies in the early 1900s, for example, it did so by jettisoning Shakespeare's language in favour of the visual language of the cinema and the musical language of the score. (It is easy to overstate the silence of silent Shakespeare – most silent films of Shakespeare's plays included intertitles, and some were accompanied by lecturers who spoke the titles or read the text of Shakespeare's play aloud.) This meant that the Shakespeare of silent film could be more international, appealing across linguistic divides. Gerolamo lo Savio's *Merchant of Venice* (1910), an Italian production, is a particularly interesting example. None of Shakespeare's language appears in the extant English intertitles. Rather, the title cards summarize plot points and introduce each new scene, necessary because lo Savio compresses the tale into a single reel. Lo Savio's production featured location shooting in Venice, emphasizing the Italian nature of the story. This adaptation shifts emphasis away from Bassanio's wooing of Portia (we never see him choose a casket) to Lorenzo's elopement with Jessica and Shylock's bond with Antonio, the latter expanded perhaps because Shylock was played by Ermete Novelli, a major theatrical star of the day.

Novelli's performance manages to convey both Shylock's public obsequiousness to Antonio and Bassanio – outwardly he is all smiles and fawning bows – and his private malice towards the two Christians, which he communicates in grimaces direct to camera. In this version it is clear that Shylock seeks to entrap Antonio from the very start, for once the deal is struck he insists upon a contract and he exults in private when Antonio leaves with his gold. Lo Savio dwells on Shylock's anguish upon learning that Jessica has left, with Novelli briefly raging like Lear. This affront is, however, not the catalyst for his revenge but simply the first of the comeuppances

Shylock will suffer, culminating in his defeat at trial. In what may be a nod to Italian feminism of the period, Portia, an imposing figure, resolves to rescue Antonio immediately upon hearing of his arrest, with Bassanio's full knowledge of her plans; she is hardly disguised at all when she appears as Balthasar before the court. There is nothing particularly clever about Shylock's defeat, for the question of blood and the pound of flesh never comes up. Instead, Shylock is convicted of conspiring against a Venetian citizen. Throughout the film, the director makes much of the decisive role letters, bonds, warrants and law books play in the plot. Though only a few frames remain of Shylock's final defeat, it's noteworthy that it takes the form of Portia writing a warrant she gives to the Duke. This adaptation may do without Shakespeare's language, but it affirms the power of texts nevertheless.

My last example, the Chinese opera *Bond* (Chinese title *Yue/Shu*), demonstrates the challenge that the globalization of Shakespeare presents for the study of Shakespeare's language.[7] *Bond* adapts *The Merchant of Venice* to the conventions of *Yuju* opera – a characteristic poetic line of seven and ten syllables, alternating passages of dialogue and song, narratives taken from folktale and history, highly codified character types sharply differentiated between good and evil, cross-dressed performances (in this case, women play many of the major male roles), and various points of action in the drama punctuated with percussion (which gives it the name *Bangxi*, or woodblock, opera). *Bond* is an especially interesting example of the recent vogue for Shake-*xiqu*, that is, adaptations of Shakespeare to Chinese opera. The *Merchant of Venice* narrative is resituated in the glory days of the Song Dynasty (960–1279), with Venice represented by the prefecture of Nisi, a fictional city based on Kaifeng, the ancient capital of the Northern Song Dynasty and a major destination on the Silk Road. The principal conflict is not between Christian and Jew, which has little historical relevance to Chinese culture, but between Cathayans (native Chinese) and Saracens (Arab Muslim merchants from the West). The play's central theme thereby becomes the tension between the ruthless pursuit of profit and the contractualism that supports it, embodied by Shylock, and the hold of other, non-economic bonds on the Chinese characters – the bond of marriage, the bond of male–male friendship, the bond of filial duty, the bond to the traditional Chinese ideals of moderation, fair dealings and recognition of mortal evanescence.

The tale is thus relevant to modern Taiwan and mainland China, in particular to the challenge its extraordinary economic growth poses to a traditional Chinese ethical framework. Setting the tale in ancient China and treating it as a parable of moral conundrums works to avoid any obvious references to contemporary Chinese ethnic or racial tensions, references that might have put the opera in conflict with political authorities.

There is much to be said about this operatic adaptation, but here I want to focus on its approach to Shakespeare's language. Of course no translation of Shakespeare into another language can preserve the particular sound texture of the original. Even so, the authors Ching-Hsi Perng and Fang Chen make an effort to remain remarkably faithful to Shakespeare's text. This is especially apparent in four scenes – Antonio's striking of a bargain with Shylock, Bassanio's choosing of the gold casket, the trial and the ring episode in the play's final scene – all of which tend to paraphrase Shakespeare's dialogue closely. In the casket scene, one immediate challenge is how to include the hint Portia slips into the song we hear as Bassanio makes his selection. The '-ed' rhyme is specific to English, and it reminds us that Shakespeare's wordplay depends upon particularities of English that defy direct translation into another language. Perng and Chen's solution involves a clever substitution. Instead of Portia supplying a song, her counterpart, the princess Tián, writes a letter to Ba (Bassanio) which tells him 'A truthful heart, who reads this letter, will / Be linked with her heart, as if by a thread' (54). Since the Chinese word for 'thread', 'qian', is a homophone for the Chinese word for 'lead', 'qiān', the letter hints at the correct answer,[8] though Ba has to be prompted to recognize it by Tián's maid, Xingyun (Nerissa).

More generally, Perng and Chen substitute Chinese points of reference for Shakespeare's Biblical and classical allusions and substitute the imagery of classical Chinese poetry for much of Shakespeare's imagery. The reply of Xia Luo (Shylock) to the judge's entreaty for mercy, recast as a song, provides a good example:

Enticing though the orchid's fragrance be,
There are those that seek the stench of odors foul.
Some have a taste for stinking tofu, see,
Some find the tender roast pig makes them howl.
And some find handsome parrots' parts

While some the pink, plump partridge do adore.
To dress in blues and greens suits some folk's hearts,
While some like reds and oranges so much more.
Reasons, ah, reasons there are millions, you know,
They differ from person to person, and so ...
(speaks) If you keep pressing for a reason, I can give you none, except that I bear him a soul-felt hate and a relentless loathing.
(sings) He's a pin in my eye, a thorn in my flesh,
Even death is too light, his soul to enmesh! (65, cf. *MV* 4.1.34–61)[9]

This passage illustrates a general principle of adaptation at work throughout *Bond*: the songs tend to be more freely and fully transposed into a Chinese repertoire of poetic images than are the prose dialogue passages. (In this example, this technique introduces an irony not in Shakespeare's original, since many of the dishes Xia mentions are Taiwanese favourites.) *Bond* features, in other words, two somewhat different types of fidelity to Shakespeare's text – one reproducing Shakespeare's dialogue with relatively close paraphrase, the other shifting the dialogue's thematic content into Chinese cultural equivalents. This approach preserves Shakespeare's cultural authority, so often located in fidelity to his text, and also makes the case that Shakespeare's story has much in common with classic Chinese folktales. Overall, the quality of Chinese in this opera – stylized, elevated, rich with poetic imagery – corresponds roughly to the nature of Shakespeare's dramatic language. This is to say, speaking very generally, the linguistic register of *Bond* might sound to a contemporary Chinese spectator much like the register of *The Merchant of Venice* sounds to a typical contemporary English spectator.

Io Savio's silent film and the opera *Bond* offer us several insights into the nature of Shakespearean adaptation. Adaptation, we've seen, necessarily involves both some elements of fidelity to Shakespeare's text and some elements of deviation from it. Those elements of deviation can be dictated by a new medium or language, by differences in artistic conventions or social mores, or by the adaptor's decision to change Shakespeare's thematic emphasis or approach to characterization. Changing Shakespeare's text is not something to be lamented. Rather, it's a creative means for accommodating *The Merchant of Venice* to new cultural or artistic environments, a way for Shakespeare's play to continue to speak to a world very different from and very much more global than the one he wrote for. It is also a means for modern artists to accommodate themselves to Shakespeare, to extend their own artistic practices and invigorate their thematic concerns by grappling with his work. Shakespeare's survival in a world of modern media and global culture depends upon the ingenuity of adaptors. But adaptation can also be a valuable lens through which to view Shakespeare's own text. Paradoxically, by deviating from the script of *The Merchant of Venice*, adaptations can draw our attention all the more to Shakespeare's choices as a dramatist. By leaving out Bassanio's selection of the lead casket, lo Savio's film may remind us of how important that sequence is in Shakespeare's version for characterizing Bassanio and, indeed, how central Bassanio is to the play. These adaptations' very differences from *The Merchant of Venice* may allow us to return to Shakespeare's original script with a fresh eye and new sorts of questions. And lastly, adaptations remind us of a central truth of reading Shakespeare – every encounter with Shakespeare's script involves some element of adaptation. We understand playscripts by imaginatively performing them in our heads. To read *The Merchant of Venice* involves envisaging how Venice and Belmont might look; how Antonio, Shylock and Portia might act; and how their words might be spoken, and as we do we adapt Shakespeare's play to our own expectations and experiences, often unconsciously. The trick is to become aware of this process, to embrace it or resist it when need be, and to develop a wider range of expectations and experiences that allow you to read a challenging text like *The Merchant of Venice* in several different ways. The goal, in short, is for you to become a versatile and critical reader. I hope this book has helped you do that.

NOTES

Introduction

1 Steve Frank, '"The Merchant of Venice" Perpetuates Vile Stereotypes of Jews. So Why Do We Still Produce It?', *The Washington Post*, 28 July 2016.

Chapter 2

1 Since this tale was not translated into English until after Shakespeare's death, it is an important piece of evidence that Shakespeare knew sufficient Italian to read it in the original.
2 *Shakespeare's Sources: Comedies and Tragedies* (London: Methuen, 1961), 51.
3 *Narrative and Dramatic Sources of Shakespeare*, ed. Geoffrey Bullough, vol. 1 (London: Routledge and Paul, 1957), 464. Bullough includes texts of both *Il Pecorone* and Richardson's translation of the *Gesta Romanorum* in his collection of sources for *The Merchant of Venice*. Bullough's eight-volume collection is a valuable resource for those interested in exploring Shakespeare's techniques of adaptation. All subsequent references to this volume will be noted parenthetically in text.
4 For example, the rare word 'insculped', spoken by Morocco in *MV* 2.7.57 and nowhere else in Shakespeare's works, also appears in Richardson's *Gesta*.
5 *A Record of Aunciept Histories, Intituled in Latin: Gesta Romanorum …. Now Newly Perused and Corrected by R. Robinson, Citizen of London* (London: Thomas Est, 1595), 99v–100r. This book is available on Early English Books Online. All subsequent references will be indicated parenthetically.
6 See William C. Carroll, '"I Knew Him in Padua": London Theatre and Early Modern Constructions of Erudition', *SEDERI* 28 (2018): 7–32.

7 This tale is recounted in Matthew 8.28–34, Mark 5.1–20 and Luke 8.26–39.

8 Barabbas is also the name of the Jewish villain in Christopher Marlowe's *The Jew of Malta* (first performed 1592), the play that almost certainly prompted Shakespeare to write a play of his own with a prominent Jewish character.

9 I'm speaking here strictly of direct Biblical citations. *The Merchant of Venice* is filled with oblique Biblical references of many sorts. For a now classic overview of this subject, see Barbara K. Lewalski, 'Biblical Allusion and Allegory in *The Merchant of Venice*', *Shakespeare Quarterly* 13 (1962): 327–43.

10 The *Oxford English Dictionary* suggests that the word comes originally from the seaport city of Ragusa (modern-day Dubrovnik), a rival of Venice in Mediterranean trade.

11 See Drakakis's long note on this allusion in his Arden edition of *The Merchant of Venice*, ed. John Drakakis, Third Arden Series (London: Bloomsbury, 2011), 398–9. Some editors have emended 'rage' to 'page', shifting the emphasis from Hercules's anger at losing to the humiliation of being beaten by a social inferior.

Chapter 3

1 For full discussions of anti-Semitic stereotypes in Shakespeare's day, see Derek Cohen, 'Shakespeare and the Idea of the Jew', in *Shakespearean Motives* (London: Macmillan, 1988), 104–18; and James Shapiro, *Shakespeare and the Jews* (New York: Columbia University Press, 1997).

2 For an extended discussion of this perspective on Shylock, see Martin Yaffe, *Shylock and the Jewish Question* (Baltimore: Johns Hopkins University Press, 1997), especially chapter 1.

3 See Karen Newman, 'Portia's Ring: Unruly Women and Structures of Exchange in *The Merchant of Venice*', *Shakespeare Quarterly* 38 (1987): 19–33.

Chapter 4

1 This chapter draws upon ideas discussed in far more detail in Frederick Turner, *Shakespeare's Twenty-first Century Economics:*

The Morality of Love and Money (Oxford: Oxford University Press, 1999), especially chapters 4 and 5; A. G. Harmon, *Eternal Bonds, True Contracts: Law and Nature in Shakespeare's Problem Plays* (Albany: State University of New York Press, 2004); Peter F. Grav, *Shakespeare and the Economic Imperative* (New York: Routledge, 2008), 83–107; Amanda Bailey, *Of Bondage: Debt, Property, and Personhood in Early Modern England* (Philadelphia: University of Pennsylvania Press, 2013); John Kerrigan, *Shakespeare's Binding Language* (Oxford: Oxford University Press, 2016), especially chapters 6 and 7; and Katharine Eisaman Maus, *Being and Having in Shakespeare* (Oxford: Oxford University Press, 2016), especially chapters 3 and 4.

Chapter 5

1 In the end, the nature of bleeding flesh becomes one means by which Portia achieves legal victory over Shylock. Shylock's inability to cut Antonio without shedding blood may refer obliquely to Jewish ritual practices for preparing meat, which require that it be drained of blood to be declared kosher. The impossibility of bloodless flesh at the trial, then, gives the lie to Jewish dietary law and, by extension, all of Jewish adherence to ritual. For a wide-ranging discussion of the resonances of the blood metaphor in the play, see Janet Adelman, 'Her Father's Blood: Race, Conversion, and Nation in *The Merchant of Venice*', *Representations* 81.1 (2003): 4–30.

2 Graham Holderness, *The Faith of William Shakespeare* (Oxford: Lion Hudson, 2017), 152–4.

Chapter 6

1 For a general discussion of racist humour, see Simon Weaver, *The Rhetoric of Racist Humour: US, UK and Global Race Joking* (London: Routledge, 2011).

2 The classic discussion of 'interpellation' is Louis Althusser, 'Ideology and Ideological State Apparatuses (Notes towards an Investigation)', in *Lenin and Philosophy and Other Essays*, trans. Ben Brewster (London: Verso, 1971).

3 For a perceptive discussion of this dynamic, see James O'Rourke, 'The Guilty Pleasures of Bigotry: Ethnic Stereotypes in Trevor Nunn's

Merchant of Venice and Dave Chappelle's Pixie Sketches', *Shakespeare* 12.3 (2016): 287–99.

4   For a fuller discussion of 'complexion' and its relationship to racial and ethnic prejudice in the play, see R. W. Desai, '"Mislike Me Not for My Complexion": Whose Mislike? Portia's? Shakespeare's? Or That of His Age?', in *The Merchant of Venice: New Critical Essays*, ed. John W. Mahon and Ellen MacLeod Mahon (New York: Routledge, 2002), 305–20.

5   The head references hint at the woman's 'maidenhead' that a successful suitor might leave with, so that the bawdy subtext is that Aragon, the unsuccessful fool, is left impotent as well.

6   Lancelet's family name, spelled 'Iobbe' in this opening speech in the earliest printed texts of the play, compounds the joke. This is another of the ironic Biblical allusions linked to Lancelet – this time to Job, the prophet who maintains his faith to God despite his many sufferings. What sets Job's tale in motion in the Old Testament is a contest between God and Satan to test Job's faith, a contest comically analogous to the conflict between the fiend and Lancelet's 'conscience'.

7   See Drakakis, *The Merchant of Venice*, 238, note 141–2.

8   For a discussion of the characteristic tone and sources of Jewish humour (which Shakespeare may be reflecting), see Jeremy Dauber, *Jewish Comedy: A Serious History* (New York: W. W. Norton, 2017).

Chapter 7

1   Philip Sidney, *An Apology for Poetry*, ed. Forrest G. Robinson (New York: Macmillan, 1970), 78.

2   Sidney, *Apology for Poetry*, 79.

3   See Drakakis, *The Merchant of Venice*, 374, 70n.

Chapter 8

1   Clarissa Sebag-Montefiore, 'If a Shakespeare play is racist or antisemitic, is it OK to change the ending?,' *The Guardian*, 3 November 2017.

2   The line also provides a performance opportunity: in Gregory Doran's 1997 production for the Royal Shakespeare Company,

Bassanio spills gold coins on the floor when he offers Shylock the 36,000 ducats at trial. The coins stayed on the floor throughout the scene as Shylock and Portia wrangled with one another, as if to underline that something other than money was at stake, and they also remained throughout the final scene as well, so that when Lorenzo speaks about gold on heaven's floor, the image takes on a dark irony.

3 For excellent overviews, you might turn to Toby Lelyveld, *Shylock on the Stage* (London: Routledge, 1961); James C. Bulman, *Shakespeare in Performance: The Merchant of Venice* (Manchester: Manchester University Press, 1991); John Gross, *Shylock: A Legend and Its Legacy* (New York: Simon & Schuster, 1993); and the section 'The Merchant of Venice in the Theatre', in *The Merchant of Venice*, Arden Third Edition, ed. John Drakakis (London: Methuen, 2010), 112–59.

4 A long-cited piece of evidence in support of this performance tradition appears in an elegy for the actor Richard Burbage. This elegy was once thought to be from the period but now understood as the work of nineteenth-century forger John Collier. However, in a recent discussion in *The New York Review of Books* (14 October 2010), Stephen Greenblatt cites as evidence a 1664 ballad by Thomas Jordan, 'The Forfeiture, a Romance', which retells the plot of Shakespeare's play. Here's the relevant passage:

> His beard was red; his face was made
> Not much unlike a witches.
> His habit was a Jewish gown,
> That would defend all weather;
> His chin turned up, his nose hung down,
> And both ends met together.

This passage appears in *The New Variorum Edition of Shakespeare*, ed. Henry Howard Furness, vol. VII, *The Merchant of Venice* (Philadelphia: J. B. Lippincott, 1888), 461–2.

5 Julia Pascal, *The Shylock Play* (London: Oberon Books, 2008), 83.

6 Tibor Egervari, *The Merchant of Venice in Auschwitz*, Unpublished manuscript, 1998, available online at http://www.canadianshakespeares.ca/anthology/auschwitz.pdf. This citation is taken from page 31.

7 A video of this production is available at the MIT Global Shakespeares website (http://globalshakespeares.mit.edu/bond-lu-poshen-2009/).

8 Ching-Hsi Perng, 'Bonding Bangzi and the Bard: The Case of *Yue/Shu* and *The Merchant of Venice*', in *Shakespeare in Culture*, ed. Bi-qi Beatrice Lei and Ching-Hsi Perng (Taipei: National Taiwan University Press, 2012), 142–3.

9 Citations from *Bond* (*Yue/Shu*) are taken from the script available at http://shakespeare.digital.ntu.edu.tw/shakespeare/view_record_other_file.php?Language=en&Type=rf&rid=TBC2009MOV043. All subsequent citations will be noted parenthetically by page number.

FURTHER READING, LISTENING AND VIEWING

Primary texts

Marlowe, Christopher. *The Jew of Malta*. Ed. James Siemon. Third edition. London: Methuen, 2009.

Robinson, Richard. *A Record of Auncient Histories, Entituled in Latin: Gesta Romanorum Discoursing Vpon Sundry Examples for the Aduancement of Vertue, and the Abandoning of Vice. No Lesse Pleasant in Reading, Then Profitable in Practise*. London: Thomas Est, 1595.

Shakespeare, William. *The Comedy of Errors*. Ed. Kent Cartwright. Arden Third Series. London: Arden Shakespeare, 2016.

Shakespeare, William. *1 Henry IV*. Ed. David Scott Kastan. Arden Third Series. London: Arden Shakespeare, 2002.

Shakespeare, William. *Henry V*. Ed. T. W. Craik. Arden Third Series. London: Arden Shakespeare, 1995.

Shakespeare, William. *The Merchant of Venice*. Ed. Charles Edelman. Shakespeare in Production series. Cambridge: Cambridge University Press, 2003.

Shakespeare, William. *The Merchant of Venice*. Ed. M. M. Mahood. The New Cambridge Shakespeare. Cambridge: Cambridge University Press, 2003.

Shakespeare, William. *The Merchant of Venice*. Ed. John Drakakis. Arden Third Series. London: Arden Shakespeare, 2011.

Shakespeare, William. *The Merchant of Venice*. Eds. Janelle Jenstad and Stephen Wittek. Shakespeare. Internet Editions. Accessed 25 January 2018. Available at http://internetshakespeare.uvic.ca/Library/Texts/MV/.

Shakespeare, William. *The Merry Wives of Windsor*. Ed. Giorgio Melchiori. Arden Third Series. London: Arden Shakespeare, 1999.

Shakespeare, William. *The Most Excellent History of the Merchant of Venice*. Ed. Annabel M. Patterson. Shakespeare Originals series. Englewood Cliffs, NJ: Prentice-Hall, 1995.

Shakespeare, William. *Much Ado about Nothing*. Ed. Claire McEachern. Arden Third Series. London: Arden Shakespeare, 2005.

Shakespeare, William. *Othello*. Ed. E. A. J. Honigmann. Arden Third Series. London: Arden Shakespeare, 1996.
Shakespeare, William. *The Sonnets*. Ed. Katharine Duncan-Jones. Arden Third Series. Revised edition. London: Arden Shakespeare, 2010.
Shakespeare, William. *Titus Andronicus*. Ed. Jonathan Bate. Arden Third Series. London: Arden Shakespeare, 2003.
Sidney, Philip. *An Apology for Poetry*. Ed. Forrest G. Robinson. New York: Macmillan, 1970.

Reference works

Blake, Norman. *A Grammar of Shakespeare's Language*. Houndsmills: Palgrave Macmillan, 2002.
Blake, Norman. *Shakespeare's Language*. Houndsmills: Palgrave Macmillan, 1983.
Bullough, Geoffrey, ed. *Narrative and Dramatic Sources of Shakespeare*. Vol 1. New York: Columbia University Press, 1958.
Dessen, Alan C., and Leslie Thompson. *A Dictionary of Stage Directions in English Drama, 1580–1642*. Cambridge: Cambridge University Press, 1999.
Shakespeare: A New Variorum Edition. Ed. Horace Howard Furness. *The Merchant of Venice*. Vol 7. Philadelphia: J. B. Lippincott, 1888.
Thomas, Vivian. *Shakespeare's Political and Economic Language: A Dictionary*. London: Bloomsbury Arden Shakespeare, 2015.

Criticism

Adelman, Janet. 'Her Father's Blood: Race, Conversion and Nation in *The Merchant of Venice*'. *Representations* 81 (2003): 4–30.
Althusser, Louis. 'Ideology and Ideological State Apparatuses (Notes towards an Investigation)'. In *Lenin and Philosophy and Other Essays*. Trans. Ben Brewster. New York: Monthly Review Press, 2001. 85–126.
Andrews, John. 'Textual Deviancy in *The Merchant of Venice*'. In *The Merchant of Venice: New Critical Essays*. Eds. John W. Mahon and Ellen MacLeod Mahon. New York: Routledge, 2002. 164–78.
Bailey, Amanda. *Of Bondage: Debt, Property, and Personhood in Early Modern England*. Philadelphia: University of Pennsylvania Press, 2013.
Bassi, Shaul, and Alberto Toso Fei. *Shakespeare in Venice: Exploring the City with Shylock and Othello*. Treviso: Editrice Elzeviro, 2007.
Belsey, Catherine. 'Love in Venice'. *Shakespeare Survey* 44 (1992): 41–53.

Bulman, James. *Shakespeare in Performance: The Merchant of Venice*. Manchester: Manchester University Press, 1981.

Burckhardt, Sigurd. '*The Merchant of Venice*: The Gentle Bond'. In *Shakespearean Meanings*. Princeton, NJ: Princeton University Press, 1968. 206–89.

Carroll, William C. '"I Knew Him in Padua": London Theatre and Early Modern Constructions of Erudition'. *SEDERI* 28 (2018): 7–32.

Cohen, Derek. 'Shakespeare and the Idea of the Jew'. In *Shakespearean Motives*. London: Macmillan, 1988. 104–18.

Cohen, Walter. '*The Merchant of Venice* and the Possibilities of Historical Criticism'. *ELH* 49 (1982): 765–82.

Coodin, Sara. *Is Shylock Jewish?: Citing Scripture and the Moral Agency of Shakespeare's Jews*. Edinburgh: Edinburgh University Press, 2017.

Cookson, Linda, and Brian Loughrey, eds. *Longman Critical Essays: The Merchant of Venice*. London: Longman, 1992.

Danson, Lawrence. *The Harmonies of The Merchant of Venice*. New Haven: Yale University Press, 1978.

Dauber, Jeremy. *Jewish Comedy: A Serious History*. New York: Norton, 2017.

Desai, R. W. '"Mislike Me Not for My Complexion": Whose Mislike? Portia's? Shakespeare's? Or That of His Age?' In *The Merchant of Venice: New Critical Essays*. Eds. John W. Mahon and Ellen MacLeod Mahon. New York: Routledge, 2002. 305–20.

Drakakis, John. 'Jessica'. In *The Merchant of Venice: New Critical Essays*. Eds. John W. Mahon and Ellen MacLeod Mahon. New York: Routledge, 2002. 145–64.

Edelman, Charles, ed. *The Merchant of Venice (Shakespeare in Performance)*. Cambridge: Cambridge University Press, 2002.

Ferber, Michael. 'The Ideology of *The Merchant of Venice*'. *English Literary Renaissance* 20.3 (1990): 431–64.

Frank, Steve. '"The Merchant of Venice" Perpetuates Vile Stereotypes of Jews. So Why Do We Still Produce It?' *The Washington Post*, 28 July 2016.

Freeman, Jane. '"Fair Terms and a Villain's Mind": Rhetorical Patterns in *The Merchant of Venice*'. *Rhetorica* 20.2 (2002): 149–72.

Freud, Sigmund. 'The Theme of the Three Caskets (1913)'. In *The Standard Edition of the Complete Psychological Works of Sigmund Freud*. Vol 12. Ed. James Strachey. London: Hogarth Press and the Institute of Psycho-analysis, 1958. 289–302.

Ghose, Indira. *Shakespeare and Laughter: A Cultural History*. Manchester: Manchester University Press, 2011.

Gilbert, Miriam. *The Merchant of Venice*. Shakespeare at Stratford Series. London: Arden Shakespeare, 2001.

Graeber, David. *Debt: The First 5000 Years*. Brooklyn: Melville House, 2011.

Grav, Peter F. '"My Purse, My Person": Conflating the Economic and the Personal in *The Merchant of Venice*'. In *Shakespeare and the Economic Imperative*. New York: Routledge, 2008. 83–107.

Greenblatt, Stephen. 'Shakespeare's Cure for Xenophobia: What "The Merchant of Venice" Taught Me about Ethnic Hatred and the Literary Imagination'. *The New Yorker*, 10/17 July 2017. Available at https://www.newyorker.com/magazine/2017/07/10/shakespeares-cure-for-xenophobia.

Gross, John. *Shylock: Four Hundred Years in the Life of a Legend*. London: Chatto and Windus, 1992.

Gross, Kenneth. *Shylock Is Shakespeare*. Chicago: University of Chicago, 2006.

Hall, Kim. 'Guess Who's Coming to Dinner: Colonization and Miscegenation in *The Merchant of Venice*'. *Renaissance Drama* 23 (1992): 87–111.

Hamlin, Hannibal. *The Bible in Shakespeare*. Oxford: Oxford University Press, 2018.

Harmon, A. G. *Eternal Bonds, True Contracts: Law and Nature in Shakespeare's Problem Plays*. Albany: State University of New York Press, 2004.

Holderness, Graham. *The Faith of William Shakespeare*. Oxford: Lion Hudson, 2016.

Holland, Peter. '*The Merchant of Venice* and the Value of Money'. *Cahiers Élisabéthains* 60 (2001): 13–30.

Hutson, Lorna. *The Usurer's Daughter: Male Friendship and Fictions of Women in Sixteenth-century England*. London: Routledge, 1994.

Hyde, Lewis. 'Usury: A History of Gift Exchange'. In *The Gift: Imagination and the Erotic Life of Property*. New York: Vintage, 1983. 109–42.

Kahn, Coppélia. 'The Cuckoo's Nest: Male Friendship and Cuckoldry in *The Merchant of Venice*'. In *Shakespeare's Rough Magic*. Eds. Peter Erickson and Coppélia Kahn. Newark, DE: University of Delaware Press, 1985. 104–12.

Kaplan, M. Lindsay, ed. *William Shakespeare: The Merchant of Venice: Texts and Contexts*. New York: Palgrave, 2002.

Kerrigan, John. *Shakespeare's Binding Language*. Oxford: Oxford University Press, 2016.

Lelyveld, Toby. *Shylock on the Stage*. Cleveland, OH: Case Western Reserve University Press, 1960.

Lewalski, Barbara K. 'Biblical Allusion and Allegory in *the Merchant of Venice*'. *Shakespeare Quarterly* 13 (1962): 327–43.

Luxon, Thomas H. 'A Second Daniel: The Jew and the "True Jew" in *The Merchant of Venice*'. *Early Modern Literary Studies* 4.3 (1999). Available at http://purl.oclc.org/emls/04-3/luxoshak.html.

Mahon, John W., and Eleanor MacLeod, eds. *The Merchant of Venice: New Essays*. Routledge, 2002.

Marx, Steven. *Shakespeare and the Bible*. Oxford: Oxford University Press, 2000.

Maus, Katharine Eisaman. *Being and Having in Shakespeare*. Oxford: Oxford University Press, 2016.

McDonald, Russ. *Shakespeare and the Arts of Language*. Oxford: Oxford University Press, 2001.

McPherson, David C. *Shakespeare, Jonson, and the Myth of Venice*. Newark: University of Delaware Press, 1991.

Muir, Kenneth. *Shakespeare's Sources: Comedies and Tragedies*. London: Methuen, 1961.

Muldrew, Craig. *The Economy of Obligation: The Culture of Credit and Social Relations in Early Modern England*. New York: St. Martin's, 1998.

Nahshon, Edna, and Michael Shapiro, eds. *Wrestling with Shylock: Jewish Responses to* The Merchant of Venice. Cambridge: Cambridge University Press, 2017.

Newman, Karen. 'Portia's Ring: Unruly Women and Structures of Exchange in *The Merchant of Venice*'. *Shakespeare Quarterly* 38 (1987): 19–33.

O'Rourke, James L. 'The Guilty Pleasures of Bigotry: Ethnic Stereotypes in Trevor Nunn's *Merchant of Venice* and Dave Chappelle's Pixie Sketches'. *Shakespeare* 12.3 (2016): 287–99.

O'Rourke, James L. 'Racism and Homophobia in *The Merchant of Venice*'. *English Literary History* 70 (2003): 375–97.

Orgel, Stephen. *Impersonations: The Performance of Gender in Early Modern England*. Cambridge: Cambridge University Press, 1996.

Patterson, Steve. 'The Bankruptcy of Homoerotic Amity in *The Merchant of Venice*'. *Shakespeare Quarterly* 50 (1999): 9–32.

Perng, Ching-Hsi. 'Bonding *Bangzi* and the Bard: The Case of *Yue/Shu* and *The Merchant of Venice*'. In *Shakespeare in Culture*. Eds. Bi-qi Beatrice Lei and Ching-Hsi Perng. Taipei: National Taiwan University Press, 2012. 135–57.

Read, Sophie. 'Puns: Serious Wordplay'. In *Renaissance Figures of Speech*. Eds. Sylvia Abramson, Gavin Alexander, and Katrin Ettenhuber. Cambridge: Cambridge University Press, 2007. 81–94.

Roth, Cecil. *A History of the Jews in England*. Third Revised edition. Oxford: Oxford University Press, 1941. 1964.

Schalkwyk, David. 'The Impossible Gift of Love in *The Merchant of Venice* and the Sonnets'. *Shakespeare* 7.2 (2011): 142–55.

Sebag-Montefiore, Clarissa. 'If a Shakespeare Play Is Racist or Antisemitic, Is It OK to Change the Ending?' *The Guardian*, 3 November 2017.

Shapiro, James. *Shakespeare and the Jews*. New York: Columbia University Press, 1996.

Shell, Marc. *Money, Language and Thought: Literary and Philosophical Economies from the Medieval to the Modern Era*. Berkeley: University of California Press, 1982.

Sinfield, Alan. 'Four Ways with a Reactionary Text'. *LTP: Journal of Literature, Teaching, Politics* 2 (1983): 81–95.

Sinfield, Alan. 'How to Read *The Merchant of Venice* without Being Heterosexist'. In *Alternative Shakespeares*. Vol 2. Ed. Terence Hawkes. London: Routledge, 1996. 122–39.

Singh, Jyotsna G. 'Gendered "Gifts" in Shakespeare's Belmont: The Economies of Exchange in Early Modern England'. In *A Feminist Companion to Shakespeare*. Ed. Dympna Callaghan. Chichester: Blackwell, 2016. 162–78.

Skinner, Quentin. 'Why Shylocke Loses His Case: Judicial Rhetoric in *The Merchant of Venice*'. In *The Oxford Handbook of English Law and Literature, 1500–1700*. Ed. Lorna Hutson. Oxford: Oxford University Press, 2017. 97–119.

Sokolova, Boika. 'Reading Morocco: Four Film Versions of *The Merchant of Venice*'. In *Shakespeare Closely Read; A Collection of Essays: Written and Performance Texts*. Ed. Frank Occhiogrosso. Madison NJ: Fairleigh Dickinson University Press, 2011. 93–115.

Turner, Frederick. *Shakespeare's Twenty-first Century Economics: The Morality of Love and Money*. Oxford: Oxford University Press, 1999.

Weaver, Simon. *The Rhetoric of Racist Humour: US, UK and Global Race Joking*. London: Routledge, 2011.

Wilders, John. *Shakespeare: The Merchant of Venice (Casebook Series)*. New York: Palgrave, 1969.

Wrestling with Shylock: Jewish Responses to The Merchant of Venice. Eds. Edna Nahshon and Michael Shapiro. Cambridge: Cambridge University Press, 2017.

Yaffe, Martin D. *Shylock and the Jewish Question*. Baltimore: Johns Hopkins University Press, 1999.

Film and television performances

Lo Savio, Gerolamo, dir. *The Merchant of Venice*. Film d'Arte Italiana. Starring Ermete Novelli, Francesca Bertini and Olga Giannini Novelli. 1911. Black and white. Available in the DVD collection *Silent Shakespeare*.

Welles, Orson, dir. *The Merchant of Venice*. CBS. Starring Orson Welles, Charles Gray and Irina Maleeva. 1969. Colour. An excerpt from this unfinished film is available on YouTube at https://www.youtube.com/watch?v=x6xBumLVBLY.

Messina, Cedric. *The Merchant of Venice*. Time-Life and BBC. Starring Maggie Smith, Frank Finlay and Charles Gray. 1972. Colour. Produced for the Time-Life/BBC Shakespeare series.

Sichel, John, dir. *The Merchant of Venice*. BBC. Starring Laurence Olivier, Joan Plowright and Jeremy Brett. 1973. Colour. Made for television, set in Edwardian England.

Gold, Jack, dir. *The Merchant of Venice*. BBC. Starring John Franklyn-Robbins, Gemma Jones and Warren Mitchell. 1980. Colour.

Zadek, Peter, and George Moorse, dirs. *Der Kaufmann von Venedig*. ZDF and ORF. Starring Gert Voss, Eva Mattes and Paulus Manker. 1990. Colour. Part of the Edition Burgtheater series, in German.

Hunt, Chris, and Trevor Nunn, dirs. *The Merchant of Venice*. BBC. Starring Henry Goodman, Derbhle Crotty and David Bamber. 2001. Colour. Television recording of a stage production for the National Theatre, London.

Selwyn, Don, dir. *The Merchant of Venice*. He Taonga Films. Starring Waihoroi Shortland, Ngarimu Daniels and Te Rangihau Gilbert. 2002. Colour. An adaptation in Maori, a native New Zealand language.

Radford, Michael, dir. *The Merchant of Venice*. Sony Pictures and MGM. Starring Al Pacino, Lynn Collins and Joseph Fiennes. 2004. Colour.

Lough, Robin, dir. *The Merchant of Venice*. Opus Arte. Starring Makram J. Khoury, Patsy Ferran and Jamie Ballard. 2015. Colour. Recording of a stage production for the Royal Shakespeare Company, Stratford-upon-Avon.

Munby, Jonathan, dir. *William Shakespeare's The Merchant of Venice*. Opus Arte. Starring Jonathan Pryce, Daniel Lapaine and Rachel Pickup. 2016. Colour. Recording of a stage production at the Globe Theatre, London.

Audio performances

Brill, Clive, dir. *The Merchant of Venice*. Arkangel Shakespeare. Starring Trevor Peacock, Julian Rhind-Tutt and Haydn Gwynne. 2005.

Edwards, Hilton, dir. *The Merchant of Venice*. Spoken Arts. Starring Hilton Edwards, Genevieve Lyons and Micheál MacLiammóir. 1959.

Kavanaugh, Peter, dir. *The Merchant of Venice*. BBC Radio 4. Starring Warren Mitchell, Martin Purvis and Samuel West. 2000.

Monette, Richard, dir. *The Merchant of Venice*. CBC Audio. Starring Paul Soles, Lucy Peacock and Peter Hutt. 2002.
Rylands, George, dir. *The Merchant of Venice*. Argo. Starring Tony Church, Margaretta Scott and George Rylands. 1960.
Smith, R. D., dir. *The Merchant of Venice*. Caedmon Audio. Starring Michael Redgrave, Nicolette Bernard and John Westbrook. 1957.
Tydeman, John, dir. *The Merchant of Venice*. Naxos. Starring Antony Sher, Roger Allam and Emma Fielding. 2008.
Welles, Orson, dir. *The Merchant of Venice*. Mercury Text Records. Starring Orson Welles, Brenda Forbes and Erskine Sanford. 1938.
Wood, Peter, dir. *The Merchant of Venice*. Caedmon Audio. Starring Hugh Griffith, Dorothy Tutin and Harry Andrews. 1963.

Adaptations for various media

Armstrong, Gareth. *Shylock*. London: The Player's Account, 1999. Play.
Badiyi, Reza, dir. 'Out of Mind, Out of Sight'. Episode of *Buffy, The Vampire Slayer*. Broadcast 19 May 1997. Television.
Bates, Margret Holmes. *Shylock's Daughter*. Chicago: C. H. Kerr, 1894. Novel.
Egervari, Tibor. *The Merchant of Venice in Auschwitz*. Unpublished manuscript, 1998. Available at http://www.canadianshakespeares.ca/anthology/auschwitz.pdf. Play.
Ericson, Ross. *Gratiano*. London: Bloomsbury, 2019. Play.
Ervine, St. John Greer. *The Lady of Belmont*. New York: Macmillan, 1924. Play.
Gurney, A. R. *Overtime*. New York: Dramatists Play Service, 1997. Play.
Hawke, Simon. *The Merchant of Vengeance*. New York: Forge, 2003. Novel.
Hinds, Gareth. *The Merchant of Venice*. Cambridge: Candlewick Press, 2008. Graphic novel.
Isler, Alan. 'The Monster'. In *Op. Non Cit*. London: Jonathan Cape, 1997. Short story.
Jacobson, Howard. *Shylock Is My Name*. London: Hogarth, 2016. Novel.
Jong, Erica. *Serenissima: A Novel of Venice*. New York: Houghton Mifflin Harcourt, 1987. Novel.
Kellerman, Faye. *The Quality of Mercy*. New York: William Morrow, 1989. Novel.
Ken, Nikai, dir. *Mirai Seiki Shakespeare #01 (The Merchant of Venice)*. Avex. Starring members of the troupe AAA. 2008. In Japanese. Television.
Leiren-Young, Mark. *Shylock: A Play*. Vancouver: Anvil Press, 1996. Play.

Lewisohn, Ludwig. *The Last Days of Shylock*. New York: Harper and Brothers, 1931. Novel.

Lu, Po Shen, dir. *Bond (Yue/Shu)*. MIT Global Shakespeares. Starring Hai-ling Wang, Yang-ling Hsiao and Hai-shan Chu. 2009. Available at http://globalshakespeares.mit.edu/bond-lu-poshen-2009/. In Chinese with subtitles. Opera.

Marowitz, Charles. 'Variations on the Merchant of Venice'. In *The Marowitz Shakespeare*. London: M. Boyars, 1978.

Melnikoff, Pamela. *Plots and Players*. New York: Peter Bedrick Books, 1989. Novel.

Moore, Christopher. *The Serpent of Venice*. New York: HarperCollins, 2014. Novel.

Pascal, Julia. *The Shylock Play*. London: Oberon Books, 2008. Play.

Perng, Ching-Hsi, and Fang Chen. *Bond (Yue/Shu)*. Unpublished manuscript, 2009. Available at http://shakespeare.digital.ntu.edu.tw/shakespeare/view_record_other_file.php?Language=en&Type=rf&rid=TBC2009MOV043. In Chinese and English. Opera.

Posner, Aaron. *District Merchants*. Washington, DC: Premiered at the Folger Theatre, 2016. Play.

Pressler, Mirjam. *Shylock's Daughter*. New York: Dial, 2001. Novel.

Rubinstein, Harold. *Shylock's End*. In *Shylock's End and Other Plays*. London: Gollancz, 1971. Play.

Schwartz, Moshe (Maurice). *Shylock and His Daughter: A Play Based on a Hebrew Novel*. New York: Yiddish Art Theatre, 1947. Play.

Tezuka, Osamu. *The Merchant of Venice*. In the Rainbow Parakeet series, 1959. In Japanese. Graphic novel.

Thomas, Polly. *The Wolf in the Water*. BBC3. Broadcast 22 May 2016. Radio play.

Tiffany, Grace. *The Turquoise Ring*. New York: Berkeley Hardcover, 2005. Novel.

Wesker, Arnold. *The Merchant*. Ed. Glenda Leeming. London: Methuen, 1983. Play.

Wilson, David Henry. *Shylock's Revenge*, 1989. Available at https://hopecorner.net/downloads/dhw15.pdf. Play.

Yong, Faye, and Richard Appignanesi. *Manga Shakespeare: The Merchant of Venice*. London: Harry N. Abrams, 2009. Graphic novel.